Flying Eagle & Indian Head Cents

FOURTH EDITION

Richard Snow

Flying Eagle & Indian Head Cents

FOURTH EDITION

4001 Helton Dr., Florence, AL 35630
whitman.com

Correspondence concerning this book may be directed to the publisher, Attn: *Flying Eagle and Indian Head Cents*, at the address above.

ISBN: 978-07948-51316 / ZT1945 08/25 / Ebook ISBN: 978-07948-53563
Printed in China.

The values shown here are not offers to sell or buy but are included only as general information. Descriptions of coins are based on the most accurate data available, but could contain beliefs that may change with further research or discoveries.

Advertisements within this book: Whitman does not endorse, warrant, or guarantee any of the products or services of its advertisers. All warranties, statements, and guarantees are the responsibility of the advertiser.

The Red Book Series™ builds on the historic *Guide Book of United States Coins* (popularly known as the *Red Book*). Each numbered volume takes a deeper look into a *Red Book* topic, with more history, more images, more data, and updated valuations from the *Greysheet* pricing team. Volume 6, *Flying Eagle and Indian Head Cents*, is just one of nearly 30 volumes in the encyclopedic Red Book Series.

For a complete catalog of numismatic reference books, supplies, and storage products, visit Whitman online at Whitman.com.

If you enjoy United States coins, visit Greysheet.com for up-to-date news, pricing, and research.

ORDER NOW

Worth every penny.

Whitman Classic® coin albums are the perfect way to organize and protect your Flying Eagle, Indian Head, and Lincoln Cents. Crafted with archival-quality materials, these durable, easy-to-use albums offer long-term protection and a professional presentation for your collection. Whether you're collecting by type, year, or variety, Whitman albums bring elegance and structure to your hobby.

Explore the full lineup at **whitman.com**.

Contents

How to Use This Book

This book studies each cent of the Flying Eagle and Indian Head types struck by the United States Mint, 1856–1909. The coins, which include major varieties, are listed by date and mintmark. Circulation-strike mintage figures are for coins struck for use in commerce; Proof mintages are for coins struck for presentation or for collectors.

Each issue's pricing chart includes the coin's unique GSID number (explained below) and values in up to nine grades per row. Most issues will have multiple pricing rows, to accommodate values for coins graded Brown (BN), Red-Brown (RB; sometimes called *Red and Brown*), and Red (RD).

1867: Circulation Strike

GSID	VG-8	F-12	VF-20	EF-40	AU-50	AU-58	MS-60	MS-63	MS-65
1308 (Brown)	$80	$105	$135	$175	$245	$340	$345	$455	$1,000
1309 (Red-Brown)	—	—	—	—	—	—	390	650	1,150
1310 (Red)	—	—	—	—	—	—	—	950	7,000

1867: Proof Strike

GSID	PF-63	PF-64	PF-65
1503 (Brown)	$300	$375	$650
1504 (Red-Brown)	525	1,000	1,200
1505 (Red)	1,150	3,100	4,400

The *Greysheet* Identification system represents unique catalog numbers for more than 275,000 items of U.S. and world coinage and paper money, and it is the bedrock of the vast CDN–Whitman database. Comprising tens of millions of records of pricing, auction prices realized, metadata, and images, it grows and changes on a daily basis. The GSID number allows the user to quickly search this database and enables seamless identification across Whitman's family of products.

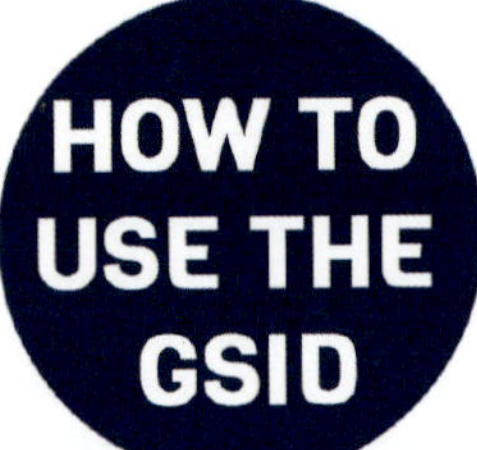

Look up your coins and currency using GSID℠ today!

Visit greysheet.com/coin-prices

Enter GSID in search box

View live results - FREE

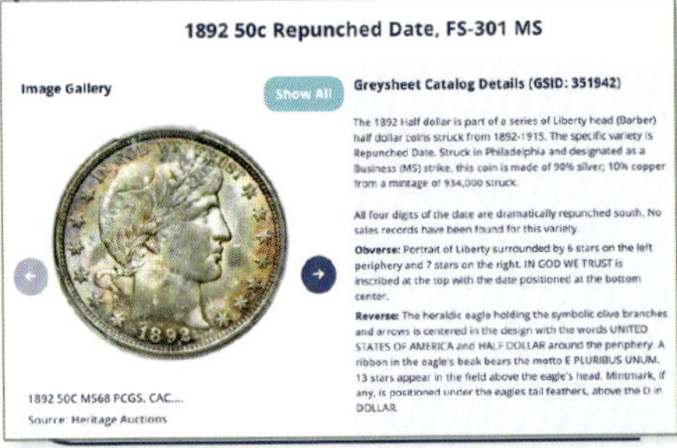

1892 50c Repunched Date, FS-301 MS

Image Gallery

Show All

Greysheet Catalog Details (GSID: 351942)

The 1892 Half dollar is part of a series of Liberty head (Barber) half dollar coins struck from 1892-1915. The specific variety is Repunched Date. Struck in Philadelphia and designated as a Business (MS) strike, this coin is made of 90% silver; 10% copper from a mintage of 934,000 struck.

All four digits of the date are dramatically repunched south. No sales records have been found for this variety.

Obverse: Portrait of Liberty surrounded by 6 stars on the left periphery and 7 stars on the right. IN GOD WE TRUST is inscribed at the top with the date positioned at the bottom center.

Reverse: The heraldic eagle holding the symbolic olive branches and arrows is centered in the design with the words UNITED STATES OF AMERICA and HALF DOLLAR around the periphery. A ribbon in the eagle's beak bears the motto E PLURIBUS UNUM. 13 stars appear in the field above the eagle's head. Mintmark, if any, is positioned under the eagles tail feathers, above the D in DOLLAR.

1892 50C MS68 PCGS. CAC...
Source: Heritage Auctions

Subscribe for pricing

Grade	CAC	CPG Value (Retail)	Greysheet Price (Wholesale)
MS66		$120,000	$100,000
MS66	CAC	$162,000	$135,000
MS65		$63,000	$52,500
MS65	CAC	$78,000	$65,000
MS64		$28,800	$24,000
MS64	CAC	$40,800	$34,000

GSID℠ is a service offered through Greysheet® that identifies and links all coins and currency in our catalog across the entire family of Whitman Brands™ products, such as the Greysheet® online pricing tool, mobile app, CDN Exchange, and much more!"

James B. Longacre
Designer of the Flying Eagle and Indian Head Cents
Portrait by Charles Daughtrey

1 Introduction

To complement my study of Flying Eagle and Indian Head cent dates and die varieties, I have invited my long-time friend Q. David Bowers to contribute an introduction to this book. He describes how these coins were designed, minted, and distributed, and offers advice for collecting them today. Dave has included new research material and updated information from his best-selling 1996 work *A Buyer's and Enthusiast's Guide to Flying Eagle and Indian Cents.*

—*Richard Snow*

Yesterday and Today

Flying Eagle cents, minted for circulation only in 1857 and 1858, and Indian Head cents, produced from 1859 to 1909, were once the most popular, most widely circulated, most plentiful coins in everyday American life. Just about every kid had a pocketful of "Indian pennies," and older folks used them as well. One-cent pieces could do a lot of things: several of them could buy a newspaper, or candy, or a streetcar ride, or entertainment—such as from a Mutoscope arcade machine. Drop a cent into the slot, turn the crank, and you would be dazzled by an automobile racing around a track, or a boxing match, or a striptease. Indian Head cents were anywhere and everywhere.

In 1909 the curtain fell. The new Lincoln cent was introduced on August 2. By this time, Flying Eagle cents had long disappeared from circulation. Within a few decades, Indian Head cents would become at first scarce in pocket change, then unusual, and by the early 1950's, startling to find.

Although many numismatists collected these coins during the era in which they were issued, most interest arose in the 1930's. In that decade, popular albums were marketed in quantity, including "penny boards" by J.K. Post, of Neenah, Wisconsin, in 1934—soon to become Whitman Publishing Company. Wayte Raymond's *Standard Catalogue of United States Coins* was launched in the

100 years ago, every pocket held a few.

same year. In 1935 the *Numismatic Scrapbook Magazine* made its debut. The hobby of collecting coins was in full swing, and Americans looked to the common cents of yesteryear.

A One-Cent Trip Down Memory Lane

The song "The Old Oaken Bucket" begins with, "How dear to my heart are the scenes of my childhood / When fond recollection presents them to view." Similarly, "Old Folks at Home," "When You and I Were Young Maggie," and other melodies evoke scenes of days gone by, of sweet 16, remembrance of things past. Somehow, the "good old days" always seem to have been simpler. In the 1930's an Indian Head cent taken from pocket change—a well-worn coin of 1871 or a fairly sharp one of 1907—with its warm, brown color, was enjoyable to view. These coins were little messengers from days gone by. Collecting them was easy enough to do, with inexpensive holders and albums. With some pleasant hunting, within a week or two most of a complete run of dates could be found. The dates in the 1860's might be worn nearly smooth, the 1877 might be missing and ditto for the 1909 San Francisco Mint coin, but most of the others could be found. In neat little rows in an album—1859, 1860, 1861, 1862, 1863, and onward—such a set was nice to own.

Today, each Flying Eagle and Indian Head cent in existence has its own story hidden between its obverse and reverse surfaces. If only it could speak!

A glittering Proof 1859 Indian Head cent might relate that Joseph J. Mickley gazed down upon it in 1860, and that T. Harrison Garrett admired it in his upstairs study in Evergreen House in Baltimore in 1880. Or, another sparkling little 1859 Proof cent might relate that J.M. Clapp took time from his activities in the oil fields of north central Pennsylvania in early October 1896, to read a slim catalog received in the mail from dealer Charles Steigerwalt, and to post a bid for this piece offered in the Henry Blair Collection auction held on October 14.

A well-worn 1879 Indian Head cent worth just a few dollars probably traveled in most states of the Union in its time, was spent hundreds of times for penny candy, saw the inside of a piggy bank or two or three, was dropped in many gum and amusement machines, and was prized many times as part of a kid's allowance—perhaps even more than a numismatist prizes it today. One can just imagine a freckle-faced, pigtailed little girl running down the street to the store to get rid of this small but quite valuable coin as fast as possible! What treasures it could buy!

Flying Eagle and Indian Head cents were the most egalitarian of all American coins in their day. Anyone could own one—and did. In 1863, when all silver and gold coins were being hoarded and the two-cent, nickel three-cent, and nickel five-cent denominations had not yet been made, the cent was the only United States coin in circulation. Remarkable!

Doubtless, today there are Indian Head cents on the ocean floor in the hull of the *Titanic*, others under the sand on the beach at Coney Island, some moldering in the sod of the Gettysburg battlefield, and still more in attics and dresser drawers. Hundreds of millions of worn Indian Head cents were withdrawn by the Treasury Department and melted. More than likely, of the 1,849,560,942 originally coined from 1859 to 1909, probably no more than about 2% to 3% are in collectors' hands today, or, say, about 37 million to 55 million, most of which are of the later dates in the series (1879 to 1909). Of course this is just an estimate.

Tens of millions of copper-nickel Flying Eagle cents (1857 and 1858) and Indian Head cents (1859 to 1864) have never been redeemed by the Treasury Department, and hundreds of millions of bronze Indian Head cents (1864 to 1909) are presently unaccounted for. Most will probably forever remain that way and, quite likely, were destroyed long ago.

Now, about some coins from that 2% to 3% that *you* might enjoy owning.

Collecting Flying Eagle and Indian Head Cents Today

Today, such coins can no longer be found in pocket change. Even an old-time piggy bank is apt to be filled with Lincoln, not Indian Head, cents. Accordingly, your source is the numismatic marketplace. By the time you buy this reference, you probably already own a copy of *A Guide Book of United States Coins* (popularly known as the *Red Book*). If not, it is a good idea to buy or borrow one. The *Guide Book* sets the context for these cents among other denominations of their era and gives a lot of basic information about all types of coins and how to collect them.

Flying Eagle and Indian Head cents have become a specialty—the two types are usually collected together—and today thousands of numismatists seek them. The great rarity in the set—if you can call it a *rarity*, for at least two thousand exist today—is the 1856 Flying Eagle cent, not a regular circulating issue, but a pattern coin. Because it looks just like the first regular issue, 1857, and has been collected for such a long time, by tradition it has been adopted into the series. Among Indian Head cents the key issue is the 1877, by virtue of its mintage of 852,500, low for the series (in comparison, more than 108 *million* were made of the 1907 cent). The 1864 bronze cent with the initial L on the headdress ribbon (for the Mint's chief engraver, James B. Longacre, who designed it) is scarce, as are the 1871, 1872, and 1909-S, among others. Interestingly, although 309,000 were minted of the 1909-S, it is easier to find than the 1877. The reason is that by 1909 many more people were collecting and saving coins than in 1877.

Magnifier (Loupe): An H.E. Harris magnifier (or *loupe*, pronounced "loop") is a common sight at coin shows. These magnifiers fold into their chrome cases to protect the lens, which is usually 10x to 16x or greater strength.

Many sources beckon as you build a collection. Coin shops are a great source and permit you to look over an extensive inventory. Shops are a great place to acquire accessories such as books, albums, and magnifiers. Two different magnifiers are ideal: one with two 4x lenses that can be used together and have a wide field of view; plus a smaller, stronger glass to see details of dates and other aspects.

Coin conventions and shows are held regularly. Periodicals such as the weekly newspapers *Coin World* and *Numismatic News*, and monthly magazines, including *Coins* and *COINage*, often available at newsstands, publicize show and convention schedules. It is always wise to double-check before traveling a long distance, as sometimes shows are cancelled. At a coin show you can browse to your heart's content, "talk coins" with collectors and dealers, and get many ideas.

The Internet offers thousands of Flying Eagle and Indian Head cents for sale. However, unless they are offered by an established numismatic firm with good professional credentials, there are many traps. Once you become experienced, then feel free to look into a "beautiful 1872 cent I found from an old estate; I don't know much about coins, but it looks nice" type of coin. Until then, deal with professionals.

If you adopt Flying Eagle and Indian Head cents as a serious specialty and pursue many of the scarce and rare items described by Richard Snow in this book, then public and Internet auctions (again, on the Internet, be cautious of non-professionals) offer many opportunities.

Determining Value

The price of an Indian Head cent depends on several factors, including its rarity, its condition (the amount of wear it has received), its eye appeal, and its popularity. As to popularity, the basic different dates in the series are all popular, as are the two San Francisco Mint cents, the 1908-S and the 1909-S. Within the dates there are many interesting *die varieties*, explained in detail in this book. These sideline varieties have different degrees of popularity. An 1872 cent with the word LIBERTY doubled in the headdress is a "gotta get one!" coin for many collectors, while a repunched date on an 1869 cent plays to a smaller audience.

The rarity or number of coins available is an important factor in valuation. A rare 1877 cent sells for much more than any of the common cents of the 1890's and 1900's.

The grade is one of the most important factors in a coin's price. Today, most collectors and dealers use the 70-point Official American Numismatic Association Grading Standards for United States Coins (laid out in a book of the same name, available from all dealers). The details for Flying Eagle and Indian Head cents are given separately in this book, but a brief outline is appropriate here.

Each grade has a number and a brief descriptor. A coin graded Good-4 (or G-4) is worn nearly smooth, but with its date and much of its lettering still readable. An Extremely Fine–40 (EF-40) coin has only light wear and all of its lettering is sharp. Uncirculated or "new" coins, called Mint State, are graded from MS-60 to MS-70. The low end of the Mint State range, MS-60, describes a coin that is nicked or has other handling marks, not from general circulation, but from storage in a bag, or otherwise being loose with other coins. An MS-70 coin is in a state of absolute perfection.

All Flying Eagle cents and Indian Head cents from 1857 to 1863 were made in copper-nickel alloy (88% copper and 12% nickel) and have a light golden appearance. Beginning partway through 1864, bronze alloy (95% copper, 5% tin and zinc) was used. Bronze cents tone naturally over a period of time from mint "red" (actually more orange) to deep brown. A bronze cent with original mint red color is abbreviated RD, such as MS-65RD, meaning that the grade is Mint State-65 and the color is red. One with a mixture of red and brown, and with significant amounts of each, is called red and brown, abbreviated RB, while one that is brown is noted as BN.

Small Details, Big Differences: An 1857 Flying Eagle cent in MS-63 will fetch a price 15 to 20 times that of the same coin in Fine condition.

Often a small difference in grade and color can make a large difference in price. This will become very understandable as you review catalog listings and various offerings of coins for sale. Since the 1980's more than 100 commercial grading or certification services have been established (most of which have disappeared from the market). These firms charge a fee to give their opinion of a coin's grade and to mark it on a sealed plastic holder (called a *slab*). Today the leading third-party grading services are PCGS (Professional Coin Grading Service, established in 1986) and NGC (Numismatic Guaranty Company, 1987), and the recently launched grading service of Certified Acceptance Corporation (CACG, 2003). These three are the only grading companies that guarantee the authenticity and grades of the coins they certify, and the vast majority of very valuable, rare U.S. coins sold at auction have been certified by one of them.

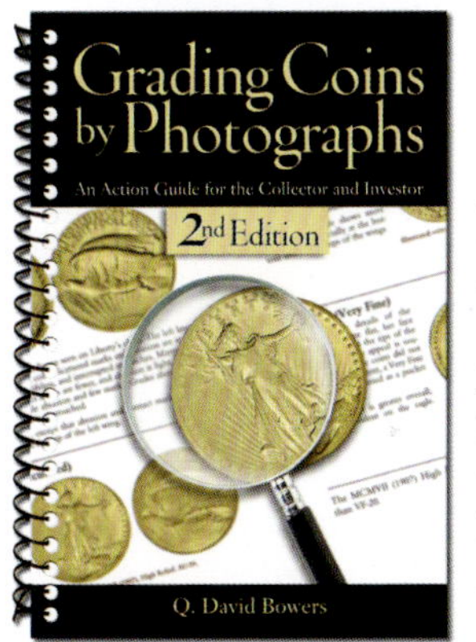

"*Grading Coins by Photographs* is a total delight, absolutely essential reading for all serious collectors. I always enjoy and learn from David Bowers's books. He has presented a tremendous amount of information on the critical issue of coin grading," notes David Hall, cofounder of PCGS and president of Collectors Universe.

Grading is a matter of opinion, and expert opinions can and do vary. Even the same certification service can view the same coin on two different occasions and assign different grades to it each time. It is best to buy the *coin*, not the label on a certified holder. A numismatist friend who has been a long-time collector can advise you in this regard, as can a trusted dealer.

Eye appeal can vary widely, even among certified coins. One MS-65RD cent of 1898 might have some annoying stains, while another might be beautiful and pristine. Generally, avoid any coin that does not look "pretty" when viewed under low-power magnification.

Enjoying Your Collection

No one is obligated to collect Flying Eagle and Indian Head cents. The reason to assemble a set is to enjoy the pursuit. The thrill of the hunt, the friendship of other collectors, and the coins themselves are all part of the game. Forming a set may well take the best part of a year. For some of the rarer issues in higher grades the quest is more challenging, and several years or more are needed. Ditto if you become interested in die varieties in addition to the regular dates.

It's a curious fact that many if not most coin collectors receive pleasure from seeking and buying coins, but do not enjoy their coins once they own them.

How can you *enjoy* a coin once you own it? For starters, use the magnifying glasses just mentioned.

Examining a Flying Eagle or Indian Head cent carefully under magnification can often yield much information and perhaps create a puzzle or two. A good way to appreciate die differences is to take an early coin in a given series and compare it to a later one in the series. For example, under magnification compare an 1860 Indian Head cent (the first year with the oak-wreath-and-shield reverse design) with one from the last year in the series, 1909. You will see differences in die relief and details and much else. Or, pick a dozen different Indian Head cents at random and look at their date numerals under a glass. Some have the date in a straight line, others curved. On some the date is small and tightly spaced, on others large and wide. As examples, the 1871 has the date in widely spaced digits curved along the bottom border, and the very next year, 1872, has small numerals, close together, and in a straight line.

Don't be in a hurry. Take your time. Look and then look again. Repunched dates, planchet defects, die breaks, die finish lines, and much more await you. These features are all discussed in the pages of this book. Among Indian Head cents there were so many different dies used that without doubt many presently unknown interesting varieties await discovery, perhaps by you!

Further, each Flying Eagle and Indian Head cent has its own Mint history (how it was struck, what alloy was used, etc.) and numismatic history (market trends, hoards, prices, etc.). The Flying Eagle and Indian Head Cent Collectors Society ("Fly-In Club") publishes *Longacre's Ledger* and is a meeting place for specialists.

If you can bring all of these aspects together—the studying under magnification of a coin's surface, knowledge of its ties with American history, and its Mint and numismatic background—each coin in your collection will come *alive*. It will no longer be simply a date in a specific grade with a market price, but it will be an object of history, art, and admiration. Don't forget the nostalgia part either—Flying Eagle and Indian Head cents as a link to history.

History of the Flying Eagle Cent

The government expressed concern in 1849 that Treasury Department profits from copper coinage had fallen sharply. This was an important consideration. While silver and gold coins of the era had nearly their full face values' worth of metal content and were minted as a service to depositors of precious metals, one-cent pieces were a profit center. They cost far less than a cent to produce, and the profit, called seignorage, translated directly to the Mint's bottom line.

Feuchtwanger Tokens: The inventor's "Feuchtwanger's Composition" tokens, struck in 1837, would later circulate during the coin shortages of the early 1840's.

In an effort to find a replacement for the 10.89-gram copper "large" cent, which was considered cumbersome to handle and too expensive to produce, the Mint experimented with reduced-diameter and lower-weight cents as early as 1850, with several "annular" (ring-shaped) designs in various metals.

The idea of a smaller-format cent was hardly new; in 1837 Dr. Lewis Feuchtwanger had spent much time and effort trying to interest Congress in adapting "Feuchtwanger's composition"—a type of "German silver" made of nickel, copper, and zinc, with a silvery appearance—to make coins. He gave each member a printed notice about his cent and its advantages and attached an example of the coin. The alloy was said to have been "clean, white and durable material, of specific value, from which coins and all articles can be advantageously manufactured as are now wrought out of silver."[1]

His proposal rejected by Congress, Feuchtwanger took matters into his own hands and caused many thousands of small-diameter tokens to be privately struck. These bore on the obverse the depiction of an eagle killing a snake, while the reverse featured a wreath and the inscriptions FEUCHTWANGER'S COMPOSITION and ONE CENT. He also produced several varieties of THREE CENTS tokens.

In 1851 and early 1852 the price of copper subsided somewhat, and within the Treasury Department urgency for a new cent was diminished. Later in 1852 and in 1853 the price rose again—at one point to 42¢ per pound. The Mint estimated that when the price was greater than 40¢ per pound (which was enough metal to make 42-2/3 one-cent pieces), a loss was sustained if the costs of manufacturing were added to the calculation. In 1853 some patterns were struck in a nickel-copper composition utilizing an 1853 quarter eagle obverse die with a pattern reverse. These pieces appeared silvery, in the manner of 1837 Feuchtwanger cents.

Momentum for a new-style cent increased sharply in 1854 and 1855 when really serious investigation began. Some of the pattern cents of these two years used an adaptation of Christian Gobrecht's flying eagle design created in 1838 for use on half dollars. Other 1854 and 1855 pattern cents featured Liberty Head designs. One particularly notable variant was made by mechanically copying the obverse of an 1854 Liberty Seated dollar (the crossbar and diagonal of the 4 did not copy, and the date appeared as *1851*).

James B. Longacre (Chief Engraver, U.S. Mint, 1844–1869)Longacre portrayed himself in this watercolor portrait, circa the 1840's. In addition to designing the Flying Eagle and Indian Head cents, his work is seen in the two-cent piece, silver and nickel three-cent pieces, the Shield nickel, several patterns, and various gold coins.

In spring 1856, James Booth, the Mint's melter and refiner, concluded that a mixture of 88 parts copper and 12 parts nickel would be ideal for a new cent. This alloy became known as *copper-nickel*. Booth suggested that a weight of 72 grains would be convenient, as this was equivalent to 80 pieces to the troy pound (although the avoirdupois, rather than troy measure, was usually employed for base metals). The resultant coins were to be of small diameter and fairly thick, to eliminate any quick-glance confusion with silver coins.

On July 11, 1856, Mint Director James Ross Snowden recommended the new format. Chief Engraver James B. Longacre was instructed to prepare patterns. Nickel came from a private mine at Lancaster Gap, Pennsylvania, the owners of which obligingly furnished free samples of the copper-nickel alloy to the Mint, from which patterns were struck. In 1863 Joseph Wharton became the owner of the mine. Afterward he used his political influence to create new denominations in nickel alloy: the three-cent and five-cent pieces of 1865 and 1866.

The New Design

Longacre's obverse design for the small-diameter copper-nickel cent depicted an eagle flying to the left, with UNITED STATES OF AMERICA around and the date below. Longacre adopted the eagle motif created by Christian Gobrecht 20 years earlier and used on the 1836 silver dollar. The national bird featured is said to have been modeled from a real eagle, Peter, once a mascot at the Mint.

The reverse motif of the new cent was not original either, but was a copy of the "agricultural" wreath containing, as usually stated, "wheat, corn, cotton, and tobacco," devised earlier by Longacre for use on the 1854 gold $1 and $3 coins. In modern literature the cotton leaves are often referred to as *maple* leaves, as the more closely resemble the latter in a botanical sense; besides, few numismatists are aware of what a cotton leaf looks like. (In the 19th century this was occasionally called a tobacco wreath, and Director Snowden called it a cereal wreath; however, cotton leaf is correct.[2]) The wreath composition, beginning at the ribbon, seems to be: tobacco, wheat, corn, cotton, and a corn ear, the last hardly true to nature.

Although the top ends of the wreath do not particularly resemble corn ears, this is what they were intended to be. Thomas K. DeLorey said, "The original wax model for the agricultural wreath, now in my possession, shows the detail of the two corn ears at the tops of the wreath as long, feathery fronds, signifying the tassel normally found on a corn ear. However, none of this detail survived the transfer to the various incarnations of this wreath, and in each case Longacre was forced to replace it with a series of dots resembling kernels of corn themselves."[3]

While the reincarnation of Peter on the Flying Eagle cent and the re-use of an old wreath created a design admired by numismatists and others, it remains a puzzle why original motifs were not used on such a momentous change in the most utilitarian of all American coin denominations.

However, at the time the "lowly" cent received very little attention in either the Engraving Department or the director's office at the Mint, despite its status as a profit-maker. This denomination was more or less taken for granted. When experiments in new and artistic motifs were undertaken, likely as not they were in precious metal denominations. Similarly, annual issues of the *Mint Report* typically devoted a great deal of space to silver and gold coins, but said very little about one-cent pieces. There were exceptions, of course.

Moreover, Chief Engraver Longacre was known for the slow pace at which he performed his work. Perhaps Snowden thought it would simplify matters if new motifs did not have to be created. Similarly and at a later time, Longacre copied his own designs and those of others to create several other issues including imitating the face of Liberty (from the 1849 $20 and 1854 $3 gold pieces) for use on the Indian Head cent, copying the shield on the 1864 two-cent piece for the obverse of the 1866 Shield nickel, and borrowing the 1859 cent laurel-wreath reverse for use on the 1865 nickel three-cent piece.

Some of the new artistic work on various coins, patterns, and medals was eventually (after October 1857) given to Assistant Engraver Anthony C. Paquet, whose contribution to the small-cent field is just now beginning to be recognized for its true importance.

Saint-Gaudens and the Flying Eagle Cent

On January 13, 1905, Mint Director George E. Roberts wrote to Augustus Saint-Gaudens, America's greatest living sculptor, asking if he would be interested in redesigning the American coinage. On January 20, 1905, the artist said he would like to explore the matter further in March during a visit to Washington, D.C.[4]

Eventually, President Theodore Roosevelt commissioned Saint-Gaudens to create new motifs for all denominations from the cent to the $20 gold piece. Working in his home-studio (now a National Historic Site) in Cornish, New Hampshire, he created motifs for the $10 and $20 gold coins before succumbing to cancer on August 3, 1907.

During the course of his work, on June 28, 1906, Saint-Gaudens wrote to President Roosevelt stating he was working on designs for a replacement of the Indian Head cent, in the process paying tribute to what he considered to be the high point in historical American coinage:

> Now I am attacking the cent. It may interest you to know that on the "Liberty" side of the cent I am using a flying eagle, a modification of the device which was used on the cent of 1857. I had not seen that coin for many years, and was so impressed by it that I thought if carried out with some modifications, nothing better could be done. It is by all odds the best design on any American coin.

Augustus Saint-Gaudens: A painting of Saint-Gaudens at work, by his friend Kenyan Cox.

Saint-Gaudens died before he completed his coinage motifs for various denominations. As it turned out, his flying eagle was indeed used for coinage, but not on the cent. Today it is familiar as the reverse of the $20 gold coins minted from 1907 to 1933.

Vermeule and the Flying Eagle Design

In his book *Numismatic Art in America* (2008), Cornelius Vermeule of the Boston Museum of Fine Arts commented on Gobrecht's design (as seen on early silver dollars and later adapted for the copper-nickel cent):

> The famous flying eagle . . . is one of the greatest symphonies of die design and cutting to be performed on any flan at any period in the history of western civilization. This is cold observation, not mere national pride.
>
> Only the most sensitive, most penetrating photograph can bring out the bold yet subtle relief and foreshortening of the bird as he flies across our vision from right front to left rear. Feathers, wing tips, beak, and curled talon are presented with a naturalistic power and precision as advanced in American numismatic art as was Benedetto Pistrucci's 1818 portrait of aged George III [on British coinage]. . . .
>
> This vision of the national bird on the wing was as magnificent a presentation in depth, detail, and silhouette as the human mind could conceive and the human hand translate into the mechanics of coining processes.

In view of the admiration that Saint-Gaudens, Vermeule, and others had for Longacre's "recycled" design borrowed from Gobrecht, and the enthusiasm collectors have for Flying Eagle cents today, perhaps it is all for the best that some other motif was not created in the 1850's at the Mint when experiments to eliminate the cumbersome large copper cent were conducted.

A few comments concerning Peter, the putative model for the Flying Eagle cent, and the engraver, Christian Gobrecht, who first translated the motif to coin form, may be of interest, followed by notes about James B. Longacre, who adapted Gobrecht's design for the 1856 Flying Eagle cent:

"Peter" the Eagle

The *American Journal of Numismatics*, Vol. 27, 1893, p. 85, reprinted this from *Harper's Young People* (similar accounts also appeared elsewhere):

> On the dollars of 1836, 1838 and 1839, and the nickel cent coins in 1856 is the portrait of an American eagle which was for many years a familiar sight in the streets of Philadelphia. "Peter," one of the finest eagles ever captured alive, was the pet of the Philadelphia Mint, and was generally known as the "Mint bird." Not only did he have free access to every part of the Mint, going without hindrance into the treasure vaults where even the treasurer of the United States would not go alone, but he used his own pleasure in going about the city, flying over the houses, sometimes perching upon lamp posts in the streets. Everybody knew him, and even the street boys treated him with respect.
>
> The government provided his daily fare, and he was as much a part of the Mint establishment as the superintendent or the chief coiner. He was kindly treated and had no fear of anybody or anything, and he might be in the Mint yet if he had not sat

> down to rest upon one of the great flywheels. The wheel started without warning, and Peter was caught in the machinery. One of his wings was broken, and he died a few days later. The superintendent had his body beautifully mounted, with his wings spread to their fullest extent; and to this day Peter stands in a glass case in the Mint cabinet. A portrait of him as he stands in the case was put upon the coins named.

In stuffed form Peter was exhibited widely including at the Treasury exhibit at the World's Columbian Exposition in Chicago in 1893. Today the bird is on view in the lobby of the Philadelphia Mint on Independence Square.

Artist Titian Peale, son of artist and museum proprietor Charles Willson Peale, was asked by Mint Director Robert Maskell Patterson to create drawings of a "lifelike" flying eagle motif for use on coinage, a departure from the perched and heraldic eagles in use for many years.

Whether Peter was actually the model for Peale and Gobrecht may never be known with certainty, but it may have been this unfortunate bird that was mentioned in a letter dated April 9, 1836, from Mint Director Robert Maskell Patterson to Secretary of the Treasury Levi Woodbury, here quoted in part. At the time, sketches were being prepared for new coinage motifs:

> The die for the reverse is not yet commenced, but I send you the drawings which we propose to follow—the pen sketch being that which we prefer. The drawing is true to nature, for it is taken from the eagle itself—a bird, recently killed, having been prepared and placed in the attitude which we had selected. The eagle is flying, and like the country of which it is the emblem, its course onward and upward. . . .
>
> It was my intention to begin the new coinage with the dollar, but it has occurred to me that it might be more proper, and more agreeable to the government, that it should be begun with the indemnity gold. Besides, it would really be a pity that six millions worth of gold coins should be spread over the country with that thing on the reverse which courtesy may call an eagle, but which nature and art refuse to recognize.

(The reference to "dies" in the first paragraph, and other such references in 1836, refer to dies rather than models, perhaps verifying that the pantograph method of model-to-hub reduction was not yet in use. A Contamin portrait or transfer lathe was installed in 1837, after which the process became mechanized. As for "indemnity gold," Patterson is referring to shipments received as indemnification from France. In addition, many gold coins of heavy weight, sometimes called "old tenor" coins, minted prior to the Act of June 28, 1834, came into the Mint and were converted to coins of the new standard, which was instituted on August 2, 1834.)

The preceding indicates that Gobrecht's flying eagle was recommended for use on gold coins rather than the silver dollar, Patterson strongly disliking the perched eagle design on current gold coins (which were of the denominations $2.50 and $5). Considering that Director Patterson liked the flying eagle, and that he served as director until July 1851, it is curious that the motif was used only ephemerally on American coinage under his watch. It is further curious that "that thing on the reverse" which Patterson detested was used on the reverse of the new Liberty Seated quarter (1838), half dollar (1839), and silver dollar (1840).

Christian Gobrecht

Christian Gobrecht (born December 23, 1785, died July 23, 1844) was an accomplished clockmaker, reed organ builder, medal-ruling machine inventor (1817), engraver of rolls for printing designs on calico, speaking doll or automaton maker, and (most important to his career) bank-note engraver and medalist.

Born in Hanover, York County, Pennsylvania, Gobrecht showed an aptitude for things mechanical by an early age. After serving an apprenticeship in clock making in Manheim (Lancaster County, Pennsylvania) he moved to Baltimore (where in 1810 he engraved an excellent portrait of George Washington for J. Kingston's *New American Biographical Dictionary*), then in 1811 relocated to Philadelphia, where he engaged in bank note plate engraving. By 1816 he was on the staff of Murray, Draper, Fairman & Company, of Philadelphia, where he prepared vignettes for currency plates ordered by various private banks. Gobrecht's signature on vignettes of this era is not known, but this is not necessarily unusual as most such works of art by various engravers were very small and not signed.

Christian Gobrecht's Dollar Design: The engraver's flying eagle would later appear on the copper-nickel cent.

Gobrecht came to the Mint in September 1835 to work as "second engraver" (not "assistant") on the staff while William Kneass held the chief engravership. Kneass had suffered a stroke in late August, and never fully recovered. By that time Gobrecht had done contract work for the Mint for more than a decade, including the production of letter and number punches. He assumed his work at the Mint with a running start, and set about creating dies from sketches prepared by Thomas Sully and Titian Peale for what we know today as the Liberty Seated coinage. After Kneass's death (August 27, 1840), Gobrecht was appointed chief engraver on December 21, 1840, although in fact Kneass had done very little work after his stroke.

Following the production of pattern silver dollars, Gobrecht's flying eagle design was used only briefly on circulating coinage for a limited number of silver dollars dated 1836 and 1839, comprising fewer than 2,000 coins totally. It was also used in modified form (with ruffed neck feathers and somewhat "lumpier" body) on pattern half dollars dated 1838 and 1839. However, when Liberty Seated half dollars in 1839 and silver dollars in 1840 were made in large numbers for circulation, Gobrecht's flying eagle motif was abandoned in favor of a traditional perched-eagle design for the reverse.

Years later in 1854, a decade after Gobrecht's death, the flying eagle from his pattern half dollars of 1838 and 1839 reappeared on copper pattern cents of this date and, shortly thereafter, on pattern 1855 cents as well. However, Peter's most famous and enduring reincarnation was on the copper-nickel, small-diameter Flying Eagle cents dated 1856, 1857, and 1858.

James Barton Longacre

Born on August 11, 1794, in Delaware County, Pennsylvania, to Peter and Sarah Barton Longacre, James Barton Longacre was chief engraver at the Philadelphia Mint from 1844 to 1869.

Young Longacre served for a short time as an apprentice to James F. Watson of Philadelphia, then continued his apprenticeship with George Murray, prolific bank-note engraver of Murray, Draper & Fairman, who at one time also employed Christian Gobrecht.

Longacre set out on his own in 1819 and engraved metal plates for bank notes and book illustrations, including for a work on signers of the Declaration of Independence and another on stage personalities, but particularly for the *National Portrait Gallery of Distinguished Americans*, of which the first of four volumes was dated 1834. This last work was published in multiple large print runs, was widely circulated, and brought great fame to Longacre and others whose work was included.

Longacre was appointed as chief engraver at the Mint on September 16, 1844, to succeed the late Christian Gobrecht. While Gobrecht had been a medalist and coin engraver of high repute, Longacre's experience in the medium of struck pieces was limited or non-existent. Certain numismatic historians (e.g., Walter Breen) have ascribed many repunching blunders to him and have called him incompetent as a coin designer and engraver. Nevertheless, the coins he designed serviced a very long span of American history. Longacre remained chief engraver until his death on January 1, 1869.

While numismatists—especially readers of the present text—may consider Longacre's memory dear for the 1856 Flying Eagle and 1859 Indian Head cents, he is also remembered for the 1864 two-cent piece, 1851 and later silver three-cent designs, the 1865 nickel three-cent piece, the 1866 Shield nickel, 1849 and later gold dollars, the 1854 $3 gold piece, and the 1850 double eagle, as well as many patterns, not the least of which are the beautiful Indian Princess pattern silver coins of 1870 and 1871, the latter issued after his death.

For a more in-depth study of James Barton Longacre, see appendix C.

Anthony C. Paquet

Anthony C. Paquet was born in the German city of Hamburg, on the Elbe River, in 1814, probably the son of Touissaint François Paquet, a bronze worker in that city. He came to America in 1848, and in the mid-1850's had an engraving shop in New York City. Unfortunately, there seems to be virtually nothing in present numismatic literature to identify tokens, medals, or any other metallic items he may have created prior to coming to the Mint.

Paquet did contract work for the Mint in early 1857, and on October 20 of that year joined the Mint staff as an assistant engraver. He remained in that post through early 1864, after which he returned to the private sector, but continued to do important commissions for the government, including two designs for Indian Peace medals. A pattern 1877 half dollar is by his hand.

Paquet furnished the letter punches for certain patterns and possibly for regular-issue coins as well, one recorded shipment arriving in late May 1857, although he could have done earlier work as well. Apparently, the same engraver made up punches for various denominations including the dime, quarter dollar, and half dollar. However, these fonts were not used at the time for circulating coinage.

Reverse Designs of the 1861 $20 Gold Piece: The regular design is at left; Paquet's is at right. The most readily noticeable difference is in the lettering style.

His coinage work at the Mint included numerous patterns as well as several regular-issue dies, among the latter being the short-lived modified obverse for the 1859 Liberty Seated half dime (Philadelphia Mint only) and the equally short-lived "Paquet reverse" for the 1861 $20 gold coins, the latter made at the Philadelphia and San Francisco mints.

Paquet died in 1882.

The Famous 1856 Flying Eagle Cent

By the mid-1850's American children and adults had grown up with the old copper "large" cents that had been in circulation ever since their introduction in 1793. The change in 1857 to the lightweight, small-diameter, lightly hued copper-nickel cent would require some education, Mint officials figured.

Franklin Pierce: The president received four specimens of the 1856 Flying Eagle cent.

Accordingly, beginning in late November 1856, approximately 1,000 or more 1856-dated pattern Flying Eagle cents were struck for distribution to newspaper editors, congressmen, and others of influence, with some coins held in reserve for distribution to numismatists. Included in the dispersal were one to each senator and representative, four to President Franklin Pierce, about 200 to the Committee on Coinage, Weights and Measures, and other pieces to Treasury Department officials.[5] However, it seem apparent that any congressman who wanted a few extra pieces had no trouble getting them. Exactly how many promotional pieces of the 1856-dated Flying Eagle cent were struck in 1856 and early 1857 is not known, and it could have been far in excess of 1,000 coins.

These initial specimens of the 1856 Flying Eagle cent were of the circulation-strike format, not Proof, and were intended to be similar in finish to what the average citizen would see when mass production of the new coin began. The "advertising campaign" was a success, and the Act of February 21, 1857, was signed into law, making the copper-nickel Flying Eagle cent a reality.

Collectors Take Notice

Word of the curious, interesting, new, little 1856 Flying Eagle cents spread, and these coins began to have a premium value among the small but rapidly growing community of coin collectors. Specimens soon traded for 50¢ to $1 each when they could be found, which was not often. By 1859, Edward D. Cogan sold a copper-nickel specimen for $2. As $2 was more than a day's pay for many people in the late 1850's, this was indeed a significant premium.

Similar Wreaths: The reverse of the Flying Eagle cent bears a resemblance to that of the $3 gold piece (first minted in 1854). Both were designed by James Longacre.

Around the same time the Mint was busily engaged in restriking rarities for collectors. In 1859, Director James Ross Snowden announced that he could supply scarce coins to numismatists who had George Washington tokens and medals to trade for them. Snowden had been director since June 4, 1853 (and would continue until he was replaced by the new president, Abraham Lincoln, in spring 1861).[6] Under his administration facilities for what became known the Mint Medal Department were set up on March 7, 1855, to provide a dedicated area for the production of Proof coins, medals, and, as it came to pass, restrikes. Beginning in 1859, Snowden, William E. DuBois, and other Mint officials kept busy augmenting the Washington Cabinet section of the Mint Collection (this display would be dedicated on February 22, 1860).

Snowden offered such numismatic delicacies as recognized rarities, Proofs, patterns, and low-mintage coins in exchange for Washington medals and other desired items. Such trades were pleasing to Mint officials and collectors alike. By this process and by selected purchases, the Washington display was increased from a nucleus of "four or five specimens" to 138 pieces by February 1860.[7]

In addition to the *few* rarities Snowden and his close associates may have made for trading for Washington pieces, thousands of other patterns, Proofs, restrikes and other coins were made and sold secretly—with no entries made in Mint records. This activity commenced with vigor in spring 1859 and continued under later directors until early 1885. All involved kept a code of silence. Occasionally, disinformation was issued by Mint spokesman W.E. Dubois.

Whatever the unrecorded circumstances may have been, during the late 1850's and early 1860's—probably from about 1858 and continuing through the early years of the Civil War—additional 1856-dated Flying Eagle cents were struck, but apparently from original obverse dies (there is no evidence that new dies were made after early 1857). The year a particular reverse die was made—1856, 1857, or 1858—made no difference as reverses bore no dates and superficially looked alike. While three of the reverse dies used to coin 1856-dated cents seem to be contemporary with 1856, a fourth is of a style first used in 1858.

At the time, it was felt by collectors that Proof was a *better* finish than Uncirculated (Mint State). Thus, all of the restrike 1856 cents were made with prooflike or even full Proof surfaces by resurfacing existing dies. However, the surface of these Proofs was not quite as deeply mirrored as would be the Proofs of the later dates 1857 and 1858.

Exactly how many Proof 1856 Flying Eagle cents were restruck is not known. A fair estimate might be 1,500 to 2,500 coins. Today, Proof 1856 Flying Eagle cents are much more plentiful than are frosty-surface Mint State coins, the latter being originals from the distribution in 1856 and early 1857 to congressmen and others. Clouding the situation are the fact that many Proof coins have been certified as Mint State and that in any event for many specimens there is no sharp delineation as to what constitutes a Mint State coin and what defines a Proof. Thus, population reports are of little help to the specialist seeking information.

As time went on, the 1856 Flying Eagle cent became one of the most popular of all United States coins. Although it is a pattern—as the design was not official until February 21, 1857—the 1856 has been "adopted" into the regular series.

Coinage in Transition

In the meantime the coinage of the soon-to-be-old-style copper large cents continued with vigor in 1856, and in January 1857, some 333,456 additional large cents were struck. Most of the latter were held back at the Mint and later melted.

The Act of February 21, 1857, abolished the large cent and provided for the production of the new format: cents made of 88% copper and 12% nickel, weighing 72 grains (with the tolerance in weight to be no greater than four grains per coin). Although not specified by law, the diameter was ultimately set at 3/4".[7]

The design of the new cent was not specified, but would be whatever the director of the Mint wanted, so long as approval was secured from the secretary of the Treasury. Accordingly, the Flying Eagle cent was created within the Mint with no congressional or other vote needed. While in its draft stages there was a provision that the new cents be legal tender up to a total of 10¢ per transaction, this proviso did not appear in the final version. This was hardly novel, as the old-style cents were not legal tender either (the Mint Act of April 2, 1792, regulating the coinage, gave legal tender status to silver and gold coins only). As cents were not legal tender, anyone including government officials could refuse to accept them!

Snowden Makes Plans

Director of the Mint James Ross Snowden wrote to Secretary of the Treasury James Guthrie on February 20, 1857, seeking approval of the new cent and explaining its features:

In anticipation of the approval by the President of the bill entitled "An Act relating to foreign coins and to the coinage of cents at the Mint," and for the purpose of submitting to you at as early a period as possible after it may be signed the question of fixing the "shape and device" for the new cent, I make this communication.

Heretofore, from time to time, I have had the honor to communicate with you in reference to the adoption of the most suitable alloy and the proper weight of the coin. These have been established in the bill in accordance with our views. I have to submit for your approval the selection of dies to be used in the coinage, and I recommend an adoption of the dies from which the enclosed specimens have been struck.

The obverse is a flying eagle with the legend "United States of America" and the date of the piece. The reverse is simply a wreath compiled of the principal staple production of our country, enclosing the denomination. The propriety, simplicity and symmetry of this arrangement I think is apparent on inspection of the coin.

The wreath is similar in design to the three-dollar gold coin, but the greater thickness of the cent enabled it to be brought out in higher and more perfect relief, and it fills more completely the face of the coin. The devices and general appearance of the cent, its thickness and smooth edge, render it so dissimilar as to prevent its being mistaken for any other denominations. The last named characteristic will enable persons . . . where there is an absence of light, to ascertain the denomination.

The weight of the piece is 72 grains or 3 pennyweights, equal to three twentieths of an ounce troy. The diameter is fifteen twentieths or 3/4 of an inch, and the thickness of the planchet is sixty-five thousandths of an inch. It will be seen that the relative proportions are most obviously variant from the other coins. Retaining nearly the thickness of the old copper cent, its diameter is but one twentieth of an inch greater than the dime. This familiarity of the portion is also relied upon as an important safeguard against mistaking it for other coins issued from the Mint.

I may add that I have caused some dies to be prepared, and if the "shape and devices" meet with your approval we will be able to commence the issue of a new cent at an early day, that is to say as soon as we can procure and prepare the materials necessary for the coinage.

I also take this opportunity to ask for instructions as to the "purchase of the materials necessary for the coinage of the cent," in accordance with the 5th section of the bill. The copper and nickel for these coins must be the best quality and free from other metals. I suggest that they be purchased in an open market on the most advantageous [terms] that they can be obtained in like manner as we have before purchased material for the copper cent. A superior quality of nickel mined and manufactured in the United States is obtainable in any desired quantity at the lowest market rate which will enable us to proceed with the coinage without delay.

I have the honor to be with great respect your faithful servant

James Snowden
Director of the Mint[8]

While this letter was being considered, the Coinage Act of February 21, 1857, became a reality and provided for the redemption of certain old coins and the issuance of the new copper-nickel cents.

On February 24, Secretary Guthrie wrote to Director Snowden to approve the new cent, but also to suggest a change:

> I have now to ask your attention to the edge of the piece, and to suggest the propriety of such attention in the die, as will render it less sharp.

To Guthrie's letter the director replied in part:

> I have noticed the remarks contained in your letter of yesterday approving the dies for the cent coinage, and will . . . have the coin changed in the manner as suggested.

Presumably, the unwanted sharp feature was simply a wire rim—or "fin" as it was called at the Mint—and no true alteration of the rim, dentils, or other design features took place.

Flying Eagle cents were struck in quantity beginning in April 1857, and were stockpiled for several weeks awaiting their initial release.

New Cents for Old Coins

A fascinating account of what happened when the new Flying Eagle cent made its debut was printed in *The Bankers' Magazine and Statistical Register*, August 1857, and was extracted from an article in *The Philadelphia Bulletin.* The time was May 25, 1857, and the place was Philadelphia:

> Every man and boy in the crowd had his package of coin with them. Some had their rouleaux of Spanish coin done up in bits of newspaper wrapped in handkerchiefs, while others had carpet bags, baskets and other carrying contrivances, filled with coppers—"very cheap and filling," like boarding-house fare.
>
> The officiating priest in the temple of mammon had anticipated this grand rush and crush, and every possible preparation was made in anticipation of it. Conspicuous among these arrangements was the erection of a neat wooden building in the yard [interior courtyard] of the Mint, a special accommodation of the great crowd of money-changers. This temporary structure was furnished with two open windows which faced the south. Over one of these windows were inscribed the words CENTS FOR CENTS, and over the other CENTS FOR SILVER. Inside the little office were scales and other apparatus for weighing and testing coin, a goodly pile of bags containing the newly-struck compound of nickel and copper, and a detachment of weighers, clerks, etc.
>
> The bags containing the "nicks" were neat little canvas arrangements, each of which held 500 of the diminutive little strangers, and each of which bore upon the outside the pleasant inscription "$5." Just as the State House bell had finished striking 9 o'clock the doors of the Mint were thrown open, and in rushed the eager crowd—paper parcels, well-filled handkerchiefs, carpet bags, baskets and all. But those who thought there was to be a grand scramble, and that the boldest pusher would be first served, reckoned without their host. The invading throng was arranged into lines which lead to the respective windows; those who bore silver had the post of honor assigned them and went to the right, while those who bore nothing but vulgar copper [old half cents and large cents] were constrained to take the left.

> These lines soon grew to be of unconscionable length, and to economize space they were wound around and around like the convulsions of a snake of a whimsical turn of mind. The clerks and the weighers exerted themselves to the utmost to meet the demands of all comers, and to deal out the little canvas bags to all who were entitled to receive them; the crowd grew apace, and we estimated that at one time there could not have been less than 1,000 persons in the zigzag lines, weighed down with small change, and waiting patiently for their turn.
>
> Those who were served rushed into the street with their moneybags, and many of them were immediately surrounded by an outside crowd, who were willing to buy out in small lots and in advance on first cost. We saw quite a number of persons on the steps of the Mint dealing out the new favorites in advance of from 30% to 100%, and some of the outside purchasers even huckstered out the coin again in smaller lots at a still heavier advance. The great majority of those who came out "made tracks" with their bags of money, and not an omnibus [horse-drawn enclosed carriage for public transportation] went eastward past the Mint for several hours that did not, like the California steamers, carry "specie" in the hands of the passengers. *[The reporter misuses the word "specie," which refers to gold and silver coinage, not copper.]*
>
> Those who made their way homeward a-foot attracted the attention of passersby by their display of specie bags, and we doubt much whether, in the history of the Mint, there was ever so great a rush inside the building, or so animated a scene outside of it. It was, in effect, at once a funeral of the old coppers and of the ancient Spanish coins, and the giving of a practical working existence to the new cents.
>
> In a few weeks the coin will be plentiful enough at par, the Spanish coins will go out at the hands of the brokers just as they already have disappeared from ordinary circulation, and as regard for the old cents there will be "nary red" to be seen, except such as will be found in the cabinets of coin collectors.

On May 25, 1857, the day that the 1857 Flying Eagle cent made its debut, Mint Director Snowden wrote to Secretary of the Treasury Guthrie:

> The demand for them is enormous. . . . We had on hand this morning $30,000 worth, that is 3,000,000 pieces. Nearly all of this amount will be paid out today. The coinage will go forward, however, at the rate of 100,000 or more pieces per day and the demand will be met as well as we can.

A "Review" of the New Cent

Not everyone loved the new Flying Eagle cent. This scathing commentary appeared in *Life Illustrated*, New York, June 27, 1857, reprinted from a recent issue of the *Albany Journal:*

> The new cent coin wins opinions anything but golden. Its color—like copper counterfeiting pinchbeck and blushing at being caught in the cheat—is the ground of objection with some. Others revile the ambiguous figure which the Mint officers interpret to mean a flying eagle, but which, to the uninstructed, resembles a table napkin, or pen wiper got up for sale at a fancy fair.

The latest objection we have noticed is that children swallow it, with great consequent irritation of the stomach and bowels, from the corrosive nature of the metals of which it is composed.

There is just one good thing in the new cent. It weighs precisely the hundredth part of a pound. People inclined to decimals may turn it to some good purpose as a convenient mode of determining fractional weights; sixpence worth is an ounce; three of them can be sent by mail for three cents more.

Those of our readers who desire to see what the new cent ought to have been in color and material, can step into the State Library and admire the beautiful collection of bronze medals of the French kings, presented by Napoleon the Little. They are nearly black. A cent of this hue could not be mistaken for a half-eagle, or a dime, while the present abortion is of a compromise tint between the two. Our Mint is the more inexcusable, because the French have, within the last three years, replaced their old and cumbrous copper coinage by one of bronze, in which the defect of weight was compensated not so much by superior value in the material as by artistic taste and elegance in the devices and execution. Their example was before us for instruction and imitation.

Who cares whether a penny is worth the hundredth part of a dollar, or only the one hundred and fiftieth? Not a soul. It is mere counter change, not designed for keeping. But our Mint is scrupulous on this. Honesty, which has deserted pretty nearly every other civil department of the federal government, still keeps a lingering foothold there. And thus it comes that an administration which sticks at no outrage upon Liberty—whose effigy is banished from the cent—insists upon mixing preposterous German silver with its copper, to the end that the purchaser of a penny may get his dirty penny's worth. So did the Pharisees pay tithes of mint, anise, and cumin, while neglecting the weightier matters of the law.

Redemption of Silver

In exchange for the new copper-nickel cents the Mint and two other Treasury branches redeemed outstanding large cents from circulation and also took in worn Spanish-American silver coins, as noted above. The silver denominations consisted nearly entirely of 1/2-real, 1-real, and 2-real pieces (the larger 4- and 8-reales coins were rarely encountered; reales were also called "bits"), primarily made at the Mexico City Mint. Director Snowden had estimated that about $3 million worth of these foreign silver coins were in circulation by early 1857. Most were severely worn, often to the point of virtual smoothness.

Up to this point, these Spanish-American silver coins had been received at Treasury offices, post offices, and government land agencies at these discounted rates:

1/16th dollar or half bit: $0.05
1/8th dollar or one bit: $0.10
1/4th dollar or two bits: $0.20

These redemptions were permitted for two years from the passage of the Act of February 21, 1857, but an extension was later granted, and coins were exchanged until the Act of June 25, 1860, ended the practice.

Spanish Dollar: Mostly minted in Mexico City, these silver coins circulated in the British colonies and, later, in the United States, up to the 1850's.

To facilitate their exchange for new one-cent pieces, the government raised the rate to par with United States coins, subject to several rules to prevent severely worn coins from being turned in. Redemptions took place at the Philadelphia Mint, New Orleans Mint, and the New York Assay Office.

1/16th dollar or half bit: $0.0625

1/8th dollar or one bit: $0.125

1/4th dollar or two bits: $0.25

Thus, $5 worth of 1/16th dollars had to weigh more than $4.30 face value worth of current silver coins (half dimes to half dollars); $5 worth of 1/8th dollars had to weigh more than $4.50 worth of silver coins; $5 worth of 1/4th dollars had to weigh more than $4.80 in silver coins.

Although the accounting was sloppy, and figures varied among reports, the *Mint Report* for the fiscal year ending June 30, 1862, gave these totals redeemed as of two years earlier, by June 30, 1860: 1/16 dollars: $114,182; 1/8 dollars: $249,330; and 1/4 dollars: $440,858. The total of $804,380 was equivalent to 80,438,000 one-cent pieces.

Coinage for Circulation

By most accounts, the new small-diameter Flying Eagle cents were a great success. More than 17 million were made for circulation in 1857, followed by more than 24 million in 1858. The old-style large copper cents soon became an anachronism. In the early and mid-1860's, millions were taken north to Canada, where they circulated actively at a time when they were no longer plentiful in everyday transactions in the United States.

However, the Mint was not satisfied with the design. Parts of the relatively large Flying Eagle motif on the obverse were opposite in the coining press from the heavy agricultural wreath on the reverse, and the demand was made at the moment of striking for metal to flow into deep orifices which could not be completely filled under normal die spacing and production conditions. The result was that some coins showed weaknesses, particularly at the eagle's head and tail.

In 1857 Mint Director Snowden suggested that the head of Christopher Columbus replace the eagle on the cent. Chief Engraver Longacre replied on July 17 that the idea was certainly entitled to consideration. However, since earlier objections had been raised against the use of George Washington's portrait on United States coinage, the portrait of Columbus would probably meet with the same problem.

Pattern copper-nickel cents were made in 1858 with a very small or "skinny" eagle on the obverse, thus obviating the metal flow problem, but this motif—which Richard Snow has elsewhere fancifully described as "a quail in the throes of death"[9] and Mint Director Snowden called an "eagle volant"[10] (a flying eagle)—was not deemed satisfactory. The lettering around the obverse border was fairly heavy in its vertical elements, somewhat similar to that associated with the work of Anthony C. Paquet on other denominations of the era, and was entirely unlike the "Small Letters" or "Large Letters" fonts used on regular issue 1858 Flying Eagle cents.

In the same year pattern Indian Head cents were produced by James B. Longacre. These had an Indian Head motif in the center of the obverse. The face of the new Liberty was copied from Longacre's 1854 $3 gold piece (and is related somewhat to his 1849 gold $1 and $20 designs), now outfitted with a ceremonial headdress.

On the reverse—designed by James B. Longacre or, alternatively, Anthony C. Paquet—a low-relief laurel wreath was used instead of the heavy agricultural wreath. The words ONE CENT were in shallow relief as well. This solved the metal-flow and striking problem.

Months after patterns had been made, Director Snowden wrote to the Treasury Department, November 4, 1858, stating that the present Flying Eagle cent coinage was not very acceptable to the general population, partly as the public was now used to seeing birds drawn from nature and not the "heraldic eagle which bears but little resemblance to the bald eagle." Snowden went on to say that the new experimental dies were in lower relief and have "an ideal head of America—the sweeping plumes of the North American Indian giving it the character of America," and that there was "a plain laurel wreath" on the reverse enclosing the denomination ONE CENT. Snowden requested that coinage commence as of January 1, 1859, as changes should not be made mid-year.[18]

Exit the Flying Eagle cent.

Columbus and Washington: Rejected from the nation's circulating coinage in the 1850's, they would later appear on commemoratives (the 1893 World's Columbian Exposition half dollar and the 1900 Lafayette dollar).

Various Pattern Cents of 1858: "Pattern cents of the year 1858 form a playground for numismatists, and in time, most of them can be collected. . . . Specialists with a technical turn of mind can investigate certain die variations and states." (*United States Pattern Coins*, tenth ed., 2024)

History of the Indian Head Cent

Mint Director Snowden described the new cent motif as "an Indian head with a falling crown of feathers."[12] Quite probably patterns of this format were available by spring 1858, for on April 12 a Mr. Howard wrote to Director Snowden:

> I have learned that a new pattern piece for the cent has been struck off at the Mint, having upon the obverse a head resembling that of the three dollar piece, and on the reverse a shield at the top of the olive and oak wreath.
>
> I beg leave to inquire of you if you will use your efforts to procure me one specimen only. For which I will give you any price you choose to ask if it is not over five dollars.[13]

Knowledge was certainly widespread by early that summer, for R. Coulton Davis (Philadelphia druggist and avid collector of pattern coins) wrote to Director Snowden on June 24, 1858, indicating that a Boston newspaper had just carried a favorable story about the proposed new Indian design.[14] On June 26, 1858, Augustus B. Sage, writing on behalf of the newly formed American Numismatic Society, contacted Snowden regarding a specimen of the new Indian Head cent for the Society and another for his own collection.[15]

The Indian Motif

In a letter dated August 21, 1858, to Mint Director James Ross Snowden, Longacre observed:

> I allude more especially to the design on the obverse. . . . Why should we in seeking a type for the illustration or symbol of a nation that need not hold itself lower than the Roman virtue or the science of Greece, prefer the barbaric period of a remote and distant people, from which to draw an emblem of nationality, to the aboriginal period of our own land? . . . Why not be American from the spring-head within our own domain?
>
> From the copper shores of Lake Superior to the silver mountains of Potosi, from the Ojibwa to the Araucanian, the feathered tiara is as characteristic of the primitiveness of our hemisphere, as the turban is of the Asiatic. Nor is there any thing in its decorative character, repulsive to the association of Liberty, with the intelligent American.[16]

On November 4, 1858, Mint Director Snowden discussed Longacre's motif in a letter to Secretary of the Treasury Howell Cobb, noting in part:

> The obverse . . . presents an ideal head of America—the drooping plumes of the North American Indian give it the character of North America . . . and that so far from being modeled on any human features in the Longacre family, or any Indians, these were based squarely on the classical profiles on ancient sculpture. . . . In any event, the feathered headdress was certainly intended in at least two instances to be that of the Indian, the artists at the Mint evidently not realizing the absurd incongruity of placing this most masculine attribute of the warrior brave on the head of a woman.

Earlier, in 1854, Longacre had used a "feathered tiara" on the new designs for the gold dollar and $3 gold piece. However, it was differently styled than the headdress, typically likened to a war bonnet, used on the 1858 and later Indian Head cents.

$3 Gold Piece (1854–1889)

Indian Head $2.50 (1908–1929)

Indian Head $10 (1908–1933)

Buffalo Nickel (1913–1938)

Oregon Trail Memorial Half Dollar (1926–1939)

$5 Silver Certificate (Series of 1899)

Sacagawea $1 Obverse (2000 to date)

Native American $1 Reverse (2009)

Native American $1 Reverse (2011)

Native American $1 Reverse (2012)

Native American $1 Reverse (2014)

Native American $1 Reverse (2015)

Native American $1 Reverse (2017)

Native American $1 Reverse (2018)

Some Other Native American Motifs in U.S. Currency: These designs exhibit varying degrees of historical/ethnological accuracy. For example, a woman (Liberty), as depicted on the $10 gold piece, would not have worn the feathered headdress of an Indian chief.

A legend arose that Longacre's daughter Sarah posed as the model, but in actuality the image is probably a composite. Longacre himself stated the facial profile was copied from a statue, *Venus Accroupie* (Venus Crouching), apparently either in a Philadelphia museum or in the Vatican in Italy.[17] The above-quoted letter from Snowden to Cobb seemingly addresses the "Sarah question" via the sentence denying the representation of "any human features in the Longacre family."

A photograph of Sarah Longacre (born on February 20, 1828, and thus hardly a little girl when either the 1854 $3 coin or the 1858 pattern Indian Head cents were made) taken on her wedding day in 1847 is inconclusive, but shows her face to be an equal or better candidate than the somewhat unlikely profile of the aforementioned Venus (both images are presented in juxtaposition in *Longacre's Ledger*, July 1992, p. 19). The attribution of the portrait will probably never be decided to everyone's satisfaction, especially absent any surviving information from Longacre stating that his daughter Sarah was the model.

With regard to the absurdity of placing an Indian chief war bonnet on the head of a maiden, history repeated itself in 1907 when Augustus Saint-Gaudens decked Liberty in a feathered headdress on the new $10 gold coin. However, ethnologically correct male Indians in headdresses were used elsewhere in the American monetary system, most notably on the $5 Silver Certificate paper currency in the Series of 1899, Bela Lyon Pratt's designs for the new $2.50 and $5 gold coins of 1908, and James Earle Fraser's Buffalo nickel of 1913.

Director Snowden wrote to Longacre on November 6, 1858, to advise that the Treasury Department had approved the new (Indian) design, the change to take effect on January 1, 1859. Longacre was to prepare the necessary dies. For the reverse die, he requested a slight modification (possibly referring to the laurel leaves, which were increased from five per cluster to six).[18]

In due course in 1859 Longacre's Indian Head design became standard on the copper-nickel cent, and 36,400,000 examples were coined for circulation. As it turned out the laurel wreath reverse was only used this year on the cent. It was not forgotten completely, however, and in 1865 it was adapted for use on the new nickel three-cent denomination.

1860: Design Modified

In late 1859, the reverse was redesigned to feature a wreath of oak leaves with olive leaves wrapped together in a ribbon at its base. A shield was added above the wreath. On December 13, 1859, Mint Director Snowden wrote to Treasury Secretary Howell Cobb:

> A modification of the devices on the reverse of the cent is desirable. I propose to introduce the shield upon the reverse. This will give it a more national character, and be a decided improvement upon the present coin.

The new oak wreath with narrow shield reverse motif may have been the work of Anthony C. Paquet, alternatively of James B. Longacre, and in any event was adapted from pattern reverses of 1858 (one with an oak wreath with an open top, and one with an oak wreath with a broad ornamented shield at its apex). The lettering ONE CENT on the 1860 issues differs from that on the 1859 cent. The Indian Head obverse design and oak wreath and narrow shield reverse remained standard in the series through its end in 1909.

Upwards of 1,000 coins were struck with the 1859 date and this new reverse design. These were not released into circulation, as nearly all appear in the market today in uncirculated condition. Perhaps the entire mintage was bought up by a member of the growing circle of coin dealers at the time. 1,000 coins would have been a $10 investment.

For an unexplained reason, the obverse design was redesigned in 1860. Undated dies from 1859 were dated 1860 until they were used up. These are called the "Pointed Bust" design. The new design is artistically a step backwards, as the details are less highly refined. This new design was used until 1864.

Too Many Cents: an "Evil"

By autumn 1860 there were too many cents in circulation, not only of the Flying Eagle type minted for commerce in 1857 and 1858, but also of the new Indian Head design first minted in 1859. An article in the *Philadelphia Press*, reprinted in the October 1860 issue of *The Bankers' Magazine and Statistical Register*, advised the following:

> We are requested to state that the Spanish and Mexican fractions of the dollar will not, after today, be received at the Mint at their nominal value, exchanged for the new cents. The main object of the law authorizing these coins to be received at their nominal value of twenty-five, twelve and a half, and six and a quarter cents [Spanish 2-real, 1-real, and half-real coins], was to retire them from circulation, and thus relieve the community from worn-out and depreciated currency, which materially interfered with our excellent decimal system of coinage.
>
> The object having in a great measure had been obtained, and the amount of cents issued being quite large, Mr. Snowden, director of the Mint, recommended that a law should be passed to repeal so much of the former law, on the subject as required these exchanges to be made. This accordingly has been done.
>
> Hereafter the new cents will only be paid out in exchange for gold and silver coins of the United States, and for the copper cent of the former issues. This regulation will undoubtedly be regarded by many of our citizens as a judicious one, inasmuch as the large issue of the new nickel cents has rendered them almost as much of a nuisance as the old Spanish currency. Many persons who have obtained for the latter, at its nominal value, much larger number of the cents than they could legitimately use, have used them to pay bills of one, two or three dollars, and as this custom has been extended, it has caused considerable inconvenience.
>
> The new regulation, by destroying the cause of the over-issue of cents, will no doubt do much to diminish the evil which has resulted from it, and it is hoped that the period is not far distant when the supply of cents will not be graded on the demand for them for use in the small transactions to which silver coins are not adapted.

More About the Flood of Cents

The same issue of *Bankers' Magazine* told more:

> There is much feeling manifested in this city at the persistence of the Philadelphia Mint coinage of cents, the market is so flooded with them. The answer of the Mint is, that there is a constant demand, to meet which they must continue to coin. This demand comes from those who care nothing for the inconvenience of the community, or who do not experience any of the evils of the great surplus of cents, and are therefore inconsiderate enough to order new pieces from the Mint to meet their payments.
>
> Banks, and a variety of other institutions and establishments which have to provide change, prefer an elegant new cent to a dirty old one, and will order from the

Mint a constant supply as fast as their stock is exhausted. Of course, as they are not obliged to receive them back, they care little how many are afloat. Thus the evil goes on increasing every day.

"In Our Youth, Our Hearts Were Touched By Fire"
(Oliver Wendell Holmes, Speaking of the Civil War)
These soldiers of the early 1850's would have grown up spending half cents and large cents (minted from 1793 onward). In 1857 their pocket change would instead include the new, smaller Flying Eagle cent, and later the Indian Head cent. Five years later, while they fought in the Civil War, all coins would become scarce, hoarded by the public. (From a painting by Henry Alexander Ogden, published by the U.S. Army Quartermaster General in 1890)

> There are 10 million cents at this moment in New York over and above the want of the community, and they serve no purpose except to rob the poor of the daily commission on their hard earnings. There is no way to get rid of them; they are sold every day at a depreciation, and immediately put into circulation to be paid out and sold over again. There is but one way to remedy the evil. Let the secretary of the Treasury order the Mint at once to stop the coinage.
>
> If there is any demand for them, orders can be filled here at this moment, at a discount of one year's interest. Congress should then give the people the privilege of exchanging them at the Mint for silver; this would at once meet the "demand" at the Mint, and the director would take care that there were not too many coined, if the surplus were allowed to go back to its source.

The *Report of the Director of the Mint*, 1860, included this commentary:

> The new cents have heretofore been issued in exchange for the fractions of the Spanish and Mexican dollar, and for the old copper cents. As the Spanish and Mexican pieces were received at their nominal value, large amounts of these coins have been brought to the melting-pot, and thus the community has been relieved from an irregular and depreciated currency. But it has required the issue of a large amount of cents, and induced a temporary redundancy of that coin in some of the Eastern cities. They are gradually, however, being distributed to all parts of our country, including a portion of the Southern states, where the copper cent was scarcely known as a circulating medium.
>
> Since the passage of the Act of 25th of June, 1860, the issues have been limited to exchanges for the copper cents, except the supplying of the government offices with the new issue, and distant parts of the country in limited amounts. In order to accelerate the process of relieving the community from the cumbrous and inconvenient copper cents, the Mint now pays the expenses of transportation on them, and will make returns in the new issues. This arrangement will tend to relieve the country from a burdensome currency, without increasing the amount of circulation of that denomination of coins.

The Situation in July 1862

The Bankers' Magazine and Statistical Register, November 1862, reported on the dramatically changed situation in Philadelphia the preceding July:

> The great feature of [July 1862] was the heavy manufacture of cents, of which 3,600,000 were made, of the value of $36,000. There was a great rush to the Mint to procure cents. The *North American* says: "At an early hour in the morning there were not less than 150 boys and men, and 31 young ladies and girls, awaiting a supply of pennies. The boys and men carried shotbags, cigar boxes, baskets, and all sorts of contrivances in which to carry off the much-needed coin. The girls principally carried neat baskets. When the distribution came to be made, the girls were first served, to the intense chagrin of the men, who had been standing on a single foot, alternately, upon the sidewalk for two or three hours. The men and boys were not attended to until the last girl had departed."

Actually, the larger part of the story was left unsaid. The Civil War was raging, and the outcome was far from certain. Some foreign countries (Britain being the prime example) dallied with the idea of recognizing the Confederate States of America, while others sided with the Union. Meanwhile, as in other times of national emergency, the public tried to squirrel away items of lasting value. In the second week of July 1862 there was a flurry of hoarding throughout the Eastern and Midwest sections of the United States. By month's end no silver coins were seen in circulation, and copper-nickel cents were "in anxious demand, and we have heard of 2% [premium] in some instances being paid for them."[19] Gold coins had not been seen in general trade since the preceding December (1861).

As a palliative Congress passed the Act of July 17, 1862, stating that ordinary postage stamps could be used as money in paying federal debts up to $5. The intent of this law was subverted soon thereafter, and the Treasury ordered a supply of privately printed notes popularly referred to as Postage Currency, although there had been no legal provision for them. Denominations were 5¢, 10¢, 25¢, and 50¢. The first of these notes had perforated edges just like stamps. (Today these are collected as part of the Fractional Currency series.) Postage Currency notes were first distributed to Army paymasters in August 1862 and to the public in September. By early 1863 about $100,000 of these notes reached circulation every day, but the demand remained unsatisfied.

Meanwhile, in New York City in mid-July 1862, there were no silver three-cent pieces, half dimes, or other coins of intrinsic value with which to buy a glass of soda or a mug of beer or a streetcar ride, unless such coins were purchased at a premium from a speculator.

The Treasury Department stopped paying out freshly minted silver and gold coins and relegated them to bank vaults or sold them at a premium (in terms of paper money) for export. Silver coins did not return to general use until the mid-1870's and were not in generous supply until 1876; gold was back in circulation beginning on December 17, 1878 (the mandated date was January 1, 1879, but this was anticipated in practice).

For more than a decade, beginning in the summer of 1862, substituting for silver coins were many privately issued items including tickets and small notes printed in values from 1¢ upward, government postage stamps placed in privately printed envelopes and brass frames (the latter known as *encased postage stamps*), and a vast flood of small one-cent-size bronze (mostly) and brass tokens, these in addition to a vast quantity of Fractional Currency bills.

Indian Head cents continued to be minted in record numbers in the summer of 1862, and from time to time quantities were released into circulation, as outlined in the newspaper report cited above. The reason why the public clamored for cents in July 1862 is that they were becoming increasingly difficult to find in circulation at the time. Many had been taken off the market, sometimes by being wrapped in paper rolls or packets of 25, 50, or 100 coins, and then stored by those who accepted them in trade. "Bus companies, theatres, and restaurants accepted these rolls everywhere. A retail store in New York received so many that the floor of the room in which they were stored collapsed."[20]

Hoarders had Flying Eagle and Indian Head cents. The public did not. By July 10, 1862, copper-nickel cents were trading at a 4% premium (in terms of paper money) in New York City, and by July 15 they cost a similar premium in Springfield, Massachusetts.[21] What a change from the glut of 1860!

In his *Fractional Money* study, 1930, p. 187, Neil Carothers commented:

> In a vain effort to satisfy the demand [for copper-nickel Indian Head cents] the Mint forced itself into a rate of production even higher than that of 1858. By the

end of July the weekly issue amounted to 1,200,000 pieces. One-third of this total was reserved for Philadelphia, the remainder going to the other large cities. No applicant anywhere received more than $5 worth.

The coinage jumped from 12,000,000 pieces in the [fiscal] year ending June 30, 1862, to 47,800,000 in the following year. Even this extraordinary value in cents, $478,000, was a small sum which contrasted with the $25,000,000 or more in silver coin that had disappeared. The demand for the cent pieces was never satisfied. The conditions in Philadelphia, which were duplicated in other cities, were described in the *Public Ledger* of July 18th [1862]:

"The difficulty among small shopkeepers, provision dealers in the markets and in the city generally, in making change, has caused an extraordinary demand for cents, and all that can be commanded at the Mint are eagerly bought. . . . Though many of those who desired cents stood in line for hours, waiting an opportunity to get into the Mint, they had to go home without them, as the supply on hand was exhausted before half the applicants were accommodated."

Carothers went on to note that these cents, called *nickels* or simply *nicks* (in an era before the nickel five-cent piece, introduced in 1866, would assume that name), were in demand because the ownership of a few cents "meant that the owner could ride rather than walk. And, for months after it meant that he could buy a postage stamp without an altercation with the clerk or a cigar without receiving in change a handful of the dealer's own manufactured currency [paper tickets or notes]."

Encased Postage

Civil War Tokens: These tokens were made in a wide range of compositions and designs. More than 10,000 different varieties have been recorded, many imitating the Indian Head cent with its headdress-clad youth. Some were political or patriotic in nature, featuring military leaders or propagating slogans. The *Guide Book of United States Coins* estimates that 50 million or more pieces were issued. (Illustrations enlarged)

The Scene from 1863 to 1866

By March 1863 the Treasury Department's so-called Postage Currency notes in values of 5¢ to 50¢ had become common in trade and, seemingly, should have alleviated the cent shortage. However, the public still preferred coins, silver and gold remained nowhere to be seen, and attention continued to be focused on the copper-nickel Indian Head cent. On March 9, 1863, the *Public Ledger* reported that in Philadelphia cents were "so scarce as to command a premium of 20%."[22]

By the end of the Mint's fiscal year on June 30, 1863, copper-nickel cents were sufficiently scarce that Director James Pollock reported that they were "scarcely to be had" in circulation, and stated that he could not guess "as to the amount of cents that will be required to meet the public demand."

Under the provisions of the Act of March 3, 1863, the federal government issued Fractional Currency notes in denominations from 5¢ to 50¢, but this distribution did not begin until October 10 of the same year. At this time the tattered Postage Currency notes began to be gradually retired. In autumn 1864 a new Fractional Currency denomination, the 3¢ note, reached circulation, but, like the 15¢ denomination introduced in 1869, it was never widely used. Fractional Currency notes (which the public called *stamps*) tended to become tattered and soiled easily and hard to stack and count.

Gradually, as privately issued bronze tokens were dumped into circulation by the millions and used for everyday change, Indian Head cents returned to commercial channels and circulated, but seemingly not in large numbers in any one place. As late as June 30, 1864, at the end of the Mint's fiscal year, Director Pollock reported, "Large quantities are hoarded, and thus kept from circulation."

Apparently, by autumn 1864 the situation eased somewhat, for little was said later in *Mint Reports* about cent hoarding. By this time the new bronze Indian Head cent was a reality. In the same year, 1864, the bronze two-cent piece was introduced to help relieve the need for pocket change, and in 1865 the nickel three-cent piece made its debut, followed by the nickel five-cent piece in 1866. Still, silver coins remained in Treasury vaults and did not circulate, not even the lightweight trimes (silver three-cent pieces). However, by 1865 and 1866 there were enough minor coins in the channels of commerce to satisfy most needs.

Bronze Cents

Copper-nickel alloy was very difficult for the Mint to use. It was extremely hard, did not strike up well, and caused rapid die wear. In 1863 Mint officials noted that the public eagerly used private tokens minted of softer bronze, and pattern Indian Head cents (Judd-299, Pollock-359) were struck in a related alloy (the Mint alloy was 95% copper and 5% tin and zinc). The new bronze Indian Head cents, minted under the Act of April 22, 1864, were of lighter weight and thinner, and struck up better than the old-style coins. By the end of May 1864, the copper-nickel cent had been discontinued, and the bronze cent had become standard.

Meanwhile on April 15, 1864, Joseph Wharton, who in 1863 had purchased the nickel mine at Lancaster Gap, Pennsylvania, and who reportedly had $200,000 invested in it, published a pamphlet, *Project for Reorganizing the Small Coinage of the United States of America*, which recommended that the use of nickel be *increased*, and denominations of 1¢, 2¢, 3¢, 5¢, and 10¢ be made with an alloy of 25% nickel and 75% copper. Wharton exercised strong influence on certain members of Congress, and at his doorstep can be directly laid the widespread use of nickel in coinage during this era including the new nickel three-cent piece in 1865 and the nickel five-cent piece in 1866—all made in accordance with his 25% nickel, 75% copper suggestion.

This same Lancaster Gap nickel source, under different ownership, had supplied nickel for copper-nickel cents from 1856 onward.[23]

The 1860's and 1870's

After 1865, quantities struck of Indian Head cents dropped significantly as the two-, three-, and five-cent coins and Fractional Currency notes took up the slack. From then through 1878 there were only a few years in which the mintage exceeded ten million: 1868, 1873, 1874, and 1875. For three years—1871, 1872, and 1877—production was less than five million annually, with 1877 registering only 852,500 coins.

By 1871 so many cents had accumulated that they had become a nuisance. Congress passed a law allowing them to be redeemed in greenbacks by the Treasury when presented in amounts of $20 or more. The Act of March 1871 provided for the melting of millions of unwanted two-cent pieces (first coined in 1864) as well as worn copper and bronze cents, with the metal to be used to strike more Indian Head cents. This piece of legislation resulted in generous mintage figures after 1872.

In 1873 the Treasury's illegal resumption of silver specie payments put a small quantity of silver coins back into commercial channels. By autumn 1876 this severely lessened the demand for minor coins, resulting in lower mintages for the cent, nickel three-cent, and nickel five-cent pieces.[24]

Small Change After the War: By 1866, hoarding was no longer a problem. Commerce was aided by several new coins in circulation (including the two-cent piece, and three-cent and five-cent pieces in nickel).

1879 to 1909

Beginning in 1879, production of Indian Head cents at the Philadelphia Mint went back above the ten million mark annually and remained there for the rest of the series through to its end in 1909. The lowest mintage of this interval was 11,765,384 (including 3,790 Proofs) for 1885, and the highest mintage and the only year to cross the 100-million mark was 1907 with a production of 108,138,618 (including 1,475 Proofs). The American economy was in a rapid-growth stage during the early 20th century, coin-operated machines were being made in unprecedented quantities, and Indian Head cents were needed in record numbers.

Until 1908, production of Indian Head cents was limited to the Philadelphia Mint. In that year 1,115,000 cents were produced at San Francisco, each coin having a tiny S mintmark below the wreath on the reverse. The first production took place on November 27, 1908.

In 1909 309,000 1909-S Indian Head cents were made, the lowest circulation-strike production in the Indian Head series.

The San Francisco Mint, 1906: When San Francisco was rocked by an earthquake in April 1906, the Mint was the only building standing for several blocks. It was up and running again by the following year, and contributed to Indian Head cent production in 1908 and 1909.

Aspects of Collecting

To build your collection of Flying Eagle and Indian Head cents you will need to participate in the marketplace. These coins as well as those in other series are easy enough to buy—just by writing a check. However, the difference between a drab collection and a great one, even within the same grades, is a matter of connoisseurship.

If you go car-buying or house-buying, the seller is not likely to tell you, "This is a tired old automobile on its final laps," or "There is so much work to be done on this building that it isn't worth it." So it is with coins. Even certified coin holders give no indication as to whether the coin within is a rare beauty or as ugly as a toad. Accordingly, it is up to *you* to be a smart buyer—if you want to.

Here are some guidelines for smart buying:

Look at the coin, not at the numerical grade or color designation, except as a starting point. If it is stained, spotted, ugly, or unappealing, don't buy it. Wait for another. You'll have a later chance. A spot-free, pristine, beautiful MS-65RD cent priced at $1,200 might be a better buy than a stained, cleaned "MS-65RD" priced at $500.

There are a lot of traps among certified coins, and even more among coins that are not certified. Some are downright ugly. Over the past 30 years the best-quality coins have likely been submitted for grading. One must assume that unless a collection has been tucked away since the 1980's, it has been considered for certified grading. If the owner decided not to have the coin certified, why? Likely it was cleaned, or had problems, and its value would have not increased by sending it in for grading.

The coins that have been graded over the past 30 years may have been strictly graded when first submitted. Over time the standards have loosened a bit. Some of these earlier-graded coins might be considered for a resubmission. As the population of certified coins gets resubmitted over and over, a few of the coins will get graded higher each time. Eventually all coins will reach the highest level of their acceptance. Some will go beyond this level and be considered overgraded. As a collector, you must weigh the grade, quality, and price to get the right value for you coin. Services like CAC and Eagle Eye Photo Seal help in identifying properly graded coins in certified holders.

Certified holders now attribute the top 100 varieties on their holders. This has created a greater market in varieties where prior to certified grading it was the area of just a few dedicated collectors. The advent of certified set registries has also increased collecting of top population coins. There can be a big price difference between a low-population coin if there are none graded higher than a coin just one grade lower.

Think independently. Don't let someone fool you into believing that all MS-65RD coins are better than, for example, MS-63BN specimens. This is not the case. There are nice coins and there are ugly coins within each grade category.

Don't be a bargain hunter. If the quality is there and the coin is *rare*, don't be afraid to pay the going rate or even more. No one ever bought the best quality for the cheapest price. This is true throughout the Flying Eagle and Indian Head cent series and is especially so among the bronze Indian Head cents of 1864 to 1909. On the other hand, among later Lincoln cents, if a coin is common in gem condition (as are, for example, Proof Lincoln cents of the past two or three decades), then finding a gem will be a snap, just about every vendor has high quality, and the effort of cherrypicking for quality will not be important. Stated another way, the discipline needed to buy a modern PF-66RD 2000-S Lincoln cent is one thing, and that needed to buy a PF-66RD Indian Head cent of 1890 is another.

Study the specific variety of the coin you intend to buy in order to learn its characteristics, its availability in various grades, and its other aspects. Fortunately for you, there is much information available on Flying Eagle and Indian Head cents—in this book and elsewhere (see the bibliography)—so you can indeed know where you are going.

Take your time. No matter how well endowed your checking account may be, allow yourself a year or two or three to put together a nice set. This will prolong the thrill of the hunt as well. No one has ever put together a *quality* collection of Flying Eagle and Indian Head cents by buying in a hurry.

A Few Words About Proofs

The Mint struck Proof Flying Eagle and then Indian Head cents, in quantities ranging from a couple dozen to several thousand. These were made by using dies with highly polished faces, striking the coins slowly on a medal press, and handling them with care afterward. The resultant coins had deeply mirrored fields.

Because these were sold at a premium to collectors, most were saved. We know that 2,350 Proof Indian Head cents were struck in 1878. Likely, 1,500 or so still survive. Some have been cleaned or tampered with, most pristine pieces have natural medium brown and iridescent toning, and others have mint red color in varying degrees. Some are beautiful to behold, others are not.

In contrast, circulation strikes were placed into commerce and soon became worn. The survival of Mint State coins is a matter of chance—a piece put away in a cast-iron bank in the 1880's, or left in a box of keepsakes, or perhaps picked out of circulation by a coin collector. In proportion to the original mintage figures, only a tiny fraction of 1% of the various issues have survived in Mint State.

As Proofs were made by a different method of manufacture, they can be considered "varieties" different from circulation strikes. Many specialists obtain one Proof and one Mint State coin for a given date. Generally, high-grade Proofs are apt to have more problems than are high-grade circulation strikes, simply because numismatists who owned Proofs often cleaned them.

Toned Proof Cents: Environmental factors can lead to a variety of beautiful surface colors.

Grading Flying Eagle Cents

The following grading guidelines are adapted from the *Official American Numismatic Association Grading Standards for United States Coins*, 7th edition.

Mint State (MS)

Coin is Uncirculated and shows absolutely no trace of wear.

1857. Graded MS-64.

MS-70. A flawless coin exactly as it was minted, with no trace of wear or injury. Must have full mint luster and natural color.

MS-67. Virtually flawless, but with very minor imperfections.

MS-65. No trace of wear; nearly as perfect as MS-67 except for some small blemish. Has full mint luster but may be unevenly toned or lightly fingermarked. A few minor nicks or marks may be present.

MS-63. A Mint State coin with attractive mint luster, but noticeable detracting contact marks or minor blemishes.

MS-60. A strictly Uncirculated coin with no trace of wear, but with blemishes more obvious than in higher grades. May have dull mint luster; color may be uneven shades.

About Uncirculated (AU)

Coin shows small traces of wear on the highest points.

1857. Graded AU-55.

AU-58 (Very Choice). Has some signs of abrasion: feathers on eagle's breast; wing tips.

AU-55 (Choice). ***Obverse:*** A trace of wear shows on the breast and left wing tip. ***Reverse:*** A trace of wear shows on the bow. ***Surface:*** Considerable mint luster is still present.

AU-50 (Typical). ***Obverse:*** Traces of wear show on the breast, left wing tip, and head. ***Reverse:***Traces of the wear show on the leaves and bow. ***Surface:*** Some of the mint luster is still present.

Extremely Fine (EF)

Coin shows very light wear on only the highest points.

1857. Graded EF-45.

EF-45 (Choice). ***Obverse:*** Wear shows on breast, wing tips, and head. All feathers are plain. ***Reverse:*** High points of the leaves and bow are lightly worn. ***Surface:*** Traces of mint luster still show.

EF-40 (Typical). ***Obverse:*** Feathers in wings and tail are plain. Wear shows on breast, wing tips, head, and thigh. ***Reverse:*** High points of the leaves and bow are worn.

Very Fine (VF)

Coin shows light to moderate even wear. All its major features are sharp.

1857. Graded VF-20.

VF-30 (Choice). ***Obverse:*** Small, flat spots of wear show on breast and thigh. Feathers in wings still show bold details. Head is worn but sharp. ***Reverse:*** Ends of leaves and bow are worn almost smooth.

VF-20 (Typical). ***Obverse:*** Breast shows considerable flatness. Some of the details are visible in feathers of the wings. Head is worn but bold. Thigh is smooth, but feathers in tail are nearly complete. ***Reverse:*** Ends of leaves and bow are worn smooth.

Fine

Coin shows moderate to heavy even wear, but its entire design is clear and bold.

F-12. ***Obverse:*** Some details show at breast, head, and tail. Outlines of feathers in right wing and tail show, with no ends missing. ***Reverse:*** Some details are visible in the wreath. Bow is very smooth.

Very Good (VG)

Coin is well worn Design is clear but flat and lacking in detail.

VG-8. ***Obverse:*** Outline of feathers in right wing ends show, but some are smooth. Legend and date are visible. The eye shows clearly. ***Reverse:*** Slight detail in wreath shows, but the top is worn smooth. Very little outline shows in the bow.

Good

Coin is heavily worn. Design and legend are visible, but faint in spots.

1858. Graded G-4.

G-4. ***Obverse:*** Entire design is well worn, with very little detail remaining. Legend and date are weak but visible. ***Reverse:*** Wreath is worn flat but completely outlined. Bow merges with wreath.

About Good (AG)

Coin's design is only outlined. Parts of date and legend are worn smooth.

AG-3. ***Obverse:*** Eagle is outlined, with all details worn away. Legend and date are readable but very weak and merging into rim. ***Reverse:*** Entire design is partially worn away. Bow is merged with the wreath.

Proof (PF)

1858, Large Letters.
Graded PF-65.

PF-60 to 70 (Proof). ***Obverse and Reverse:*** Gem PF-65 coins have very few hairlines, and these are visible only under a strong magnifying glass. At the PF-67 level or higher there should be no evidence of hairlines or friction at all. PF-60 coins can be dull from repeated dipping and cleaning (remember, hairlines on any Proof were caused by cleaning with an abrasive agent; they had no hairlines when struck). At PF-63 the mirrorlike fields should be attractive, and hairlines should be minimal, best seen when the coin is held at an angle to the light. No rubbing is seen. PF-64 coins are even nicer.

Grading Indian Head Cents

Mint State (MS)

Coin is Uncirculated and shows absolutely no trace of wear.

1864. Graded MS-63.

MS-70. A flawless coin exactly as it was minted, with no trace of wear or injury. Must have full mint luster and natural color.

MS-67. Virtually flawless, but with very minor imperfections.

MS-65. No trace of wear; nearly as perfect as MS-67 except for some small blemish. Has full mint luster but may be unevenly toned or lightly fingermarked. A few minor nicks or marks may be present.

MS-63. A Mint State coin with attractive mint luster, but noticeable detracting contact marks or minor blemishes.

MS-60. A strictly Uncirculated coin with no trace of wear, but with blemishes more obvious than in higher grades. May have dull mint luster; color may be uneven shades of brown.

About Uncirculated (AU)

Coin shows small traces of wear on the highest points.

AU-58 (Very Choice). Has some signs of abrasion: hair above ear; curl to right of ribbon; bow knot.

AU-55 (Choice). ***Obverse:*** Only a trace of wear shows on the hair above the ear. ***Reverse:*** A trace of wear shows on the bow knot. ***Surface:*** Considerable mint luster is still present.

AU-50 (Typical). ***Obverse:*** Traces of wear show on the hair above ear, and curl to right of ribbon. ***Reverse:*** Traces of wear show on the leaves and bow knot. ***Surface:*** Significant mint luster is still present.

Extremely Fine (EF)

Coin shows very light wear on only the highest points.

1861. Graded EF-45.

EF-45 (Choice). ***Obverse:*** Wear shows on hair above ear and curl to right of ribbon, and on ribbon end. The diamond design and letters in LIBERTY are very plain. ***Reverse:*** High points of the leaves and bow are lightly worn. ***Surface:*** Traces of mint luster still show.

EF-40 (Typical). ***Obverse:*** Feathers are well defined and LIBERTY is bold. Wear shows on hair above ear, curl to right of ribbon, and ribbon end. Most of the diamond design shows plainly. ***Reverse:*** High points of the leaves and bow are worn.

Very Fine (VF)

Coin shows light to moderate even wear. All its major features are sharp.

VF-30 (Choice). ***Obverse:*** Small, flat spots of wear on tips of feathers, ribbon, and hair ends. Hair still shows half of details. LIBERTY is slightly worn and letters are generally sharp. ***Reverse:*** Leaves and bow are worn but fully detailed.

VF-20 (Typical). ***Obverse:*** Headdress shows considerable flatness. Nearly half of the details still show in hair and on ribbon. Head is slightly worn but bold. ***Reverse:*** Leaves and bow are almost fully detailed.

Fine

Coin shows moderate to heavy even wear, but its entire design is clear and bold.

F-12. ***Obverse:*** Some details show in the hair and feathers. Ribbon is worn smooth. LIBERTY normally shows with no letters missing. ***Reverse:*** Some details are visible in the wreath and bow. Tops of leaves are worn smooth.

Very Good (VG)

Coin is well worn Design is clear but flat and lacking in detail.

VG-8. ***Obverse:*** Outline of feathers show but some are smooth. Legend and date are visible. Some letters in LIBERTY show; any combination of two full letters and parts of others is sufficient. ***Reverse:*** Slight detail in wreath shows, but the top is worn smooth. Very little outline shows in the bow. Rim is complete.

Good

Coin is heavily worn. Design and legend are visible, but faint in spots.

1894. Graded G-4.

G-4. ***Obverse:*** Entire design is well worn with very little detail remaining. Legend and date are weak but visible. ***Reverse:*** Wreath is worn flat but completely outlined. Bow merges with wreath. Rim is incomplete in spots.

About Good (AG)

Coin's design is only outlined. Parts of date and legend are worn smooth.

AG-3. ***Obverse:*** Head is outlined, with nearly all details worn away. Legend and date are readable but very weak and merging into rim. ***Reverse:*** Entire design is partially worn away. Bow is merged with the wreath.

Proof (PF)

1868. Graded PF-64RB.

PF-60 to 70 (Proof). ***Obverse and Reverse:*** Gem PF-65 coins will have very few hairlines, and these are visible only under a strong magnifying glass. At any level and color, a Proof with hairlines likely (though not necessarily) has been cleaned. At PF-67 or higher there should be no evidence of hairlines or friction at all. Such a coin is fully original. PF-60 coins can be dull from repeated dipping and cleaning and are often toned iridescent colors. At PF-63 the mirrorlike fields should be attractive, and hairlines should be minimal. These are easiest to see when the coin is held at an angle to the light. No rubbing is seen. PF-64 coins are even nicer.

Seeking High-Quality Flying Eagle and Indian Head Cents

With a firm understanding of grading we go on to some other aspects of Flying Eagle and Indian Head cents, mainly those of the surface appearance. These and other considerations are, of course, all interrelated so far as market value and desirability are concerned.

For the best use of your money, determine to be a connoisseur. Along the way it is important to know what *not* to buy as well as what you should acquire. Thomas Edison is said to have made 500 non-working light bulbs before *the* light bulb was invented in 1879. If you consider 20 coins before buying *the* coin, you have accomplished much.

Cleaning

Immersing a brown-toned Indian Head cent in silver dip or another cleaner will make it "brilliant," perhaps a bright orange somewhat similar to what it looked like when first minted, but to the expert's eye, ever so slightly paler and not quite the "right" hue. Cleaning a bronze coin strips the surface of its toning and makes chemically active copper metal even more susceptible to atmospheric effects. Most dipped pieces soon become blotchy or unevenly colored. Most mottled and stained Proof bronze cents in certified holders marked "BN" or "RB" have probably been cleaned. Some blotchy "RD" coins may represent recently dipped pieces that have been certified, but which changed color within the holders.

As a connoisseur you must avoid blotchy coins. Most advanced specialists would agree that a run of nicely matched, brown-toned AU-55 cents is much more desirable than a far costlier collection of blotchy MS-63RB pieces. *Quality* is the key word that you as a connoisseur should always keep in mind. *Quality* first, *price* second.

The "secret" to success in buying is simply to avoid coins that are stained and ugly, even if the price is a bargain. Let someone else buy them. The popular coin publications are filled with all sorts of claims and offers, and all too often that bargain "gem brilliant Uncirculated" or "selected brilliant Uncirculated" proves to be a scrubbed-up About Uncirculated coin. Or, that certified PF-64RB cent may indeed be PF-64, but so spotted that it is ugly as sin, and will be something you'll always regret buying, no matter how much of a "bargain" it is.

Bill Fivaz has commented: "Don't buy a problem. It will always be a problem. It doesn't get any better, and it could get worse!"[33]

Similarly, Richard Snow has remarked, "There is no price *too low* for a problem coin."[34]

"Good" Cleaning

And yet, some cleaning and techniques can improve a coin's surface. A bright unnatural orange coin that has been dipped will retone a nice brown if it is exposed to the atmosphere, such as on a windowsill under a little wire basket to prevent it from slipping away. Or, a mixture of sulfur powder and mineral oil applied with a cotton swab may do the trick. This is not a suggestion for you, but merely an indication of what can be done to bring back the latent beauty of a cent that has been made ugly. Dr. Sheldon in *Early American Cents* gives some good advice.

A *copper-nickel* cent that is stained or blotched, if it is in a higher grade, may sometimes be dipped with good effect. However, repeated dipping will yield only a dull, unattractive surface, a coin with no "life."

Dipping a *bronze* Indian Head cent usually lessens its value from the outset.

Brushing a circulated bronze coin with a camel's hair brush may remove dust and impart a glossy surface. Again, consult Dr. Sheldon on this one.

Acetone (a volatile solvent available at drug and hardware stores, and which must be carefully used) or plain old soap and water can be used effectively to remove dirt and verdigris from the surface of an Indian Head cent.

In all in instances, do your experimenting with a common, cheap bronze Lincoln cent, not a numismatically valuable older coin.

A Bit of Philosophy

If you are knowledgeable about the problems and pitfalls, you will buy coins more effectively, and the pleasures of making a good buy will be more exciting, more real. If you buy that MS-65RD Indian Head cent and know full well what the grading game is about, then you are home free. If you have looked at 16 coins and have passed them by, and finally have found Coin No. 17, the sparkling gem you've been hoping for, you will be happy and satisfied. You'll really appreciate what you have, just as Edison realized the importance of Light Bulb No. 501.

On the other hand, if you buy a coin described as MS-65RD, but are not sure whether the price is right or what the coin should look like or whether quality is important, but are relying simply upon someone else's sales pitch or the inducement of a low price, the day of reckoning awaits you.

There are pleasures in collecting Flying Eagle and Indian Head cents, and these pleasures are *delicious* once you have some knowledge. There is an Unclouded Sky in numismatics if you are a connoisseur. Become a connoisseur, a smart buyer, and you'll have a really great time.

Four Steps to Success

An important aspect for you to know, but not at all treated in the wide marketplace, is that for any Proof Flying Eagle or Indian Head cent to be other than gem grade, say PF-65 or better, it has been subject to some handling. If it has *hairlines,* this is because the coin has been *cleaned.* However, the grading services are inconsistent as to how they handle this. Generally, an Indian Head cent with hairlines, for example, will be graded less than PF-65, and assigned some grade such as PF-62 or PF-63. If the cleaning is severe, it might be called PF-60. A correct listing would be as follows: "PF-62 due to hairlines from cleaning." Some services will return a coin ungraded if it has been *severely* cleaned; others may put a "net grade" on it. There is little consistency in this regard. The problem is not as acute with circulation strikes, as the mint luster will often mask hairlines.

Any Flying Eagle or Indian Head cent, if as brilliant as when first minted, with a bright edge, is a coin that has been dipped (immersed in a liquid silver cleaner or chemical metal brightener). Any such coin, if held by the most careful of numismatists and their successors, that has come down to the present day will *always* show some light toning. This is reflected by examining coins held in old-time collections, such as the T. Harrison Garrett and James M. Clapp collections assembled in the 19th century.

Then there is the matter of sharpness of strike. Some cents are flat in areas, while others have the needle sharpness denoted as *Full Details* (FD), with every feature defined. Flying Eagle cents often have some lightness on the eagle's head and tail feathers, less often on the reverse wreath. Indian Head cents often have indistinct detail at the tips of the headdress feathers, this being particularly true of the copper-nickel issues from 1859 to 1864. Certified holders say *nothing* about strike—weak, average, or with Full Details. It is up to *you* to determine this! Tracking down these features can be a pleasant endeavor.

You can see that grading-service nomenclature such as MS-63 and PF-67 doesn't tell you much if you really want to be a connoisseur. Instead, you need to apply your own expertise and thinking.

Some time ago, for Whitman, I devised the following four-step process for successful collecting. It has caught on with a number of readers who have applied it to their own fields of interest. Adapted for the present text, here it is:

Step 1: Observe the Numerical Grade

You are holding a coin in your hand. Should you buy it? Your first step is to look at the assigned grade of the coin, or, if you are familiar with grading, to assign your own number. Experienced collectors and dealers will often share their opinions with you. Without being an annoyance, see if you can "ask around" for help.

If you are just entering numismatics, you would do well to only consider coins that have been certified by the four leading grading services—ANACS, ICG, NGC, and PCGS. All but ICG publish population reports delineating the coins that have passed through their hands. Retail price information for many commercially graded coins can be found in many places, in particular *The Certified Coin Dealer Newsletter*. However, the *Newsletter* states that prices listed there are only for average-quality coins.

The grade listed on a certified coin holder, or noted by a dealer on a cardboard or other holder, is simply the *starting point* in the buying process. This is one of the most important concepts for success.

When you visit a coin shop or a convention, or contemplate a catalog or Internet offering, have an approximate grade in mind for each coin you are seeking. If you are looking for a rare 1877 Indian Head cent, and have $1,000 to spend, there is not much sense asking to see MS-65 or other high-grade coins. Nor is there any reason to waste your time looking at well-worn pieces in G-4 grade. These are the market prices from the listings given later in this book:

1877 cent: G-4: $625 • VG-8: $800 • F-12: $1,200 • EF-40: $2,200 • AU-50: $2,600 • MS-60: $3,400 • MS-63: $4,000

At a coin show, or when sending a "want list" to a dealer, ask to see coins in the range of VG-8 to F-12 as these are more or less in the price range you want to pay.

No matter what grades you ask for, reject any coins that seem to be overgraded. This comment is made with the realization that you will need some experience, for lacking this, you will not know accurate grading from inaccurate. The best way to gain experience is to visit a coin show or a coin shop and look through as many Flying Eagle and Indian Head cents as you can. This might range from a few Flying Eagle cents to dozens or even hundreds of Indian Head cents. Stocks of Proofs are apt to be smaller. Today the Internet offers some at-home opportunities. While the grade may be hard to figure out from a low-resolution Internet image, and coins can be turned in the light and photographed to make them look more attractive than they really are, other aspects such as sharpness can be discerned.

Read the *Official ANA Grading Standards for United States Coins.* Spend time looking at cents, preferably in person, perhaps with this book in your hand. If you do this at a show or in a shop, it is good form to advise the dealer what you are doing—seeking education—and to make a courtesy purchase of a coin or a book or two. In less time than you realize, you will learn the fundamentals of grading.

Step 2: Determine First-Glance Eye Appeal

Now, the process becomes easier! At this point take a quick glance at the coin. Is it "pretty"? Is the toning (if present) attractive, or is it dark or blotchy? Is the coin stained? If it is brilliant, is it attractively lustrous, or is it dull and lifeless? Are there black spots here and there on the surface? Here the Internet can offer many opportunities for education. When buying from a dealer or on an Internet listing, insist on a return privilege if *for any reason* you do not like the coin. If the vendor does not want to offer this privilege, find another seller.

If the coin is not attractive, then reject it and go on to look at another. Even if the price seems to be a super-bargain, cast the coin aside. Stop right here, and go back to Step 1 with another coin. An ugly coin graded as MS-65RD or PF-63RB is still ugly, and would not be bought by a connoisseur for *half* of the current market price! Do not be tempted by overgraded and/or ugly coins offered at "below wholesale" prices. Keep your wallet in your pocket. The good news is that attractive Flying Eagle and Indian Head cents do exist, and in fair numbers. However, they need some scouting to find.

If the coin is attractive to your eye, then in some distant future year when time comes to sell it, the piece will be attractive to the eyes of other buyers—an important consideration. Now, with an attractive coin in hand, you have a candidate *for your further consideration.*

Step 3: Evaluate Sharpness and Related Features

At this point you have a coin that you believe to be more or less in the numerical grade assigned on the ANACS, ICG, NGC, or PCGS holder, or in a dealer's holder of another type, or, if you are in the fast lane, determined by your own experience. You also have for consideration one that has passed your test for excellent eye appeal.

The next step is to take out a magnifying glass and evaluate the coin's sharpness. Here, one rule does not fit all, but general guidelines apply. For a Flying Eagle cent, check the head and tail of the eagle. If those features are needle-sharp (with Full

Details), then look at the rest of the coin. For an Indian Head cent, the tips of the headdress feathers are the first place to look, after which you need to check the rest of the coin. Full Details coins are much more plentiful in the Flying Eagle and Indian Head cent series than, for example, among Indian Head / Buffalo nickels, Standing Liberty quarters, or Liberty Walking half dollars.

To determine sharpness, you must examine the coin! There is *no* alternative unless you enlist a trustworthy dealer or friend to do this for you, and share your guidelines.

Also check for surface quality. Is the luster satiny or frosty, with full sheen—or is the coin struck from overused dies showing metal flow and granularity? Again, certified holders reveal nothing about this. Is the planchet of good quality, or is it rough? Generally, Proofs are more sharply struck and present fewer difficulties than do circulation strikes.

If the coin you are considering buying has passed the preceding tests, it is ready *for further consideration.* Chances are good that you are holding a very nice coin in your hand!

Step No. 4: Establish a Fair Market Price

If you've done everything right, you have a Flying Eagle or Indian Head cent that is correctly graded, of superb eye appeal, and sharply struck (a realistic goal for all basic dates in the series). Now, to the price you should pay.

For starters, use one or several handy market guides for a ballpark estimate. Unlike many other specialties, nearly all issues in the Flying Eagle and Indian Head cent series are actively traded, and there is no lack of information. This book includes market values for every coin, in several grades.

Now comes the fun part: If the coin is common enough in a given grade, with sharp strike, with fine planchet quality, and with good eye appeal, then the market price is very relevant, as you can shop around. If a coin is common in the grade you want, and with all other desired features, and you have ascertained that the market price level is about $700, then there is no sense paying $800 or $950. Wait until you find one at or near $700. On the other hand, chances are good that you will not find a problem-free coin for, say, $500 or $600. If something is offered to you for *below wholesale,* this simply means that any dealer wanting to buy a choice coin will not buy *this* one—and, accordingly, it is available for less!

You are *very lucky* in that for Flying Eagle and Indian Head cents, hardly anyone looks at sharpness and overall quality. Ninety or more out of every hundred buyers consider only the certified grade. This is amazing, but true. You are also lucky that each and every issue does exist with Full Details. Bide your time until you find them. When you do, the market premium will be modest or even non-existent over a typical coin of lower quality.

2

Flying Eagle Cents (1856–1858): Analysis by Date and Mint

Designer: *James B. Longacre.* **Weight:** *4.67 grams.* **Composition:** *.880 copper, .120 nickel.* **Diameter:** *19 mm.* **Edge:** *Plain.* **Mint:** *Philadelphia.*

1856

Circulation-Strike Mintage:
800 (estimated)

Proof Mintage:
1,500 (estimated)

1856 Cent Production: The 1856 Flying Eagle cent was first produced in late 1856 and early 1857 as a pattern coin, to persuade Congress to drastically change the cent coinage from the large copper pieces then in circulation to a small copper-nickel coin. As this was the first use of this metal for the United States' coinage, trials were needed to both test the striking qualities of the alloy and demonstrate the utility of the new coin to the congressmen who were then writing what would become the Mint Act of February 21, 1857.

The original production was minted in both Proof and circulation strikes, with the vast majority being circulation strikes. U.S. Mint correspondence shows that at least 634 pieces were officially distributed to President Franklin Pierce, Treasury Secretary James Guthrie, and members of Congress. Initially, Pierce was presented with four examples and Guthrie was given four, with two more placed in the Mint Cabinet. It is unknown if these were a special striking in Proof format.

It is to be assumed that a simulated press run at normal speed was conducted to test the new alloy, size, and design. In late 1856 a relatively large run of circulation-strike coins was produced. Early the next year Secretary Guthrie received 200 of this test run and 100 more were sent to the chairman of the Ways and Means Committee, Representative Lewis Davis Campbell. Over the next few weeks, members of the Senate received 62 pieces and at least 264 were sent to the House of Representatives. Undoubtedly, Director James Ross Snowden held extra pieces at the Mint for personal distribution to employees. As far as anyone at the Mint was concerned, this initial production of the 1856 Flying Eagle cent was purely a pattern striking, meant for official purposes. However, the changeover to the copper-nickel small cent would create many new coin collectors, many attempting to assemble complete date sets of the now discontinued large cents.

When the new 1857-dated copper-nickel cents flooded into circulation on May 25, 1857, rumors about the rare 1856-dated copper-nickel cents prompted people to look through their change for the coin. The prices of extant examples skyrocketed. Soon it was trading for 200 times its face value—in an era when $2 was a workingman's daily wages. The first coin-collecting boom in this country had begun.

This new interest in collecting was not lost on the officials at the Mint. Director Snowden was writing a manual on Washington tokens and medals, soon to become a popular collecting subject. He was interested in acquiring any pieces not presently in the Mint's holdings. To augment this collection, he struck additional 1856 copper-nickel cents and began to sell them to collectors in 1859. Almost all of these additional pieces were struck in Proof, a format desired by collectors at the time.

It is unknown what price the Mint charged for these newly struck pieces, but auction records show a drop in prices for 1856 copper-nickel cents, down to 25 cents. Perhaps since the rarity of the 1856 copper-nickel cent was not firmly established, buyers were unwilling to stretch on purchasing the coins.

It is possible that the additional 1856 copper-nickel cents were first made in a single large batch in 1859, but we have no way of knowing when they were last struck. We can surmise that not all were immediately distributed, as the Mint's surplus of 1856 cents kept the price below $2 well into the 1870's. No records were kept regarding the mintage of these pieces.

Survivability: The original 1856 Flying Eagle cents were distributed to members of Congress. Mint employees also kept some of this issue. The James B. Longacre estate had 11 pieces. When the estate was auctioned in 1870, these coins brought $1 each. As these were popular trading items for coin dealers, they were kept mostly in decent shape over the years. Non-collector owners, such as congressmen, probably spent the circulated examples that are encountered today. Today the average grade of the original striking period is About Uncirculated, with high grades of Mint State being very scarce. Coins grading below Very Fine are also very difficult to find, since few circulated for very long periods.

The restrikes from 1858 to 1860 likewise went into collections where they were cared for by their owners. However, quite a number of worn examples are found today. These pieces probably entered circulation during the Civil War, when the Mint was desperate to supply the nation with cents. I imagine the unsold examples could have inadvertently been mixed with a regular shipment of cents. Very worn examples are occasionally seen and must have stayed in circulation well into the 1870's.

Collecting Challenges: All 1856 dies seem to have been prepared carefully with a Proof finish. Examples of what we call Mint State today usually have semi-prooflike fields, but evidence of normal striking conditions, such as weak strikes and strike doubling. The challenge for today's collectors is in determining which coins are Proof and which are Mint State. By comparing the striking quality of known die pairs in the order of their use it is known that the majority, if not all, of the coins distributed to Congress were from what is called the Snow-3 die pair.

The biggest challenge facing collectors is being able to afford an 1856 Flying Eagle cent. Presently, even coins worn down to Good will cost $6,000 or so. Many collectors desire the Mint State version more than the Proof because they were minted during the original striking period. Prices over the years have escalated for Mint Sate pieces due to this extra demand. Collectors must decide if a PF-65 would be a better buy than an MS-63.

Prospective purchasers should study the series before purchasing any 1856 Flying Eagle cent offered. My *Flying Eagle and Indian Cent Attribution Guide, Vol. 1*, 3rd edition (2014), details the various striking periods and their formats in great detail. In general, the die pairs known as Snow-3 are mostly Mint State coins from the original striking period and are easily distinguished by the repunching on the 5 in the date. The majority of the Proofs are from the die pair known as Snow-9. These have a centering dot on the reverse under the upper-left serif of the N in CENT. There are other die pairs, but these are rare, and of interest only to the specialist.

1856, Repunched 5, Snow-3 **1856, Reverse Center Dot, Snow-9**

Over the years, grading services have had difficulty with correct attributions on the format of 1856 Flying Eagle cents. Not until the release of the Snow attribution guide in 2000 were the details of the striking formats clearly presented. Since then, ANACS has attributed each format accordingly. In the 13 years prior to the release of the book PCGS and NGC graded many Mint State pieces as Proof and many Proofs as Mint State. This problem confused collectors and created problems for these grading companies, rendering population reports useless. Presently, they have both decided to grade all 1856 Flying Eagle cents with a PR designation. Today this is a hotly debated topic among collectors.

Collecting Circulated Pieces: The optimal collecting grade for circulated coins is EF-40. Clearly, this is the most expensive coin in the collection of Flying Eagle and Indian Head cents. Many collectors ponder the need to include this coin, as it technically is a pattern and was not officially released for circulation. However, the great historical importance of this coin has caught the fancy of enough collectors to warrant a significant premium. There will be a slight premium for the Snow-3 die pair over the Snow-9, but not as much as is seen for high-grade specimens. After a brief time in circulation it is not possible to determine whether a coin started out as a Proof or a circulation strike, so collectors are less inclined to pay great premiums for the Snow-3 in these grades.

The best criterion for choosing a circulated 1856 Flying Eagle cent is the eye appeal of the coin. You should select one with few problems and no evidence of cleaning.

Collecting Mint State Pieces: The optimal collecting grade for Mint State coins is MS-63. These are usually from the Snow-3 die pair. Because they have been shown to be from the original striking period (distributed to congressmen), they are under very high demand. They were made in smaller numbers than the Proof issues.

It is important to find an example with a good strike. Many of these Mint State coins show strike weakness on the eagle's head and tail. The surfaces are usually satiny with the fields slightly prooflike. Weakness on the eagle's breast feathers is normally evident and should not be a concern.

Values for the Snow-3 die pair have risen dramatically over the past decade. A record price of $172,500 was set for a PCGS MS-66 Snow-3 at the 2004 Florida United Numismatists show sale by Heritage Rare Coin Galleries. This is the finest Snow-3 graded Mint State by PCGS. To show the dramatic price rise, consider that this same coin sold a year earlier, at the 2003 FUN show sale, for $103,500. In 1997 my firm, Eagle Eye Rare Coins, had sold this coin for $45,000.

Collecting Proof Issues: The best value for the money is probably a PF-63 or PF-64, which are presently in the $20,000 to $24,000 range. Quality for the grade is a key issue when selecting a coin to add to your collection. An attractive high end for the grade PF-63 is a much better coin to purchase than a low-end PF-64. The majority of Proofs are from the Snow-9 die pair described above. These will have very sharp details on the design elements, and squared rims. The surfaces will not be deeply mirrored like other Proofs from this period, but on unimpaired examples there should be some reflectivity. The mintage of the Proofs is estimated to be no fewer than 1,500 pieces. This is a very large quantity of Proofs to be struck during this era, especially since they are all struck from one die pair. The Proof mintage of any other coin up to this time was no more than 500 pieces. This high level of production took its toll on the quality of the Flying Eagle cent Proofs. Later-die-state coins show die cracks and evidence of repeated polishing of the dies. This quality issue has added confusion to the Proof status of these coins.

1856: Circulation Strike

GSID	VG-8	F-12	VF-20	EF-40	AU-50	AU-58	MS-60	MS-63
15310	$8,750	$10,000	$11,000	$12,000	$13,500	$15,000	$19,000	$29,000

1856: Proof Strike

GSID	PF-60	PF-63	PF-65
15311	$16,500	$19,000	$33,500

Varieties

Presently ten die pairings have been described and listed with Snow numbers. These are enumerated in *The Flying Eagle and Indian Cent Attribution Guide, Volume 1 (1856–1858)*. Adventurous collectors have targeted the Snow-1, "Tilted ONE CENT" and Snow-4 "Low Leaves Reverse" as interesting (and rare) varieties. Some collectors have attempted to acquire complete die-pair sets. Although no one has yet accomplished this feat, one collector (Dr. Thomas Fore) has come close.

1857

Circulation-Strike Mintage:
17,450,000

Proof Mintage:
485 (traditional estimate; possibly as low as 50)

1857 Cent Production: Soon after the Mint Act of February 21, 1857 was enacted, production began on the regular-issue 1857 Flying Eagle cent. By May 25, the official release date, the excitement of the populace overwhelmed the U.S. Mint. Two special outdoor booths were set up in the Mint yard to accommodate the massive demand. In addition to the novelty of the new coin, the rush to get the new cent was augmented by the mandate that they be exchanged for the old copper cents and half cents, which were to be slowly removed from circulation. The cents were mostly paid out in bags of 500 pieces.

Up until 1860, certain foreign silver coinage, mostly Spanish coins minted in Mexico, was legal currency in this country. The new Mint Act called for the removal of these coins in exchange for the new cents or federal silver coinage. Most people chose to exchange for silver, even at a discount.

The shape of the lettering on these new dies was slightly altered, most noticeably on the O in OF, which is oval shaped. Some of the undated dies from 1856, which had a somewhat squared O in OF, were dated 1857 and used for this production. This creates two minor types of 1857 Flying Eagle cents: Type of 1856 and Type of 1857. The Type of 1857 is far more common and is usually not considered a variety.

1857, Type of 1856

1857, Type of 1857

Survivability: This issue was initially heavily saved because of its novelty. One of the effects of the redemption for old coppers is that many people may have obtained large quantities at one time. It was difficult to spend cents for anything but small purchases, so enterprising individuals would bundle the coins up into 25¢, 50¢, and $1 bags. Lack of wear from personal contact may have contributed to their survivability. Within six years they were withdrawn from circulation, along with all the other hard currency, during the Civil War. After 1863 they came back into circulation and stayed there in quantity until the redemption program of the 1870's. After 1880, they began to be curiosities in circulation.

The coins remaining today are in either very low grade (below Fine) or Mint State. Problem-free Extremely Fine and About Uncirculated coins are very difficult to locate.

Collecting Challenges: These coins are available readily enough that collectors should be patient to find attractive examples with good strikes and few problems. The Type of 1856 design is of fairly minor importance and was not well known until the 1980's. As such it is not included in any of the popular albums made for circulated coins, or in Whitman's *Guide Book of United States Coins* (the *Red Book*). Even so, some specialists desire to acquire an example.

Collecting Circulated Pieces: The optimal collecting grade for circulated coins is EF-40. Examples in Good to Fine are very plentiful. The higher-grade examples are fairly expensive, but the price is based on demand for a popular coin, so they tend to be easily resold at a price close to retail. On the other hand, low-grade examples are plentiful enough that their resale value is much lower than their retail price.

Collecting Mint State Pieces: The optimal collecting grade for Mint State coins is MS-64. Examples in this grade are very popular and in high demand. They are also widely available, so it is important to search out quality pieces. Because of price resistance, examples in MS-63 and lower are in demand if they are attractive. MS-64 examples offer the best value for the money spent. Prices for MS-65 are much higher than for MS-64 because of the demand for "gem" sets against a small supply of available pieces. Beware of lower-quality MS-65 coins that may in fact be no better than the nicer MS-64 examples available. A patient collector will be rewarded with a beautiful example of this popular design.

Collecting Proof Issues: Proof examples are very well struck and have very deep mirror fields. These are some of the most beautiful Flying Eagle cents made. All Proof 1857 cents come from the Type of 1857 dies. A few prooflike examples of the Type of 1856 design are known, and can be confused as Proofs. Some have even been mistakenly certified as Proofs.

The Proofs are much rarer than the published mintage suggests. The *Red Book* lists an estimated mintage of 485 pieces; however, nowhere near those numbers are known today. Perhaps no more than 50 were struck. Unimpaired specimens in PF-63 or higher are easily five-figure coins. Needless to say, this is one of the toughest dates in the series.

1857: Circulation Strike

GSID	VG-8	F-12	VF-20	EF-40	AU-50	AU-58	MS-60	MS-63
15313	$27	$40	$55	$90	$180	$350	$675	$1,250

1857: Proof Strike

GSID	PF-60	PF-63	PF-65
15314	$4,750	$6,250	$31,000

Varieties

This is one of the more popular dates with variety collectors. Two design types, Type of 1856 and Type of 1857, are available to collectors should they desire to acquire them.

The top varieties for this date are the multi-denominational clashed dies: Snow-7, Snow-8, and Snow-9. These have imprints on the die, called *clash marks*, which are caused not by the opposing die, but by a totally different denomination! Snow-7 has obverse clash marks from the obverse of a $20 gold piece! Snow-8 shows reverse clash marks from the reverse of a Liberty Seated quarter dollar. Snow-9 shows clash marks from the obverse of a Liberty Seated half dollar. These three varieties are widely collected as a set.

There are no fewer than 11 known doubled dies, some of which, like the Snow-3, Snow-4, and Snow-15, are quite dramatic. There are a few repunched dates known as well, including one on the Type of 1856 design. One interesting variety, S-16, shows the base of all four digits punched into the eagle's neck feathers, twice!

1857 Multi-Denominational Clashed Dies: Snow-7, -8, -9

These three varieties, clashed dies from denominations totally unrelated to the cent, are some of the most interesting among all United States coinage! In general, clashed dies are not rare, nor are they very interesting or collectable to most collectors. However, these clash marks are produced from dies other than the Flying Eagle cent and as such have great appeal with collectors.

Clashed dies are produced when dies impact each other. A reversed impression of each die is left on the opposing die. All coins later struck from these dies will show the marks as a slightly raised shelf. This may happen during the setup of the dies in the press. If the dies are initially set too close, the dies will clash during the startup of the press. This is commonly seen in the Indian Head Cent series. On the obverse the clashes are usually in the form of a jagged gear-shaped shelf by the forehead of Lady Liberty. This is from the impression of the inside of the wreath from the reverse die. The reverse will likewise show the clash impression from the forehead and nose inside the wreath, by the O in ONE. Collectors take these typical clash marks as normal artifacts of coin production and place little added interest in them. The clash marks described here, however, are much different.

The study of these coins has been ongoing by many specialists since they were first identified. In 1977 an 1857 quarter dollar with strange clash marks on its reverse was sent to Tom DeLorey, editor of *Coin World's Collector's Clearinghouse*, for identification by Jesse Perrotta. The coin was correctly identified as having clash marks from the reverse die of a Flying Eagle cent. At the same time, purely by chance, Bill Fivaz sent DeLorey another 1857 clashed die coin. This time it was a Flying Eagle cent with a clash on its obverse from a half dollar (Snow-9). DeLorey's findings were subsequently published in *Coin World* under the title "Was Mischief Afoot in 1857 Die Clashes?" The strange clash marks were ascribed to the possibility that someone at the Mint was making mismatched coins with various denominations. Today we call these types of coins *mules*. They have been surreptitiously produced in the past, most recently in 2000 with the Sacagawea dollar / Washington quarter coins.

Nearly a decade later, Bill Fivaz, who owned a clashed quarter and the Snow-9 half dollar clash, was told of a Flying Eagle cent with clash marks on its reverse from the reverse of a half dollar! After buying that coin and studying it, he discovered that it was not clashed with a half dollar, but with a quarter! It was the missing link to the quarter clashed with the cent in his collection. Today this variety is classified as Snow-8.

The last one of the known 1857 clashed dies to be discovered was the Snow-7 $20 clashed obverse. Bill Fivaz also brought this one to light, but he did not claim to be the discoverer. David McCann later was identified as the initial finder.

One theory, of a surreptitious "Midnight Minter," has undergone some rethinking as these coins and their manufacture have been studied further. An alternate theory has emerged, due mainly to research by Chris Pilliod, whose article "What Error Coins Can Teach Us About Die Settings" appeared in the April 1996 issue of *The Numismatist*. This article used striking errors to determine if a given die was used in the upper position in the coining press (called a hammer die) or if it was in the bottom position (called an anvil die). Pilliod showed that the Flying Eagle series had its die setting opposite from the 1857 quarter dollar, half dollar, and double eagle dies.

Series	Hammer Die	Anvil Die
Flying Eagle Cent	Reverse	Obverse
Liberty Seated Quarter	Obverse	Reverse
Liberty Seated Half	Obverse	Reverse
Liberty Head Double Eagle	Obverse	Reverse

The significance of this is apparent when it is noticed that the various clashed die varieties show combinations that are predicted by Pilliod's research. All show either obverse/obverse or reverse/reverse combinations. Also consistent with this is the observation that the designs are aligned right side up, rather than rotated 180 degrees as is seen on normal clashed dies. In light of Pilliod's study and the fact that no actual coins exist from these die combinations, Q. David Bowers concluded in his *Buyer's and Enthusiast's Guide to Flying Eagle and Indian Cents* that these clashed dies were not the product of surreptitious behavior at the Mint at all. It was suggested that these were caused by accident during the changing of the dies during normal coinage production. In the course of changing the dies from one denomination to another, the collar would have to be removed as well as the two dies. This would allow the press to actually cycle with two denomination dies. It may have been a common practice to cycle the press once to seat the dies in the press.

The following is the probable scenario of their production, by Bowers.

Producing the Snow-7 Double Eagle Clashed Die

It is 1857, and a coining press has been used recently to strike $20 gold pieces. A $20 obverse die is in the hammer position and a $20 reverse die is in the anvil position. It is desired to strike Flying Eagle one-cent pieces using this press, to fill the great demand for this new coin. The public is starved for them, and there are shortages for a long time after the first release of the new Flying Eagle cents on May 25, 1857.

The $20 reverse die in the anvil position is removed and replaced with a one-cent Flying Eagle obverse die. With the newly fitted one-cent obverse die in place in the anvil, opposite the $20 obverse still in place in the hammer position, the press is run through a cycle, and the $20 obverse die in the hammer position strikes the one-cent obverse die in the anvil position. Clash marks occur on both obverse dies.

The clashed $20 obverse die is removed from the press and put in storage, and a new reverse die for a one-cent piece is put in the hammer die position. Cents are struck, each of which shows the clash mark of a $20 die on its obverse.

1857, Snow-7

Whether $20 pieces were ever struck from the now-damaged obverse $20 die is not known; none have been identified thus far by numismatists.

Producing the Snow-9 Half Dollar Clashed Die

It is 1857, and a coining press has been used recently to strike Liberty Seated fifty-cent pieces. A fifty-cent obverse die is in the hammer position and a fifty-cent reverse die is in the anvil position. It is desired to strike Flying Eagle one-cent pieces using this press, again to fill the demand for this new denomination.

1856, Variety 3 gold dollar

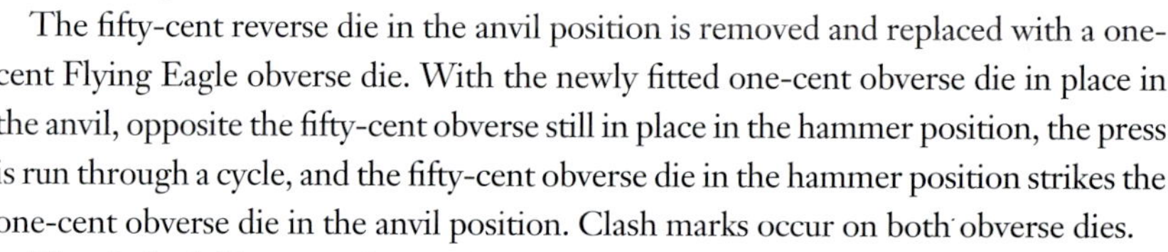

The fifty-cent reverse die in the anvil position is removed and replaced with a one-cent Flying Eagle obverse die. With the newly fitted one-cent obverse die in place in the anvil, opposite the fifty-cent obverse still in place in the hammer position, the press is run through a cycle, and the fifty-cent obverse die in the hammer position strikes the one-cent obverse die in the anvil position. Clash marks occur on both obverse dies.

The clashed fifty-cent obverse die is removed from the press, put in storage, and a new reverse die for a one-cent piece is put in the hammer die position. Cents are struck, each of which shows the clash mark of a fifty-cent die on its obverse.

Whether 1857 half dollars were ever struck from the now-damaged obverse fifty-cent die is not known; none have been identified thus far by numismatists.

1857, Snow-9

1857 Liberty Seated half dollar

Producing the Snow-8 Quarter Dollar Clashed Die

It is later in 1857, and a coining press has been used recently to strike 1857 Flying Eagle cents. Now, either the demand for cents has eased, or the demand for quarter dollars has taken precedence. A one-cent reverse die is in the hammer position and a one-cent Flying Eagle obverse die is in the anvil position. It is desired to strike Liberty Seated quarter dollars using this press.

The one-cent Flying Eagle obverse die in the anvil position is removed and replaced with a quarter dollar reverse die. With the newly-fitted quarter dollar reverse die in place in the anvil, opposite the one-cent reverse still in place in the hammer position, the press is run through a cycle, and the one-cent reverse die in the hammer position strikes the quarter dollar reverse die in the anvil position. Clash marks occur on both reverse dies.

The clashed one-cent reverse die is removed from the press, and put in storage (thus there is the possibility, however remote, that this die could have been used in 1858 in addition to in 1857), and a new obverse die for a quarter dollar is put in the hammer die position. Liberty Seated quarter dollars are struck, each of which shows the clash mark of a one-cent die on its reverse. Later, the clashed one-cent wreath reverse die is combined with a Flying Eagle obverse, and Flying Eagle cents are struck showing quarter dollar clash marks on the reverse; made in the ordinary manner.

Other multi-denominational clashed dies have been found—an 1864 two-cent piece with a reverse clash from the obverse of an Indian Head cent; an 1868 three-cent piece with obverse clash marks from the reverse of an Indian Head cent; and an 1870 Shield nickel with its obverse clashed with the obverse of an Indian Head cent—so this type of variety is not specific to 1857.

1857 quarter

1857 cent

1857, Snow-8, composite

1858 Large Letters

Circulation-Strike Mintage:
12,300,000 (estimated, out of 24,600,000 total)

Proof Mintage:
100 (estimated)

1858, Large Letters, Cent Production: The high output needed to replace 64 years of large copper cent coinage continued unabated in 1858. The Mint was having problems striking up the coins in the hard copper-nickel alloy. The dies tended to deteriorate more quickly than normal. New, shallower-relief dies were made for both the obverse (Small Letters) and the reverse (Low Leaves) to help extend the die life.

Survivability: Although scarcer today than the 1857 cents, these were distributed much more widely and are found more often in lower grades. At the time of the Civil War coinage shortage (from the summer of 1862 to early 1863), these were largely removed from circulation, only to reappear after the war. Any high-grade examples were probably held back from circulation at this time. By the time of the coinage redemption of the 1870's most were called in and melted. The remaining pieces are either very worn or in very high grade. Problem-free EF and AU coins are very scarce.

Collecting Challenges: These are a bit scarcer than the 1857 issue, mainly because collectors have divided the issue between the two obverse design types. The optimal collecting grade for this date is MS-64. Coins in this grade are plentiful enough that quality pieces should be sought out.

Few collectors are aware of the reverse design changes made this year to help improve the die life. The type carried over from 1857 is a high-relief design, called *High Leaves* because the inner leaves are closer to the base of the C and T in CENT. The new lower-relief design, used this year only, is called *Low Leaves*. (See illustrations on next page.) Both can be found paired with the Large Letters obverse. Coin albums, which have changed little since the 1960's, do not carry holes for these reverse types mentioned in the *Red Book*. Collector interest in reverse designs may shift the current lack of demand. If awareness increases, then specialists will need two examples of the 1858 Large Letters cent instead of just one.

Collecting Circulated Pieces: The optimal collecting grade for circulated coins is EF-40. Examples in low grades are plentiful and do not offer the best value because of a low resale percentage. These may be difficult to find problem free, so a bit of patience is advised. Adventurous collectors may try and acquire both reverse types as well.

Collecting Mint State Pieces: The optimal collecting grade for Mint State coins is MS-64. These are generally more readily available than lower grades as the cheaper pieces are bought up quickly. MS-65 gems are very tough to locate. Some examples come with prooflike fields and are worth a premium.

High Leaves Reverse (Type of 1857).

Low Leaves Reverse (Type of 1858).

Collecting Proof Issues: The estimated mintage of 80 reported in the *Red Book* is a low estimate based on year sets sold that year. The actual mintage is probably 100 or more, as a few extra pieces, probably numbering only 20, were struck for some pattern sets made this year.

The Proofs of this year are usually exceptional with deep mirror fields and outstanding strikes. The 1858 Large Letters Proofs are paired only with the High Leaves reverse.

1858, Large Letters: Circulation Strike

GSID	VG-8	F-12	VF-20	EF-40	AU-50	AU-58	MS-60	MS-63
15315	$27	$40	$55	$90	$180	$350	$675	$1,250

1858, Large Letters: Proof Strike

GSID	PF-60	PF-63	PF-65
15317	$4,750	$6,250	$17,000

Varieties

The major variety of this year is the 1858, 8 Over 7, which is so popular it is given a separate listing in this guide. There is another lesser-known 1858, 8 Over 7, overdate (Snow-7), which is also a doubled die. There are six other obverse doubled dies known, most of which are available for a moderate premium, if found.

Some of the Low Leaf reverse dies are found with minor doubling as well. Two repunched dates are known, one of which (Snow-4) is very wide, and is also a doubled die!

Collectors might not be aware that prior to 1909 all dates were added to coinage dies separately from the rest of the design elements. This is why doubled dies affect the design and letters but not the date, while repunched dates affect only the date.

1858, Small Letters

Circulation-Strike Mintage:
12,300,000 (estimated, out of 24,600,000 total)

Proof Mintage:
200 (estimated)

1858, Small Letters, Cent Production: The Small Letters design was an attempt to lower the relief of the Flying Eagle design. It is believed that Assistant Engraver Anthony C. Paquet supplied the letter punches for this variety. The obvious difference is the smaller letters, which are similar to a font used on some medals ascribed to Paquet's hand. Whitman's *Red Book* describes the difference as having the AM in AMERICA separated, which is a very easy way to describe the differences. The eagle was also modified slightly, although most collectors key in on the lettering style. As this was also the last year of the Flying Eagle motif, the Small Letters can be considered a one-year design change.

Large Letters

Small Letters

There is no record as to when the letter style was changed, but it was used extensively on pattern issues of this year, so perhaps it was initially a pattern design made early in the year that was found acceptable to be put into regular production the same year. If so, the Small Letters dies may have been used side by side with any Large Letters dies made at the beginning of the year.

It is interesting to note that the Mint increased the die spacing to maximize the longer die life promised by the shallower design. As a result, many more Small Letters coins are found weakly struck. It is not unusual to find these coins with an anomaly called strike doubling, which is caused by a shifting of the dies at the time the coins are struck. The result is a slight doubling around some of the design elements, including the date and letters. Many collectors confuse this doubling with the highly prized doubled dies. In the Flying Eagle series, true doubled dies will be seen only in the eagle and letters, not the date, which is added to the die in a separate process. A Flying Eagle cent with doubling on the letters and date is most likely a strike-doubled coin, and not worth an added premium.

Survivability: There is no information regarding the release of these coins. It is believed that they were first issued side by side with the Large Letters cents until those dies were used up. Today, we find no overwhelming scarcity of the Small Letters design over the Large Letters design. As such, the estimated mintage for both the Small Letters and Large Letters designs is given as half the total mintage.

As with all the copper-nickel cents, these were popular and circulated widely. By 1860, their presence in circulation was overwhelming. It was not uncommon to bundle the cents in 25- and 50-coin bags. During the coinage crisis of the Civil War, these coins were totally removed from circulation. In 1863, they quickly returned to circulation where they stayed until the redemption period of the 1870's. Most of the issue was melted at this time. The coins that survived are either median Mint State grades that never returned to circulation after the war or very well-worn coins that stayed in circulation until the 1880's.

Collecting Challenges: These are widely available in low grades and in moderate Mint State grades (such as MS-63). It is difficult to find fully struck examples, but it is better to be patient and wait for the right coin to present itself than to quickly fill a hole in your album with a weakly struck example.

There were two reverse styles used this year: High Leaves and Low Leaves (see also 1858, Large Letters). Both are found paired with the Small Letters obverse, with the High Leaves reverse a bit harder to find. If collectors start adding all four die combinations (including the two Large Letters combinations) to their sets, the added demand should push the value of all 1858 Flying Eagles slightly higher.

High Leaves Reverse (Type of 1857). **Low Leaves Reverse (Type of 1858).**

Collecting Circulated Pieces: The optimal collecting grade for circulated coins is EF-40. As low-grade examples are quite plentiful, it would be advisable to purchase higher-grade examples with original uncleaned surfaces. Selecting a well-struck example is also desirable for an attractive collection. The overwhelming demand for this issue is in the About Uncirculated grade, and as such, their prices have advance steadily over the years.

Collecting Mint State Pieces: The optimal collecting grade for Mint State coins is MS-64. This is the toughest Flying Eagle cent (of the regular issues) to locate in top condition. The prices in Mint State are not much higher than those of the 1858 Large Letters or even the 1857. Some prooflike pieces exist, which are quite attractive and command an added premium.

Collecting Proof Issues: Proof Flying Eagle cents are some of the most attractive coins in numismatics! They all are rare, so when examples become available, they are very expensive or sell very quickly. Most if not all of the Proof issues were struck to be included in a 12-piece pattern set the Mint sold to collectors between 1858 and 1860 (see below).

There are prooflike Mint State examples that may be confused for actual Proof coins. True Proofs should have deeply mirrored fields and superb strikes. The 1858 Small Letters Proof is found with both the High Leaves (rare) and Low Leaves reverse. Few collectors attempt to acquire both types, mainly due to the cost.

1858, Small Letters: Circulation Strike

GSID	VG-8	F-12	VF-20	EF-40	AU-50	AU-58	MS-60	MS-63
15316	$27	$40	$55	$90	$180	$350	$750	$1,400

1858, Small Letters: Proof Strike

GSID	PF-60	PF-63	PF-65
15318	$5,250	$8,750	$26,500

Varieties

A few scarce repunched dates are known for this year. Only one obverse doubled die is known. All other reported obverse doubled dies have proven to be strike-doubled coins, which garner no additional premium. Some of the Low Leaves dies show reworking on the denomination—these are doubled dies, but are really too minor to attract much attention.

Patterns

The Mint was busy this year trying to increase the die life and striking quality of the cents. In addition to the Small Letters obverse, which was put into production, two other obverse designs were tested: a Small Eagle and an Indian Head design. These were struck together with four reverse wreaths, including the regular wreath then in production, the Plain Oak Wreath, the Oak Wreath With an Ornamented Shield, and the Laurel Wreath.

The Mint produced 12-piece sets of all these die combinations (11 pieces with the regular-issue Small Letters Flying Eagle cent). This became a staple of the Mint's sales (along with the 1856 Flying Eagle cent) and about 150 to 200 sets were produced and sold over the next few years. Some combinations, such as the 1858 Indian Head / Laurel Wreath die combination, were struck in larger quantities to satisfy demand. Today, many advanced collectors are interested in assembling this set. Some examples of these pattern coins are found in circulated grades.

1858, 8 Over 7

Circulation-Strike Mintage:
Unknown (estimated 100,000)

1858, 8 Over 7, Cent Production: This very popular variety was created when a leftover 1857 obverse die was repunched with an 1858 date. Apparently some perfectly usable dies were available at the end of the year and, rather than be discarded, their dates were repunched with the 1858 date. Sometime in the middle of the striking run, the obverse die was taken out and resurfaced, removing evidence of the overdate. These later-die-state pieces are passed over by knowledgeable collectors and may sell only at a slight premium.

The die has some interesting attributes that can make identification easier. There is a remnant of a numeral 1 punched in the field directly between the date and the eagle. This looks like a small triangular dot. This die also has what is called a *broken wing tip* on the eagle's right wing. This broken wing tip is found on a number of other 1857 dies as well, so this is a design deviation, called a hub variety, and is not unique to the 1858, 8 Over 7 die.

1858, LL Snow-1

Versions of the 8 Over 7 are listed in most major guides, including the *Red Book*. The Strong Overdate variety is called the 1858 LL Snow-1, or simply 1858 S-1. The Weak Overdate variety is called Snow-7.

Survivability: These were released into circulation as normal 1858 Large Letters cents and circulated with all the other cents. There was no collector knowledge of the variety at the time and all that have survived today have done so mainly by chance. Perhaps only 2,000 pieces exist in all grades. Of these, perhaps only 300 or so would qualify as early-die-state pieces with the overdate showing clearly.

1858, LL Snow-1, Mid-Die State details

Collecting Challenges: If paying full price, it is important that you select early-die-state coins with the 7 clearly showing. Certification does not guarantee an early-die-state coin. Because of its rarity in high grades, collectors must sacrifice quality, or face missing out on acquiring an example.

Nearly all examples are struck with the dies skewed, or out of parallel alignment. This causes the area by the eagle's tail and the opposing area of the wreath (upper left reverse) to be very weakly struck.

Collecting Circulated Pieces: The optimal collecting grade for circulated coins is VF-20. Low-grade examples may still be found unattributed as overdates. If paying full price, a collector should select an example with significant detail remaining. Late-die-state pieces without the 7 showing should be avoided unless the premium is very small.

Collecting Mint State Pieces: The optimal collecting grade for Mint State coins is an early-die-state example in MS-63. Fewer than 100 Mint State pieces are known to exist. Of these, perhaps 35 or so would qualify as early-die-state pieces. The strength of the overdate feature is very important. The earliest die states have the overdate very bold. These are now denoted as "Strong" on PCGS holders. Later, the dies were ground down and the overdate feature fades to almost nothing. These are denoted as "Weak" by PCGS. Other grading services may denote them as Early Die State (EDS) and Late Die State (LDS). Many may not be designated at all. In this case you should critically inspect the coin and determine which it is. The "Strong" designated coins will bring much stronger prices in the marketplace. Those designated "Weak" or those on which the overdate cannot be easily seen should get only a small premium over the regular non-overdate examples.

All examples show slight to strong weakness on the eagle's tail and the opposing area on the reverse, the wreath at the upper-right quadrant. This is due to the die being slightly skewed. This weakness should be overlooked as it is an unavoidable problem.

1858, 8 Over 7: Circulation Strike

GSID	VG-8	F-12	VF-20	EF-40	AU-50	AU-58	MS-60	MS-63
15322 (Strong)	$130	$195	$310	$525	$950	$1,750	$4,250	$8,250
213475 (Weak)	—	—	200	235	290	430	750	1,300

1858, 8 Over 7, LL Snow-1

1858, 8 Over 7, LL Snow-7

3

Indian Head Cents, (1859–1909): Analysis by Date and Mint

Copper-Nickel, Laurel Wreath Reverse, Without Shield (1859)

Variety 1 (Copper-Nickel, Laurel Wreath Reverse, 1859): **Designer:** *James B. Longacre.* **Weight:** *4.67 grams.* **Composition:** *.880 copper, .120 nickel.* **Diameter:** *19 mm.* **Edge:** *Plain.* **Mint:** *Philadelphia.*

Copper-Nickel, Oak Wreath Reverse, With Shield (1860–1864)

Variety 2 (Copper-Nickel, Oak Wreath With Shield, 1860–1864): **Designer:** *James B. Longacre.* **Weight:** *4.67 grams.* **Composition:** *.880 copper, .120 nickel.* **Diameter:** *19 mm.* **Edge:** *Plain.* **Mint:** *Philadelphia.*

Bronze, Oak Wreath Reverse, With Shield (1864–1909)

Variety 3 (Bronze, 1864–1909): **Designer:** *James B. Longacre.* **Weight:** *3.11 grams.* **Composition:** *.950 copper, .050 tin and zinc.* **Diameter:** *19 mm.* **Edge:** *Plain.* **Mints:** *Philadelphia and San Francisco.*

1859

Circulation-Strike Mintage:
36,400,000

Proof Mintage:
800 (estimated)

1859 Cent Production: Production of the copper-nickel cent had always been a problem for the Mint. In attempting to extend the life of the dies, various design changes were tested in 1858. Both the obverse and reverse were altered to a lower relief, but this was still not satisfactory. The problem was that the head and tail of the eagle were directly opposite the wreath details on the reverse. In an effort to fix this problem, the Mint tried a smaller eagle on patterns, but this was also deemed unsatisfactory. The Indian Head design was also tested in 1858 and was found to be superior to the Flying Eagle. The head was centrally located on the coin and did not interfere with metal flow into the reverse die.

The design is not an American Indian, but "Liberty" in an Indian headdress. The reverse design selected is a plain olive wreath circling the denomination. However, the wreath has long been called *laurel* in the literature, following a tradition started by Mint Director J.R. Snowden in 1860.

The production of cents this year set a record for all United States coins up until that time. It was surpassed in the Indian Head cent series up to 1880 only by the 1863 issue.

Survivability: Given the high mintage, these have survived in reasonable quantities. The issue circulated for only three years before being pulled out of circulation during the Civil War coinage crisis. In 1863 they reappeared and circulated in quantity for ten more years before the wholesale withdrawal and melting of most copper-nickel cents in the 1870's. By the 1890's they were rare in circulation. Merchants who thought them a nuisance due to their greater thickness over the bronze cents had constantly removed them and returned them to the banks.

Examples are plentiful in grades Very Fine and below. Mint State examples are also widely available, but are premium priced due to type set collector demand.

Collecting Challenges: This date is easily found, but premium priced. Collectors should choose examples with exceptional strikes: full feather tips and sharp diamond detail on the lower ribbon. Many coins are of a later die state with mushy details. While later-die-state coins may not be unattractive, a sharp early-die-state coin is worthy of a premium.

Collecting Circulated Pieces: The optimal collecting grade for circulated coins is EF-40. These are easily found in most grades. Sharp strikes and crisp details are preferred but difficult to find.

Collecting Mint State Pieces: The optimal collecting grade for Mint State coins is MS-64. These can be found easily in moderate grades, but high-quality coins with crisp details are very hard to locate. Cherrypicking for quality is important for this date, since the prices are usually a bit more advanced than those of other dates of similar rarity, due to the type collector pressure.

Collecting Proof Issues: As a one-year design, it is under heavy demand. All are quite expensive for their rarity. Most are attractive, with cameo examples occasionally available. About 25% of gems show some cameo contrast. The recommended grade is PF-64 or PF-65. Collectors are advised to keep an eye out for coins with exceptional visual appeal.

1859: Circulation Strike

GSID	VG-8	F-12	VF-20	EF-40	AU-50	AU-58	MS-60	MS-63	MS-65
1289	$18	$24	$50	$145	$215	$370	$430	$875	$2,700

1859: Proof Strike

GSID	PF-63	PF-64	PF-65
1467	$1,900	$2,450	$4,250

Varieties

The Snow-1 has a full bold repunched date, and is a very rare and hotly contested variety. An MS-65 example sold for more than $12,000 at auction in 2001. Five other less-prominent repunched date varieties are known and bring moderate premiums.

1859, Repunched Date, Snow-1

1859, Shield Reverse

Circulation-Strike Mintage:
1,000+

Proof Mintage:
Likely not made in Proof format

1859, Shield Reverse, Cent Production: In late 1859, Mint Director Snowden requested a new reverse for the cent. The design was to be of a more patriotic character, as he noted in a letter to Treasury Secretary Howell Cobb on December 13.

> A modification of the devices on the reverse of the cent is desirable. I propose to introduce the shield upon the reverse. This will give it a more national character, and be a decided improvement upon the present coin.

As many as 1,000 examples were struck, and some were sent to the Secretary. The remainder of the small issue with us today is mostly in uncirculated condition. These have variously been listed as patterns (Judd-228) and regular issues in the past. Today these are still referenced as patterns, but more and more collectors of high-grade Indian Head cents include them in their collection of regular issues. This variety is an interesting addition to a collection, but you can decide whether it fits your collecting goal.

Survivability: Most of this mintage has survived in Mint State.

Collecting Circulated Pieces: Very few pieces are available in circulated grades—perhaps fewer than 50. The optimal collecting grade for circulated coins is EF-40, but fewer than a dozen exist in this grade.

Collecting Mint State Pieces: The majority of these pieces survive in Mint State in MS-63 and MS-64. MS-63 is the optimal collecting grade. Some pieces exist in MS-65 or better, but these are more difficult to acquire.

Why Are These Cents Called Patterns?: The question remains: Why are these pieces listed as patterns? It is unlikely that a design alteration like this would require the mint to produce so many examples. Typically, a few examples to show the design are all that is necessary for the purpose of deciding to make the change, as Howell Cobb did. Also these coins have the look and feel of a regular press run ready to be issued for circulation. In an 1860 book by Mint Director James Ross Snowden, *The Mint Manual of Coins of All Nations*, the first description of these coins is given. Snowden wrote: "Near the end of the year another pattern cent was struck. This is the same as the cent of 1860." Apparently Snowden himself thought these were patterns. It is possible that this entry was made while they were in the development stage, before the larger scale production was made.

It is possible that the entire issue was purchased at one time by a dealer with good connections to the mint. A mintage of 1,000 coins would only be $10 face value. This could explain why very few ever made it into circulation.

1859, Shield Reverse: Circulation Strike

GSID	VG-8	F-12	VF-20	EF-40	AU-50	AU-58	MS-60	MS-63	MS-65
12332	—	—	—	—	—	$1,200	$1,250	$1,750	$3,500

1860, Rounded Bust

Circulation-Strike Mintage:
19,566,000 (estimated, out of 20,566,000 total)

Proof Mintage:
1,000 (estimated)

1860, Rounded Bust, Cent Production: Mintage levels lowered a bit this year, as the quantity of cents in circulation was becoming satisfactory.

Survivability: This issue saw only two years of circulation before being put away during the Civil War coinage crisis. By the 1870's the copper-nickel cents were being recalled and melted. Survivors either escaped retrieval from circulation at that time and are found well worn today, or were never returned to circulation after the war and are found in high grades.

Collecting Challenges: This issue is common. Selecting an attractive coin for the grade desired is important. Look for a sharp strike and an early die state.

Collecting Circulated Pieces: The optimal collecting grade for circulated coins is AU-50. Look for well-struck pieces. Low-grade examples below Fine are readily available and should be purchased only if problem free.

Collecting Mint State Pieces: The optimal collecting grade for Mint State coins is MS-64. This date is readily found in most grades. Select a problem-free example.

Collecting Proof Issues: The mintage represents 1,000 Proof coins produced, with 450+ being melted, or released into circulation, due to poor sales. As such, these coins are much scarcer than their minted quantity would suggest.

This issue was poorly made, with a large percentage of examples seen struck only once. These will have average strikes and slightly rounded outer edges. Many examples described as prooflike were struck from the Proof dies and may have originally been part of the Proof issue. For this reason gems are very rare. Cameo contrast is virtually non-existent on this issue. The optimal collecting grade for Proofs is PF-64.

1860, Rounded Bust: Circulation Strike

GSID	VG-8	F-12	VF-20	EF-40	AU-50	AU-58	MS-60	MS-63	MS-65
1291	$18	$22	$49	$70	$110	$180	$240	$480	$1,250

1860, Rounded Bust: Proof Strike

GSID	PF-63	PF-64	PF-65
1470	$875	$2,250	$3,100

Varieties

There are three very minor repunched dates known for this year.

1860, Pointed Bust

Circulation-Strike Mintage:
1,000,000 (estimated, out of 20,566,000 total)

1860, Pointed Bust, Cent Production: The Pointed Bust portrait is the design used for all Indian Head cents dated 1859. *Pointed Bust* refers to the pointed left tip of the neckline, as opposed to the later Rounded Bust design. This bust was used on some 1860-dated cents, which could also be correctly called *1860, Type of 1859*. These were produced when as many as ten undated obverse dies made in 1859 were dated with the 1860 date punch and put into production. They are possibly the first Indian Head cent issues with the new reverse. The long-overlooked design difference is as significant as the 1864 With L and 1864 No L design change.

Pointed Bust

Rounded Bust

The difference in the shape of the bust truncation may have been noted first in 1971 by Don Taxay, in *Scott's Comprehensive Catalogue and Encyclopedia of U.S. Coins*. In 1988 Walter Breen called it to collectors' attention in his popular *Complete Encyclopedia of U.S. and Colonial Coins*. Since then, there has been a steady increase in the number of pieces known as more and more collectors find them in dealers' inventories, priced as regular Rounded Bust examples. Today they are priced similarly to the 1859 Indian Head cent in most grades.

Perhaps because of its relatively recent popularization, the standard coin-collecting albums do not typically have openings for this design. If this changes, and if collector interest increases, demand should rise to absorb all examples found, with premiums rising if more fail to show up.

Survivability: These were not recognized as a separate design until the late 1980's, so surviving examples were not saved for this reason. Most might have been saved because they were the first coins of the new reverse design. Today most examples are well worn.

Collecting Challenges: This issue is usually well struck and when high-grade examples are found they can be very pretty. Collectors used to be able to find these unattributed, but that is getting more and more difficult.

Collecting Circulated Pieces: The optimal collecting grade for circulated coins is EF-40. These are sometimes difficult to locate. Prices should presently be only a moderate premium over the Rounded Bust design, about what 1859 Indian Head cents sell for. As demand increases, this may change. To reap a small reward, even if you do not need this date, be on the lookout for it being offered as the typically found Rounded Bust cent.

Collecting Mint State Pieces: The optimal collecting grade for Mint State coins is MS-63. These are presently quite scarce in Mint State grades, with premiums rising from three to six times the price of a Rounded Bust example. These are usually quite attractive.

1860, Pointed Bust: Circulation Strike

GSID	VG-8	F-12	VF-20	EF-40	AU-50	AU-58	MS-60	MS-63	MS-65
1290	$34	$40	$75	$110	$210	$340	$375	$725	$2,900

VARIETIES

One very minor repunched date is known.

1861

Circulation-Strike Mintage:
10,100,000

Proof Mintage:
1,000 (estimated)

1861 Cent Production: The 1861 cent had the lowest mintage of the copper-nickel series. It commands a higher premium over other dates because of this reported mintage, not actual scarcity, as these were widely saved during the Civil War coinage crisis. By 1860, the record production of copper-nickel cents had all but flooded commercial channels. The Mint produced the coins this year solely to replace old copper cents that were redeemed.

Survivability: The entire issue was essentially withdrawn from circulation in the summer of 1862. After the war, these circulated for a few more years before being redeemed by the Mint during the 1870's. Many high-grade examples are known due to the wartime hoarding.

Collecting Challenges: Collectors of Civil War memorabilia put added demand on the 1861 to 1865 cents. Still, the coins are relatively readily available and affordable. Seek out attractive and problem-free examples.

Collecting Circulated Pieces: The optimal collecting grade for circulated coins is AU-50. Due to the survivability of this issue, Extremely Fine and Very Fine pieces are easily found but are of course typically priced higher than others of the era. The lower production seemed to affect the lowest grades the most, as their scarcity is more in line with the lower mintage. They are available, but at a higher premium.

Collecting Mint State Pieces: Due to the widespread hoarding during the Civil War, high-quality examples are widely available, although at a premium over the other dates.

A group of 15 to 30 pieces of exceptional quality, which came on the market many years ago, has made this one of the more common dates in the copper-nickel series in gem condition. One of these pieces, graded MS-68 by PCGS (still the only MS-68 for the copper-nickel series), sold at auction for $54,625 in January 2003.

Collecting Proof Issues: This is the key date in the Proof series, partly due to low mintage, but also because of poor quality of the dies and poor striking quality. The reverse die in particular had very shallow mirrors. Most have rounded outer edges. Gems with cameo contrast are nearly impossible to locate.

Most of the original mintage of 1,000 pieces remained unsold and might have been destroyed, or were simply released into circulation. It may be that only a few hundred pieces survived.

1861: Circulation Strike

GSID	VG-8	F-12	VF-20	EF-40	AU-50	AU-58	MS-60	MS-63	MS-65
1292	$34	$47	$70	$110	$155	$180	$240	$480	$1,250

1861: Proof Strike

GSID	PF-63	PF-64	PF-65
1473	$1,900	$3,500	$5,750

Varieties

There are only a few minor varieties of this year. On a few dies produced from a defective hub, the tops of the letters ES in STATES show some deterioration which progresses throughout the series until the design is reworked to the 1864 With L style. Some advanced collectors attempt to collect these for every year.

1862

Circulation-Strike Mintage:
28,075,000

Proof Mintage:
550 (estimated)

1862 Cent Production: With the hope of a quick end to the war diminishing, silver and gold coinage quickly vanished from general circulation. The only coin that circulated was the copper-nickel cent. Seeing demand for the cent increase, the Mint shifted most of its production from silver and gold coins to the cent. Speculators who sold them at a slight profit to merchants mostly bought up this large production.

Survivability: Most of this issue circulated briefly and then were removed from general circulation during the Civil War coinage crisis peaking in summer 1862. At the end of the war, these came out again and circulated until the redemption of the 1870's. Most examples are in higher than average condition.

Collecting Challenges: These are very popular as the predominant coin in use during the Civil War. Examples are plentiful, so collectors are advised to find problem-free pieces in as high a grade as their collecting parameters allow.

Collecting Circulated Pieces: The optimal collecting grade for circulated coins is AU-50. Examples in all other grades are easily obtainable.

Collecting Mint State Pieces: The optimal collecting grade for Mint State coins is MS-65. These are widely available in all grades up to MS-65. They are difficult to find with early die states and full strikes. Full-strike pieces should have full feather tips as well as full diamonds on the lower ribbon.

Collecting Proof Issues: This is the most common date to find in the copper-nickel Proof series. One reason for this higher quality may be that all unsold examples were saved and resold to collectors at some later time, possibly after the war. Examples are of very high quality and collectors are advised to buy PF-64 and higher grades. Cameo examples exist, but not in great quantities.

1862: Circulation Strike

GSID	VG-8	F-12	VF-20	EF-40	AU-50	AU-58	MS-60	MS-63	MS-65
1293	$13	$16	$32	$60	$95	$155	$210	$415	$1,050

1862: Proof Strike

GSID	PF-63	PF-64	PF-65
1476	$875	$1,550	$2,000

Varieties

A few varieties with misplaced digits exist. There are no major varieties.

1863

Circulation-Strike Mintage:
49,840,000

Proof Mintage:
460+

1863 Cent Production: Both the Union and the Confederacy were drained emotionally and financially due to the horrific battles of the Civil War, by 1863 entering its third year. The resulting fear had chased all federal silver and gold coinage into hiding, with the cent following in mid-1862. Still, the Mint pounded the cents out in record numbers. Eventually, with coinage substitutes (such as Fractional Currency notes) entering circulation, the cent lost its premium and started to be seen in commerce again.

Survivability: These survived in their original condition until the end of the war, when they reentered circulation. During the recoinage redemption of the 1870's a large percentage of the mintage was melted, but because the mintage was so great, even a small percentage of survivors left a large quantity of coins for today's collectors. These are easily found today in excellent condition.

Collecting Challenges: Collectors are advised to search out well-struck examples from early-die-state dies. This issue is very easy to find otherwise.

Collecting Circulated Pieces: The optimal collecting grade for circulated coins is AU-50. Examples in all the lower grades are very easy to locate. Avoid problem pieces.

Collecting Mint State Pieces: The optimal collecting grade for Mint State coins is MS-65. This date is easily found in all grades. Select coins with extra eye appeal. True gems with sharp details are slightly difficult to locate.

Collecting Proof Issues: Although similar in mintage to 1862, this issue is about twice as rare. Examples tend to be quite attractive with perhaps 40% qualifying for cameo status. The optimal collecting grade for Proofs is PF-65.

Bronze Tokens and Cents: This year saw the quantity of privately minted cent-sized copper tokens increase dramatically in major cities such as New York, Cincinnati, and Chicago. These Civil War tokens are collected extensively and offer an interesting sidelight to the federal coinage of the era.

The success of these tokens inspired the Mint to produce its own bronze cent. An interesting and historical pattern (Judd-299) was produced this year with the regular dies in bronze. These patterns make an affordable and interesting addition to collections as an early beginning to the full-scale production of bronze cents the next year.

1863: Circulation Strike

GSID	VG-8	F-12	VF-20	EF-40	AU-50	AU-58	MS-60	MS-63	MS-65
1294	$13	$16	$32	$60	$95	$155	$210	$415	$1,050

1863: Proof Strike

GSID	PF-63	PF-64	PF-65
1479	$875	$1,550	$2,400

Varieties

A few minor repunched dates are known for this date. The best variety is the reverse doubled die, Snow-10. This doubled die is popular, but not well known. This creates a possibility for cherrypicking overlooked varieties. Few dealers (or collectors for that matter) check the reverse dies for varieties.

1864, Copper-Nickel

Circulation-Strike Mintage:
13,740,000

Proof Mintage:
370 (estimated)

1864 Copper-Nickel Cent Production: Due to inaction on the part of Congress, the Mint was required to continue striking the copper-nickel cents in 1864. They were bought up by speculators and offered to the public only at a premium, even though their bullion value never reached a point where it was profitable to melt them down. These coins traded at a premium because the alternatives in circulation were worse. Merchants and their customers had to deal with paper money that seemed to lose value every week. Small change was made with postage stamps, Fractional Currency notes, and private copper tokens. When it came to silver and gold, any holder of federal coins could expect to get favorable discounts from merchants for using them instead of the alternatives. The copper-nickel cents were last struck in May.

Survivability: Almost all 1864 cents were removed from circulation as soon as they were released. After the war, they came out and circulated extensively for about ten more years. Examples that escaped the recoinage redemption of the 1870's may have circulated for another 20 more years. (For a record of minor coins redeemed from 1871 to 1881, see page 102.)

Collecting Challenges: This is one of the toughest dates in the copper-nickel series to find with attractive eye appeal. As such, collectors should put more effort into finding this date with a sharp strike and attractive luster.

Collecting Circulated Pieces: The optimal collecting grade for circulated coins is EF-40. Examples are typically mushy with average strikes. Searching for early-die-state examples will take some patience.

Collecting Mint State Pieces: The optimal collecting grade for Mint State coins is MS-64. These typically lack eye appeal. Many are struck with worn dies and exhibit a grayish color. Search out examples with better luster and a sharp strike.

Collecting Proof Issues: These tend to be of a very high quality. They are a bit more common than the Proof cents of 1863, probably due to a higher survivability rate. High-grade coins usually come with deep mirrors. Cameo contrast is available on about 50% of these.

The year sets sold by the Mint were usually produced early in the year. Therefore most sets contained only one cent, the copper-nickel cent.

1864, Copper-Nickel: Circulation Strike

GSID	VG-8	F-12	VF-20	EF-40	AU-50	AU-58	MS-60	MS-63	MS-65
1295	$32	$39	$45	$90	$130	$195	$260	$470	$1,250

1864, Copper-Nickel: Proof Strike

GSID	PF-63	PF-64	PF-65
1482	$875	$1,750	$2,500

Varieties

There are only a few minor repunched dates known. A defective digit punch has what looks like repunching under the horizontal bar of the 4. Since the defect is on the punch, many dies show this feature.

1864, Bronze, No L

Circulation-Strike Mintage:
34,000,000 (estimated)

Proof Mintage:
300 (estimated)

***Bronze* or *No L*:** These are typically called either 1864 No L or 1864 Bronze cents. Older collectors and grading services are accustomed to labeling this as *Bronze*. This separates these coins from the copper-nickel cents. The design change to the 1864 With L is assumed. In the past ten years it has been also listed as the No L, which separates the coin from the With L issue. The change from the copper-nickel alloy is assumed.

1864, No L, Cent Production: On April 22 a bill authorizing the change to a bronze cent was signed into law. This law also made the use of all private coinage illegal. The first bronze cents were produced on May 13 and released into circulation on May 20. There was no reason to make new dies for this coinage, as the Mint still had on hand many of the dies made at the beginning of the year for the copper-nickel cent coinage.

The coins were an immediate success. This cent composition remained basically unchanged, except for the emergency issues of World War II, until 1982, when it was changed to copper-coated zinc.

Survivability: These coins were released into circulation and stayed there for quite a while. They were only removed from circulation when they became too worn or damaged to be useful as coinage. Today they are mostly found in Very Good condition or lower.

Collecting Challenges: This issue is a one-year type, but this seems to be overlooked by most type collectors. As such, type collector demand is not a big factor in the pricing of these coins. These were mostly struck with dies used to strike the copper-nickel cents earlier in the year, and most coins show mushy details with numerous die clashes. Only about one in 30 coins was struck from fresh dies. The new dies produced crisp early-die-state pieces, which will have very sharp details. While many collectors will overlook die state when selecting coins, it may be important enough to spend the extra time to locate these. It may not cost much more, and the eye appeal of these pieces will more than make up for the time spent looking.

Collecting Circulated Pieces: The optimal collecting grade for circulated coins is AU-50. The vast majority is found in low grade so it is important to buy the best you can for your budget. Early-die-state pieces may occasionally be found, and should be bought when encountered.

Collecting Mint State Pieces: The optimal collecting grade for Mint State coins is MS-65RB. This is one of the most common issues of the Civil War years. In Mint State this date is no more common than any of the copper-nickel issues, but it can be found at a much lower price. Finding examples with eye appeal is recommended. Common, early-die-state pieces are very hard to find, as are ones with even red-brown color. Pieces with full mint red color are hard to find with eye appeal. Trying to find an early-die-state example is quite a challenge.

Collecting Proof Issues: The typically reported mintage is 150, but this is unreasonably low. While this issue is quite scarce, it always seems to be available. More than 200 examples have been recorded graded by ANACS, NGC, and PCGS combined. Even with duplicate submissions it seems unlikely that the mintage is anywhere near 150. A more realistic estimate may be 300. This issue is found mostly brown or with very little red present. Examples with even color with deep mirrors are most desirable for the issue. Full red examples are very difficult to find and are very expensive. Examples with cameo contrast are extremely rare and are usually priced with a significant premium.

1864, Bronze, No L: Circulation Strike

GSID	VG-8	F-12	VF-20	EF-40	AU-50	AU-58	MS-60	MS-63	MS-65
1296 (Brown)	$24	$30	$55	$75	$90	$120	$130	$190	$525
1297 (Red-Brown)	—	—	—	—	—	—	—	290	725
1298 (Red)	—	—	—	—	—	—	—	495	1,600

1864, Bronze, No L: Proof Strike

GSID	PF-60	PF-63	PF-67
2980	$260	$310	$1,750
2982 (Cameo)	—	415	2,500
2983 (Deep Cameo)	—	—	12,000

Varieties

The best variety is the Snow-4 doubled die, with the doubling most prominent on LIBERTY. It was discovered in 1991 and is widely known, yet few examples have turned up. Very few examples are known. This is a coin that can make your day if you find one. There are only seven other varieties reported, mostly minor repunched dates. The other standout variety for this date is Snow-11, which has circular lathe lines over the face on the obverse.

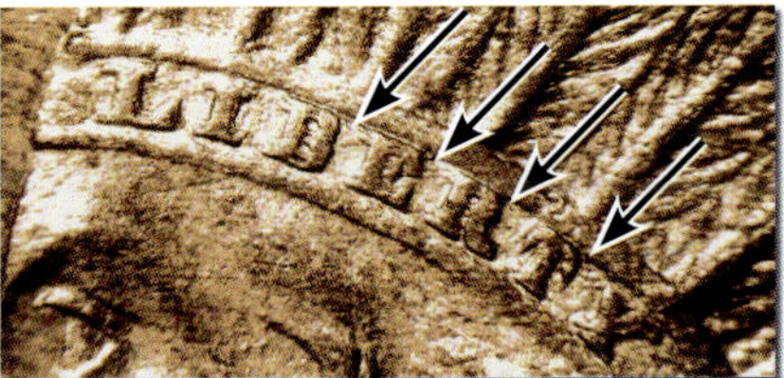

1864, No L, Doubled-Die Obverse, Snow-4

1864, Circular Lathe Lines, Snow-11

An 1864 two-cent piece variety is known with clash marks from the obverse Indian Head cent die! This raises the question: does an 1864 Indian Head cent exist with the corresponding two-cent piece clash marks? None have yet been found.

1864, Two-Cent Clash, composite

1864, Two-Cent Clash, detail

1864, Bronze, With L

Circulation-Strike Mintage:
5,000,000 (estimated)

Proof Mintage:
20 (estimated)

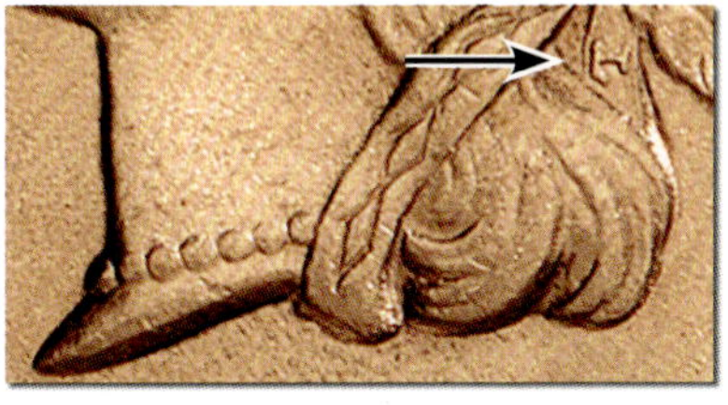

1864, With L, Cent Production: The new With L design is found on all Indian Head cents from this issue onwards. The redesign by Mint Engraver James B. Longacre is sharper than the No L design. Longacre added his initial L on the lower ribbon between the last feather and the hair curl. The bust point is narrow, similar to the 1859 issue. This feature may be used to attribute worn examples that no longer show the L; however, the premium is small in lower grades if the L does not show.

It is unknown when the design was put into production. It is likely that the new dies were made in time for the changeover to bronze in May and used side by side with the previously made No L dies. As such there is no way of knowing exactly how many coins were produced. The estimate of five million is based on the ratio of survivors compared to the No L pieces.

It is not known when this design change was reported to collectors. The rare Proof issue of this year was restruck for collectors sometime around 1870, so it is probable that it was known at that time. In the 1906 Leeds sale by Henry Chapman, lot #1213 was a single 1864 With L cent described as "Unc. Bright Red," which sold for $20. By this time they were considered rare.

Survivability: These were released into circulation alongside the No L issue and were not recognized as special by collectors for a very long time. Most are well worn.

Collecting Challenges: Many come sharp and pleasing, and it should not be too difficult to find attractive specimens.

Collecting Circulated Pieces: The optimal collecting grade for circulated coins is EF-40. Date collectors did not retrieve these from circulation until many years after their issuance, so it is difficult to find examples above Very Good. Prices for choice pieces above Very Fine are high, but do not increase significantly between grades, so it may not cost a collector much more to purchase a higher-grade coin.

Collecting Mint State Pieces: The optimal collecting grade for Mint State coins is MS-64RB. These are usually available, but never cheap, unless the coin has problems. This issue offers a great value in full red, as long as the coin has no problems such as spots, or eye appeal issues such as streaky toning.

Collecting Proof Issues: This is the rarest date in the Proof series. Apparently 20 examples were struck and most are traced today. Two die pairs struck nine pieces in 1864. An additional 11 examples were struck with another die pair sometime around

1869. The attributes of the different dies are described fully in the *Flying Eagle and Indian Cent Attribution Guide*, 3rd edition (2014). For a summary, see pages 85 and 86.

For many years, the only coins offered as Proofs were those described by Walter Breen in his *Encyclopedia of U.S. and Colonial Proof Coins*. In 1984 Breen announced the discovery of a new die pair. Ten years later, I first announced that the die pair Breen originally described as the true Proof were in fact struck much later than the date on the coins. The evidence came from the reverse dies, which were the same as those used on regular-issue Proofs and pattern cents from 1868 to 1871. Die-state analysis pinpointed production in 1869 or 1870. The second die discovered by Breen was found to have the same reverse as the regular 1864 copper-nickel Proofs. This confirmed that there were two striking periods: 1864, and 1869–1870. I discovered a third die pair in 1997, also from the first striking period.

The reason for their existence is not documented. The coins from the first striking period are found struck on both copper-nickel (unique in each die pair) and bronze planchets. They were probably struck at the same time, around the changeover to bronze planchets in May 1864. Perhaps they were struck as patterns of the new dies.

The second issuance came during the "Linderman" restriking period, 1867 to 1869, which was one of the times of active striking of collector issues at the Mint during the tenure of Mint Director Henry R. Linderman. Examples are known struck in aluminum, which was not regularly used until 1868. This issue was surely made to satisfy collector demand.

The 1864 With L Proof has excited collectors over the years. Two examples were in the estate of Mint Engraver James B. Longacre, which was sold by M. Thomas and Sons on January 21, 1870 (lot 247). The auctioneer described these as "thin die" (the No L style was conversely described as "thick die"). The pair brought $17. Prices have escalated ever since.

These coins seldom appear on the market, and usually set records when they do. In the 1960's prices were around $3,000. Sale prices in the 1970's were in the $5,000 to $10,000 range. In 1987, a superb red gem from the Norweb collection sold for $47,300. Soon after, in 1988, Breen's discovery piece sold for $44,000.

In Bowers and Merena's January 1999 Rarities sale, a PF-65RB from the first striking period set a record price for an Indian Head cent when it sold for $96,000. In the June 2002 Long Beach sale by Heritage Auctions, another example of the first striking period graded PF-64RD set another record when it sold for $132,000.

1864, Bronze, With L: Circulation Strike

GSID	VG-8	F-12	VF-20	EF-40	AU-50	AU-58	MS-60	MS-63	MS-65
1452 (Brown)	$90	$150	$195	$245	$325	$420	$430	$550	$1,200
1453 (Red-Brown)	—	—	—	—	—	—	625	825	1,500
1454 (Red)	—	—	—	—	—	—	—	1,200	4,000

1864, Bronze, With L: Proof Strike

GSID	PF-63	PF-64	PF-65
1718 (Brown)	$31,000	$41,000	$65,000
1719 (Red-Brown)	36,000	45,500	78,000
1720 (Red)	78,000	108,000	144,000

Varieties

There are many repunched dates known for this year. Presently 20 are described. Snow-1, -2, -3, and -7 show dramatic repunching on the 18 in various directions. The others are rather minor. Many collectors are interested in varieties of this year. A nearly full variety set was sold as part of the Larry R. Steve collection at the premier auction of American Numismatic Rarities (ANR), July 25, 2003. Larry R. Steve amassed the largest collection of Flying Eagle and Indian Head cent varieties in high grade ever assembled. In 1990, he co-founded the Flying Eagle and Indian Cent Collectors Society, serving as the first editor of its journal, *Longacre's Ledger*, and later, as president. Steve co-wrote a very useful book with Kevin Flynn: *Flying Eagle and Indian Cent Die Varieties*, in 1995. Selected sections of his collection were sold by American Numismatic Rarities in 2003. The balance of his collection was disbursed privately soon after.

1864 With L Proof Die Pairs: A Summary

Die Pair 1 (PR1)

Obv. 1: (B) *The date numeral 1 is directly under the bust point. Thin denticles are at 3:00 and 9:00.*

Rev. K: Nearly perfect dies. Only minute die lines in field at 1:00 confirm that these are from the same die as used on some 1864 No L Proofs.

Presently only seven examples are known. Examples from this die pair have occasionally been classified as pure copper die trials, Judd-358. It is now believed that most or all are actually struck in bronze. The difference between this obverse and Die Pair 3 is very minor. PR1 has the left edge of the base of the 1 between two denticles, while PR3 has it over the left half of a denticle. Some examples, known only through low-quality photographs in auction catalogs, may actually be PR3.

The dies are quite well made. The only identifying feature of the reverse are seemingly insignificant die-polish lines which were shown to match both this reverse and the 1864 No L PR2 only by direct comparison. In this case it is important in proving that the PR1 and PR3 were actually struck in the year of issue.

Additional examples from this die pair were also struck in aluminum, which was unavailable in quantity until 1868.

The ownership of the coin Breen mentions as being stolen has been settled. Some coins from different dies, which are not Proof, have been certified in the past.

Die Pair 2 (PR2)

Obv. 2: (B) *A long, raised die line on the neck runs diagonally from NE to SW just under the jaw. The date is far to the right of the bust point.*

Rev. 1868A: There are numerous light, crisscrossing die lines in the field. Heavy die lines off the olive leaves at 8:00 run towards the rim at 9:00.

This reverse die has very heavy and distinctive die-polishing lines. This reverse die is also found on the 1868 aluminum pattern and 1870–1871 Proofs. It is of a similar die state as some Proof issues of 1868 (Rev. A). The 1870 and 1871 issues are of a later die state. This reverse is also found on 1863 With L patterns and a minority of 1865 Proofs, all of which must have been produced on or after 1868.

Die Pair 3 (PR3)

Obv. 3: (LH) 864/864 (w). *Minor repunching is visible under high magnification. Very similar to Obv. 1; compare the date position.*

Rev. K: Same die as PR1, 1864 No L PR2. Minute die lines are in the field at 1:00.

This coin, presently thought unique, was discovered in the "Pennsylvania Estate," a collection assembled by a well-known numismatist in the 1930's to 1950's. The collection was incredible in that it had two gem Proof 1864 With L cents. This coin has set records every time it has changed hands.

1865

Circulation-Strike Mintage (Plain 5 and Fancy 5):
35,429,286

Proof Mintage (Plain 5):
500+ (estimated)

1865 Cent Production: In 1863, the older copper-nickel cents came out of hiding and circulated side by side with the new bronze cents, two-cent pieces, nickel three-cent pieces, nickel five-cent pieces, and paper Fractional Currency notes (in 3¢, 5¢, 10¢, 15¢, 25¢, and 50¢ denominations). This array of minor coinage and coinage substitutes was, to say the least, annoying to merchants and their customers. The redemption of outdated coins and paper was an important reason for the issuance of the three- and five-cent nickel coinage this year and next.

The cents this year were struck in record numbers also to assist in replacing the non-current coinage and paper money. The entire issue stayed in circulation for as long as fifty years.

Two date varieties are known and are collected today as separate dates by many collectors. The Plain 5 date type has a banana-shaped top to the 5. The Fancy 5 date type has a sharp hook-shaped top to the 5. The Plain 5 is slightly scarcer, was produced first, and includes the Proof issue. The Fancy 5 was used on a slightly larger quantity of dies. No Fancy 5 Proofs were struck.

Plain 5

Fancy 5

Survivability: This is the most readily available cent of the 1860's. These circulated for a long time, as there was not enough collector interest to save them until after the turn of the century. Most are in grades below Fine. Most high-grade survivors were saved by chance.

Collecting Challenges: Most specialists attempt to collect both the Plain 5 and Fancy 5 dates. Finding well-struck examples without problems should be the main focus for the collector.

Collecting Circulated Pieces: The optimal collecting grade for circulated coins is AU-50 for both the Plain 5 and Fancy 5 date styles. These are usually available, so selecting visually appealing coins would be advised. Avoid coins with significant contact marks or scratches, or those that have been cleaned.

Collecting Mint State Pieces: The optimal collecting grade for Mint State coins is MS-65RB for both the Plain 5 and Fancy 5 date style. These are usually available, but finding an even-colored example with a good strike is difficult. Full red gems are very difficult to find without problems. The Plain 5 is much harder to find in gem full red.

Collecting Proof Issues: Proofs are available in the Plain 5 date style only. This is one of the tougher dates in the early Indian Head cent series. Its rarity is equal to that of the 1864 No L, but it is typically priced lower because it is not a one-year type. It usually is found with streaky red-brown colors. Full red examples are very hard to locate, especially without spots and problems. Cameos are very rare.

1865, Plain 5: Circulation Strike

GSID	VG-8	F-12	VF-20	EF-40	AU-50	AU-58	MS-60	MS-63	MS-65
1302 (Brown)	$20	$32	$45	$65	$95	$130	$135	$235	$725
1303 (Red-Brown)	—	—	—	—	—	—	—	390	850
1304 (Red)	—	—	—	—	—	—	—	775	2,400

1865, Fancy 5: Circulation Strike

GSID	VG-8	F-12	VF-20	EF-40	AU-50	AU-58	MS-60	MS-63	MS-65
1299 (Brown)	$20	$32	$40	$55	$80	$95	$110	$210	$650
1300 (Red-Brown)	—	—	—	—	—	130	145	325	850
1301 (Red)	—	—	—	—	—	—	—	525	2,600

1865, Plain 5: Proof Strike

GSID	PF-63	PF-64	PF-65
1493 (Brown)	$390	$520	$775
1494 (Red-Brown)	650	1,000	1,750
1495 (Red)	775	2,500	6,250

Varieties

The Plain 5 varieties are very popular. The Snow-2 variety has a very wide repunched date with a 1 digit visible under the 8! S-1 and S-3 are also bold repunched dates, which get good premiums. Six other more minor repunched dates are collected.

Among the Fancy 5 varieties is a very bold reverse doubled die, Snow-2. This is very rare and worth a very significant premium. Many dealers overlook this variety because it is on the reverse. This creates an opportunity for collectors. S-1 used to be known as an 1865/4 overdate, but its overdate feature was discovered to be a digit punch defect, which shows up on two-cent pieces as well. Eight other repunched dates are known. One variety has a concentric raised die line through the feathers, which is puzzling to collectors and experts alike. Such varieties make collecting fun!

1865, Fancy 5, Doubled-Die Reverse, Snow-2

1866

Circulation-Strike Mintage:
9,826,500

Proof Mintage:
725+ (estimated)

1866 Cent Production: By 1866, the bronze cents were becoming well entrenched in commercial channels. The large production of the new three-cent nickel and five-cent nickel coins helped replace these denominations of Fractional Currency notes and the old copper-nickel cents in circulation. The need for cents diminished to the point that the Mint could direct its efforts to producing the new nickel coins.

Survivability: Collectors did not save this cent at the time of issue, except for Proofs. Between 1871 and 1875 most of the issue was turned in and melted at the Mint, making it scarce afterwards (see further discussion under 1871). This date is not widely available except in well-worn condition. High-grade examples that did survive the 1870's meltdown did so only by chance.

Collecting Challenges: This is the first in a series of scarcer dates that runs until 1878. A collector requiring a challenge can attempt to collect the 1866 to 1878 dates in what could be called a "Reconstruction era" set.

It is very difficult to find problem-free examples. Many attractive coins in the Very Fine to About Uncirculated grades have been processed (wire-brushed, called whizzing) to simulate mint luster. This was a common practice by dishonest elements of the hobby in the 1960's and 1970's. Collectors should learn how to spot the strange luster pattern on these whizzed coins and avoid them at all costs. (See appendix D for more on altered coins.)

Collecting Circulated Pieces: The optimal collecting grade for circulated coins is VF-20. Examples with full detail on the feather tips and diamond area are worth premium prices. Depending on the price, some minor problems such as hits and scratches may be acceptable. Expect to pay a premium for a problem-free example.

Collecting Mint State Pieces: The optimal collecting grade for Mint State coins is MS-64RB. Many of these coins come with streaky toning, which may not be a problem for red-brown coins, but for full red coins it may be a reason for rejection. Well-struck examples are not particularly tough to find. Coins with great eye appeal are worth their price. Full red coins are very tough and in high demand. Beware of chemically brightened coins, especially coins that are not certified by a top-tier grading service.

Collecting Proof Issues: The 1866 Proof issue is very scarce. Only one die pair struck this issue. The cheek area of the portrait always shows some roughness, which may have been caused by the obverse die being allowed to rust slightly. This is not a grade-limiting feature. Full red examples are very rare and will attract serious competition if problem free. Gem examples are usually available, for a price. Many may have been undergraded in the past due to the facial roughness.

1866: Circulation Strike

GSID	VG-8	F-12	VF-20	EF-40	AU-50	AU-58	MS-60	MS-63	MS-65
1305 (Brown)	$75	$95	$135	$170	$245	$365	$390	$525	$1,100
1306 (Red-Brown)	—	—	—	—	—	—	—	650	1,300
1307 (Red)	—	—	—	—	—	—	—	1,400	7,500

1866: Proof Strike

GSID	PF-63	PF-64	PF-65
1498 (Brown)	$300	$375	$525
1499 (Red-Brown)	525	850	1,250
1500 (Red)	1,250	2,000	3,000

Varieties

One of the top varieties in the Indian Head cent series is the Snow-1, an obverse doubled die that has a bold doubled LIBERTY. In addition to the doubled die, it has a base of a numeral 1 boldly sticking out of the necklace, and the tops of other digits in the denticles. This is a great variety with strong collector demand. Another very minor doubled die is known. There are 13 repunched dates known for this date, some very pronounced. Due to the high premiums this date receives, some varieties may not be worthy of an additional premium.

1866, Doubled-Die Obverse, Snow-1

1867

Circulation-Strike Mintage:
9,821,000

Proof Mintage:
625+ (estimated)

1867 Cent Production: This is another lower-mintage date, similar in rarity to the 1866. The Mint put most of its resources into the production of the new nickel five-cent piece. The nickels' mintage was nearly three times the mintage of cents in 1867. Together with the dwindling production of two-cent and three-cent pieces, the Mint was producing mostly minor coinage this year in an effort to replace tattered Fractional Currency notes issued during the Civil War (although new notes were still being made in large quantities).

Survivability: These were minted in a high enough quantity that they did not initially attract collector interest, except for the Proof issue. Starting in 1871, the cent coinage in circulation began to be recalled and melted by the Mint (see the discussion under 1871). The targets were the old copper-nickel cents, but even freshly minted bronze cents were taken in and melted. The lower-mintage dates 1866 to 1870 were among the hardest hit in this recoinage effort. The Mint continued redeeming bronze cents up until 1875. Any in high grade today survived purely by chance.

When premiums of Mint State coins soared in the 1960's, this date was a target of processors who would wire brush, or *whiz*, Very Fine to About Uncirculated coins to make them look Mint State. A large percentage of available examples in these grades were destroyed.

Collecting Challenges: Searching for problem-free examples will be difficult. Most collectors tend to settle on pieces in a grade lower than average for their set, with the hope of finding the right coin later. Be prepared to pay a good premium for attractive examples in any grade.

Collecting Circulated Pieces: The optimal collecting grade for circulated coins is VF-20. Most collections that started with Grandma's box of old coins will have a bent or corroded example to represent this date. Selecting a problem-free coin with adequate detail is important. Collectors soon realize that extra money spent on an attractive coin is money well spent. When it comes time to sell, nice coins will sell easily, perhaps for a healthy profit.

Collecting Mint State Pieces: The optimal collecting grade for Mint State coins is MS-64RB. Many coins are found struck on planchets which have lighter and darker patterns, similar to the look of woodgrain. This is caused when the tin and zinc alloy in the ingot is not fully mixed. When the ingot is rolled out, the small pockets of alloy get stretched into streaks, which quickly turn dark after the planchets are cut out and struck. This type of toning is acceptable for red-brown coins, but it will prevent a coin from staying full red. For this reason, the already scarce Mint State example of this date is very rare in full red.

Collecting Proof Issues: Proofs of this year typically show good mirrors and average quality. Gems are very hard to find, especially with full red color. Cameo contrast is very hard to find on this issue. Perhaps only 5% of Proofs PF-64 and higher might qualify as cameo.

1867: Circulation Strike

GSID	VG-8	F-12	VF-20	EF-40	AU-50	AU-58	MS-60	MS-63	MS-65
1308 (Brown)	$80	$105	$135	$175	$245	$340	$345	$455	$1,000
1309 (Red-Brown)	—	—	—	—	—	—	390	650	1,150
1310 (Red)	—	—	—	—	—	—	—	950	7,000

1867: Proof Strike

GSID	PF-63	PF-64	PF-65
1503 (Brown)	$300	$375	$650
1504 (Red-Brown)	525	1,000	1,200
1505 (Red)	1,150	3,100	4,400

Varieties

The 1867, 67 Over 67 (Snow-1) is a very bold repunched date that is widely collected by date-set collectors. It is worthy of a very good premium. There are other minor varieties known for this date, but these have much weaker collector interest. Varieties on scarce-date issues have to be very bold and interesting for collectors to be willing to pay an additional premium over an already pricey coin.

1867, 67 Over 67, Snow-1

1867, 67 Over 67: Circulation Strike

GSID	VG-8	F-12	VF-20	EF-40	AU-50	AU-58	MS-60	MS-63	MS-65
1455 (Brown)	$180	$235	$360	$725	$950	$1,300	$1,550	$2,400	$4,000
1456 (Red-Brown)	—	—	—	—	—	—	—	3,000	5,250
1457 (Red)	—	—	—	—	—	—	—	—	29,000

1868

Circulation-Strike Mintage:
10,266,500

Proof Mintage:
600+ (estimated)

1868 Cent Production: The Mint continued to put most of its attention on producing the five-cent nickel and the one-cent piece. The two-and three-cent pieces were still being made in sizable quantities, but their totals were nowhere near the amount minted for the one- and five-cent coins. The coinage of cents was not much greater in quantity than in 1866 and 1867.

In Congress this year, Mint Director Linderman promoted a bill that called for the abolishment of all other coinage below 25 cents, to be replaced by nickel coinage in one-cent, three-cent, and five-cent denominations. The three-cent piece and five-cent nickel were already established, but the idea of changing the cent to nickel failed in the Senate and lost favor when James Pollock replaced Linderman the next year.

Survivability: This issue was not considered scarce until well after the coinage melts of 1871 to 1875 (see the discussion under 1871). Any high-grade survivors were kept from being melted only by chance. Most of this mintage today is in grades lower than Fine. Many surviving Very Fine to About Uncirculated coins were destroyed during the 1960's when unscrupulous people took these coins and wire-brushed them to simulate mint luster.

Collecting Challenges: Selecting problem-free coins will be difficult. Search for well-struck pieces with good eye appeal and expect to pay a premium for these coins.

Collecting Circulated Pieces: The optimal collecting grade for circulated coins is VF-20. These are mostly found in grades below Fine. Finding attractive well-struck coins in choice circulated condition is difficult. Stay away from problem coins with heavy scratches or corrosion, unless they are offered at a gift price.

Collecting Mint State Pieces: The optimal collecting grade for Mint State coins is MS-64RB. These are available in quantities similar to those of the 1866 and 1867 coins. All three dates should be priced similarly, except in grades MS-65RD or higher, as more 1868 pieces are available in this grade. Selecting quality pieces is difficult, as many of these suffer from poor strikes. Expect to pay a premium for very attractive examples.

Collecting Proof Issues: These are found in similar quantities as the 1866, 1867, and 1869 issues. Examples tend to be red-brown in color, as many planchets have streaky toning due to improperly mixed alloy.

About 15% of this issue is found with the reverse rotated 170 degrees from normal. These are possibly from a group of Proofs struck a year or two after the date on the coin. This was a period when the Mint was striking many collector coins of earlier dates.

1868: Circulation Strike

GSID	VG-8	F-12	VF-20	EF-40	AU-50	AU-58	MS-60	MS-63	MS-65
1311 (Brown)	$80	$105	$135	$195	$260	$325	$330	$440	$775
1312 (Red-Brown)	—	—	—	—	—	—	—	500	1,200
1313 (Red)	—	—	—	—	—	—	—	1,300	4,750

1868: Proof Strike

GSID	PF-63	PF-64	PF-65
1508 (Brown)	$350	$430	$775
1509 (Red-Brown)	405	575	1,000
1510 (Red)	650	1,500	3,250

Varieties

There are three doubled dies known for this year. Snow-1, with doubling on the lower ribbon and the designer's initial, L, receives the highest premium, but is relatively unknown outside of specialist collectors. Five varieties featuring repunched dates are known as well, but all are rather minor.

1869

Circulation-Strike Mintage:
6,420,000

Proof Mintage:
600+ (estimated)

1869 Cent Production: With an original mintage lower than those of the 1866 to 1868 cents, the 1869 issue is obviously rarer. Mintages for the cent, two-cent piece, nickel three-cent piece, and nickel five-cent piece all drop this year and continued to drop over the next few years.

Survivability: Between 1868 and 1869, more than three million bronze cents and two-cent pieces were turned in to the Mint for melting. A flaw in the Mint Act of April 22, 1864 failed to give any redemption clause for the coins. At that time the cent was given a 10¢ legal tender limit, and that was lowered to only 4¢ the next year. The banks could refuse to take the cents in from merchants and, as Carothers notes, many likely did. As a result, the Mint was the buyer of last resort and obliged itself to buy and melt the coins. This was done without any authorization from Congress, but it helped to solve the oversight.

The effect of this was the wholesale melting of all the bronze issues. Many of the recently issued coins went straight back to the Mint to be melted. Over the next ten years, more than 55 million bronze cents were melted; these mass meltings have had a great impact on the availability of this date as well as all others of the era.

Collecting Challenges: This is a very tough date to find, in all grades. Few collectors realize how rare this date really is. Its price has climbed steadily over the years. With little supply of quality pieces available, it will probably continue to appreciate. Expect to always pay a premium for attractive pieces.

Collecting Circulated Pieces: The optimal collecting grade for circulated coins is F-12. Most examples are a very low grade. Finding problem-free examples in Very Fine condition or better is very difficult. Examples with problems such as scratches, cleaning, and rim dents are mostly what collectors will encounter. Try and hold out for original coins without serious problems.

Collecting Mint State Pieces: The optimal collecting grade for Mint State coins is MS-64RB. Although this grade is very scarce, there are usually examples available in the same proportion as for the 1866 to 1868 dates. These coins were saved only by chance, and in very small quantities. On such small scale, the chance survival of even a 50-piece roll would alter the pricing structure between these dates. However, such an occurrence is very unlikely for coins of this era. Full red examples, although scarce, are a bit more readily available than earlier dates.

Collecting Proof Issues: This issue was struck in the same mintage range as the 1866 to 1868 issues. Most have a mottled red-brown look, with average mirrors. Gem red examples are difficult to find. Most of this issue comes with light die-polishing lines in the fields. Die-polishing lines, sometimes confused with *hairlines*, are transferred to every coin struck from that die and are raised on the coin. Hairlines are fine scratches on the surface of a coin and are remnants of some kind of cleaning or wiping of the coin after it is struck.

1869: Circulation Strike

GSID	VG-8	F-12	VF-20	EF-40	AU-50	AU-58	MS-60	MS-63	MS-65
1314 (Brown)	$130	$230	$290	$455	$550	$675	$775	$900	$1,500
1315 (Red-Brown)	—	—	—	—	—	—	—	1,150	2,450
1316 (Red)	—	—	—	—	—	—	—	1,300	3,250

1869: Proof Strike

GSID	PF-63	PF-64	PF-65
1513 (Brown)	$850	$1,000	$1,250
1514 (Red-Brown)	950	1,300	1,600
1515 (Red)	1,150	1,600	2,800

Varieties

The so-called 1869, 69 Over 68 issue was believed to be an actual overdate in the 1950's and 1960's. As overdates receive great demand from collectors, it soared in value more than the regular non-overdate coins. It was added to coin albums and reported in pricing guides. However, this changed in 1970 when researchers at the American Numismatic Association reported that the overdate was actually only a repunched date, 1869, 69 Over 69. The makers of coin albums have since relabeled their product with 1869, 69 Over 69.

1869, 69 Over 69, Snow-3

Collectors still search for an example of this coin, and fill the void with the Snow-3 variety, which has a bold 69 Over 69 repunching. S-3 is common enough in high grades of Mint State to satisfy collector demand, but it is very difficult to find in circulated grades, especially in Extremely Fine or About Uncirculated.

There are 15 other repunched date varieties known for this date, some of which show doubling on the 9 only. The Snow-1 variety has a boldly repunched 18 and is quite scarce. Most of the other repunched dates are minor and attract little premium.

1869, 69 Over 69: Circulation Strike

GSID	VG-8	F-12	VF-20	EF-40	AU-50	AU-58	MS-60	MS-63	MS-65
331610 (Brown)	$155	$275	$350	$500	$575	$725	$775	$900	$1,500
331611 (Red-Brown)	—	—	—	—	—	—	—	1,150	2,450
331612 (Red)	—	—	—	—	—	—	—	1,300	3,250

1870

Circulation-Strike Mintage:
5,275,000

Proof Mintage:
1,000+ (estimated)

1870 Cent Production: In 1870 the reverse design was changed slightly. The new design features a bold ONE CENT denomination. The previous design had a shallower denomination, with the N in ONE being especially shallow. A growing number of collectors seek both reverse designs for this year as well as for 1871 and 1872.

Shallow N (Type of 1869)

Since reverse dies do not have dates, the Mint had a number of Shallow N dies on hand at the time, perhaps from the prior year. The Mint reworked many of these dies with the Bold N design, creating numerous doubled-die reverse varieties—a situation similar to the 1878, 7 Over 8 Clear Doubled Feathers Morgan dollar.

Bold N / Shallow N

The production of all minor coinage was in a decreasing trend during this era. The main reason for this cutback was the lack of a redemption clause in any of the issuing legislation. The nickel and bronze coinage was beginning to accumulate in commercial channels.

Bold N (Type of 1870)

Survivability: This issue was not saved to a great extent. Most of the coins were returned to the Mint over the next few years, during the 1870's recoinage (see 1871 for further discussion). Without any authority from Congress, the Mint accepted nickel and bronze issues, which had been jammed in bank vaults in ever growing numbers, and melted them down to make new coins. The 1870 cents were most likely at the top of the heap of coins being returned to the Mint. Any that survived in circulation are today found in mostly very low grades. The few high-grade examples that are available survived mainly by chance.

Collecting Challenges: As with all dates of this era, finding attractive problem-free coins will be difficult, though most are well struck. Shallow N reverse coins are slightly scarcer than those with the Bold N reverse, but not enough to warrant a premium.

Collecting Circulated Pieces: The optimal collecting grade for circulated coins is VF-20. Higher grades will be very difficult to find. Lower grades are usually available. Avoid problem pieces, such as cleaned, scratched, or corroded coins. These are discounted in general, but usually not enough to make them good buys.

Collecting Mint State Pieces: The optimal collecting grade for Mint State coins is MS-64RB. These coins are typically red-brown, with even-colored pieces particularly difficult to find. Many come with streaky toning due to an improperly mixed alloy in the planchets. Full red coins are rare, and collectors should beware of chemically altered pieces impersonating original full red coins.

When originally struck, all bronze coins are full red. The heat of striking creates a molecular shell, which somehow blocks any change in the color. When the acids in your hands come in contact with the surface of the coin, this layer is destroyed and the coin will start to turn brown. When a coin is cleaned, it is also susceptible to turning a brown color within a short period of time. For this reason, it is very important that any full red coin not have any indication of having been cleaned in the past.

Collecting Proof Issues: Proofs are usually found with medium mirrors. It seems that the dies were not polished very deeply to begin with. Any deep-mirror examples should be worthy of a significant premium. Cameo examples are rare; perhaps only 5% of high-quality examples qualify.

This date in Proof is found with the Shallow N reverse, in use from 1868, as well as a new Bold N reverse. There is a growing general collector interest in the reverse types.

1870, Shallow N: Circulation Strike

GSID	VG-8	F-12	VF-20	EF-40	AU-50	AU-58	MS-60	MS-63	MS-65
285617 (Brown)	$150	$215	$285	$480	$575	$725	$725	$825	$1,650
285625 (Red-Brown)	—	—	—	—	—	—	—	1,150	2,750
285633 (Red)	—	—	—	—	—	—	—	1,300	4,100

1870, Bold N: Circulation Strike

GSID	VG-8	F-12	VF-20	EF-40	AU-50	AU-58	MS-60	MS-63	MS-65
1317 (Brown)	$135	$195	$260	$435	$525	$650	$675	$750	$1,500
1318 (Red-Brown)	—	—	—	—	—	—	—	1,000	2,500
1319 (Red)	—	—	—	—	—	—	—	1,200	3,750

1870: Proof Strike

GSID	PF-63	PF-64	PF-65
1518 (Brown)	$650	$850	$1,250
1519 (Red-Brown)	800	1,150	2,750
1520 (Red)	1,000	1,400	3,250

VARIETIES

Due to the reverse design change, and the subsequent reworking of the dies, there are at least 23 reverse doubled dies known. Some are very dramatic, but most are very minor. The most dramatic varieties are the misplaced dates (MPD). Snow-5 shows a bold 0 digit sticking into the field under the date. S-8 shows the remnants of multiple digits above the denticles, possibly as many as eight. Both garner premiums greater than five times normal value.

One popular variety, dubbed the *Pickaxe*, has die damage by the last feather, which looks like a miner's axe. It is relatively common, being paired with at least five different dies.

Above all these in significance are the reverse design varieties: the Shallow N and Bold N. These are gaining in popularity with date collectors, as their existence becomes more widely known.

An 1870 Shield nickel variety is known with clash marks from the obverse Indian Head cent die! This gives rise to the question: does an 1870 Indian Head cent exist with the corresponding Shield nickel clash marks? None have yet been found.

1871

Circulation-Strike Mintage:
3,929,500

Proof Mintage:
960+ (estimated)

1871 Cent Production: The Mint Act of March 3, 1871, provided much-needed authorization for the Mint to redeem the nickel and bronze coinage that was clogging up commercial channels. Because these coins didn't have a bullion value close to their face value, and because their legal-tender status was limited, banks had nowhere to go to turn in excess coinage. Now the Mint was given the legal authorization to do what it had been doing for the past few years anyway.

Bold N

Shallow N

In the decade following, more than 31 million copper-nickel cents from 1857 to 1864 were melted. By 1909, about half the original mintage of copper-nickel cents was turned in and destroyed.

More than 55 million bronze cents were melted in the years following 1871. The metal was reused to make more cents. This seemingly wasteful cycle of redeeming older coins and recoining the metal into new coins went on until 1874, when the Mint started reissuing older coins alongside the new pieces.

The Shallow N reverse is found on a small number of coins from this date. As collector appreciation increases, this is becoming a very high–premium coin.

Survivability: This is one of the rarest dates in the series. Most new 1871 cents went though a quick round trip from the Mint, to the banks, and then back to the Mint for recoinage. As a result, most survivors are coins that escaped into circulation and stayed there for a long time. Most are in very low grades.

Collecting Challenges: Problem-free examples are very difficult to locate; however, a majority of this issue is found well struck. Select attractive examples. The Shallow N reverse is very scarce, but dealer awareness is presently low. This may offer an opportunity for collectors.

Collecting Circulated Pieces: The optimal collecting grade for circulated coins is F-12. Most examples are in very low grades. Searching for quality within the grade desired is important. Examples in Extremely Fine and About Uncirculated are very hard to locate and are always in demand. Avoid problem pieces with pitted surfaces, heavy scratches, or dents. Don't forget to check for the very scarce Shallow N reverse.

Collecting Mint State Pieces: The optimal collecting grade for Mint State coins is MS-63. These are typically well struck, but attractive examples are particularly elusive. Most are dull red-brown, with more brown than red. Coins with even color and vibrant luster, regardless of color, are very desirable. Many collectors prefer solid brown coins compared to streaky red-brown pieces.

Collecting Proof Issues: These typically come with moderate mirrors and red-brown coloration. It seems that no example of this date comes with the crisp, early-die-state detail that can be found on other dates in previous years. The coins always have an over-polished look rather than the fine polishing and sharp contrast seen on Proofs of other years. As a result, Proofs of this date are very rare with cameo contrast.

Both Shallow N and Bold N reverses are found for this date in Proof format. Neither is worth a premium, as collector awareness is very low. Also, there is a scarce date variation with the numerals 7 and 1 touching. These are usually poorly made and may be mistaken for circulation strikes.

1871, Shallow N: Circulation Strike

GSID	VG-8	F-12	VF-20	EF-40	AU-50	AU-58	MS-60	MS-63	MS-65
285634 (Brown)	$135	$215	$255	$575	$775	$950	$1,000	$1,900	$3,750
285638 (Red-Brown)	—	—	—	—	—	—	—	2,250	4,750
285637 (Red)	—	—	—	—	—	—	—	3,450	8,750

1871, Bold N: Circulation Strike

GSID	VG-8	F-12	VF-20	EF-40	AU-50	AU-58	MS-60	MS-63	MS-65
1320 (Brown)	$130	$195	$235	$490	$575	$675	$725	$850	$1,750
1321 (Red-Brown)	—	—	—	—	—	—	—	1,000	2,250
1322 (Red)	—	—	—	—	—	—	—	2,250	6,500

1871, Shallow N: Proof Strike

GSID	PF-63	PF-64	PF-65
376393 (Brown)	$750	$1,000	$1,500
376394 (Red-Brown)	875	1,100	2,000
376395 (Red)	1,150	1,600	3,000

1871, Bold N: Proof Strike

GSID	PF-63	PF-64	PF-65
1523 (Brown)	$750	$1,000	$1,500
1524 (Red-Brown)	875	1,100	2,000
1525 (Red)	1,100	1,500	2,700

Varieties

The scarce Shallow N reverse offers a challenge for collectors, and the premium for these has been increasing as collector awareness increases. An MS-65RB example sold for $13,000 in 2005. The Shallow N dies are given variety designations Snow-4 or Snow-5. The S-5 has a misplaced digit variety on the obverse. There are only a few other die varieties. The variety with the 7 and 1 touching, S-2, is very rare.

The Recoinage of the 1870's

When the cent was changed to bronze in 1864 it was deemed necessary to add a legal-tender limit to the authorizing legislation. At first it was 10¢, but shortly after it was dropped to only 4¢. This did little to ensure the cent's circulation—necessity and convenience alone made the new coins successful. However, by actually stating a legal-tender limit, rather than just releasing them into circulation, the banking establishments could point to a reason to refuse them in larger quantities. As the Mint's production of cents exceeded the demand in the late 1860's the coins started to accumulate with no legal outlet.

To remedy this situation, the Mint Act of 1871 authorized the Mint to redeem minor coinage (all coins previously minted in copper and nickel alloy, five cents and below) and to reissue the cents. Accordingly, the Mint took in millions of these minor coins and melted them all. The reissued coinage up until 1874 was in the form of newly minted cents.

Below is the record of bronze cents redeemed and reissued, including the quantity of copper-nickel cents redeemed and melted. It seems that in 1874 someone decided that the redeemed cents could just as easily be reissued without being melted and recoined. The coinage of cents during the 1870's was heavily influenced by this decision. In 1877 alone, enough cents were redeemed and reissued to make the mintage of new coins almost unnecessary.

Record of Minor Coins Redeemed, 1871–1881			
Year	Copper-Nickel Cents Redeemed	Bronze Cents Redeemed	Bronze Cents Reissued
1871	8,569,848	7,275,091	
1872	5,751,073	5,635,999	
1873	2,641,157	2,661,362	
1874	3,015,870	4,051,908	372,500
1875	2,204,701	3,937,872	3,926,000
1876	3,106,895	5,932,723	5,599,500
1877	2,870,433	9,908,148	9,821,500
1878	1,993,125	8,213,999	8,242,500
1879	870,342	3,515,327	3,357,500
1880	577,130	3,626,501	3,342,000
1881	81,393	765,395	1,132,500
Totals	31,681,967	55,524,325	35,794,000

Source: National Archives; reprinted in Steve/Flynn 1995

1872

Circulation-Strike Mintage:
4,042,000

Proof Mintage:
950+ (estimated)

1872 Cent Production: These cents were struck in quantities similar to those of 1871. Aside from the 1877, this is the toughest date to find today. The planchets made from the recoinage melt were not of a consistent quality. Most coins of this date are streaky due to uneven alloy mixes. Many examples were poorly struck or are found with missing detail due to some liquid, such as machine oil or water, getting on the planchet or dies.

A minority of these coins was struck with the Shallow N reverse (see 1871). This is becoming a well-known design change that is increasing in value as specialists become more familiar with its existence.

Survivability: The ongoing recoinage effort created a crazy situation where the recently issued coinage was being sent back to the Mint to be melted and struck into new coins. As soon as the new coins reached the banks, many may have been piled on top of older coins that were scheduled to be shipped back to the Mint. As a result, most of this issue was melted soon after its production.

Examples that survived are usually very low-grade pieces. It is very difficult to find problem-free coins. In the past, many examples in the Very Fine to Extremely Fine grades were wire-brushed to simulate mint luster. These whizzed coins were dangerous to collectors until the advent of certified grading. Many coins were ruined in the process of being whizzed.

Collecting Challenges: It is very difficult to find attractive, problem-free examples. Most are poorly struck, or are struck through machine oil. Any attractive problem-free example should be considered for your collection. Some collectors target this date for investment potential. One Detroit collector, Carl Herkowitz, spent 25 years buying problem-free examples of this date. Even so, he had a difficult time finding more than 200 pieces. His hoard contained 22 Mint State examples, 20 About Uncirculated, 50 Extremely Fine, 50 Very Fine, 50 Fine, and 20 Very Good. His hoard was sold from 2003 to 2005. Only one example in this group had a Shallow N reverse, and it was bought already attributed as such. Hoards of high-quality pieces like these do not cause concern about price drops if they were to be sold—on the contrary, if large groups of rare coins enter the market at once, they excite collectors and prices may actually rise.

Collecting Circulated Pieces: The optimal collecting grade for circulated coins is F-12. This is one of the toughest dates in the series to find in attractive shape, without any problems. Consider dropping strict standards on strike and light hits to acquire this date. These are very rare when properly graded in Extremely Fine and About Uncirculated. Some collectors attempt to find the Shallow N reverse as well as the typically found Bold N reverse.

Collecting Mint State Pieces: The optimal collecting grade for Mint State coins is MS-63RB. It is very difficult to locate with a full strike. Many are missing detail, usually on the reverse, due to machine oil or water resting on the planchet or on the dies. Coins that were struck through liquid will have good strikes on one side and missing details on the other. Weakly struck coins will have missing detail on both sides.

This issue will be mostly streaky red-brown, due to improperly mixed alloy. Full red coins are very rare. This is the toughest date to find in MS-65RD.

A growing number of collectors attempt to acquire both reverse types. The Shallow N is about ten times rarer than the Bold N.

Collecting Proof Issues: Proofs of 1872 are much more readily available than high-grade Mint State coins. As a result, many substitute the less expensive Proof in their collections of Uncirculated coins, although the different texture may be distracting to most collectors.

1872, Bulging T

These are a bit more readily available than 1871 and earlier dates, but because of date collector pressure they receive similar prices. While they tend to be red-brown, they are not as streaky as other dates. This makes finding attractive examples a bit easier. Proofs of this date are quite scarce in full red, and gems are very tough.

It is difficult to find deep mirrors on this issue and examples with full cameo contrast are rare.

A new Bold N reverse die with a distinctive bulging right pennant of the T in CENT is found on all Proof issues. This die was used intermittently until 1878.

1872, Shallow N: Circulation Strike

GSID	VG-8	F-12	VF-20	EF-40	AU-50	AU-58	MS-60	MS-63	MS-65
285641 (Brown)	—	—	—	$480	$575	$800	$875	$1,000	$2,500
285643 (Red-Brown)	—	—	—	—	—	—	—	1,950	3,300
285645 (Red)	—	—	—	—	—	—	—	3,500	11,000

1872, Bold N: Circulation Strike

GSID	VG-8	F-12	VF-20	EF-40	AU-50	AU-58	MS-60	MS-63	MS-65
1323 (Brown)	$150	$235	$365	$480	$575	$800	$875	$1,000	$2,500
1324 (Red-Brown)	—	—	—	—	—	1,150	1,250	1,900	3,100
1325 (Red)	—	—	—	—	—	—	—	3,250	10,500

1872, Bold N: Proof Strike

GSID	PF-63	PF-64	PF-65
1528 (Brown)	$650	$1,000	$1,700
1529 (Red-Brown)	800	1,150	2,050
1530 (Red)	950	1,900	4,400

VARIETIES

At least three different Shallow N dies were used this year. The die pairs without obverse varieties are listed as Snow-4. Shallow N dies paired with obverse varieties are listed as S-13 (repunched date) and S-14 (bold misplaced digit). There are a number of minor repunched dates, but because of the high price of this date, premiums are small.

A small part of the D in UNITED started to deteriorate on the hub starting this year. (The hub is the undated steel positive used to make dies for coinage. A hub can be used over many years since it does not carry the date.) This hub deterioration, resulting in a "broken D," is an interesting aspect to trace over the next few years, but its coins do not warrant a premium.

1873, Closed 3

Circulation-Strike Mintage:
2,500,000 (estimated, out of 11,676,500 total)

Proof Mintage:
1,100+ (estimated)

***Closed* or *Close*:** The "closed" 3 on 1873 coinage is not really closed, but nearly so. Harry X Boosel popularized *Closed 3* when he shared his affection for the date in a series of articles called "1873–1873," published in book form in 1960. For many years, the *Red Book* and Whitman's Bowers Series (now the Red Book Series) erred on the side of accuracy with the term *Close 3*. As of the 79th edition of the *Red Book*, however, Whitman has returned to *Closed 3*, in keeping with modern collector usage.

1873, Closed 3, Cent Production: On January 18, Chief Coiner A.L. Snowden submitted a formal complaint that the 3 in the dates on all the coinage dies was too close and could easily be confused for an 8. New date punches with a more open 3 were made and put into use on all the remaining dies to be made. There is no way to accurately record how many coins were struck from the dies made prior to the change. After the Open 3 dies were prepared, it is probable that both date styles were struck simultaneously. The mintage given here is estimated from the surviving percentage of Closed 3 coins compared to Open 3 examples.

1873, Closed 3

1873, Open 3

Survivability: About 25% of all 1873 Indian Head cents have the Closed 3 date style. These seem to be about as readily available as the 1872 issue, which has a higher mintage. The pace of the redemption of cents slowed a bit in 1873 and 1874, so more of this issue survived. These pieces stayed in circulation for a long time.

Collecting Challenges: The 1873 Closed 3 cent is very difficult to find unattributed, as its desirability has been known for many years. Expect to pay a premium about double the price of the Open 3. Look for attractive problem-free pieces. Many collectors add both the Closed 3 and Open 3 digit styles to their collections; however, if only one example is desired, collectors usually choose the less expensive Open 3. This keeps demand a bit lower than it would otherwise be.

Collecting Circulated Pieces: The optimal collecting grade for circulated coins is VF-20. Most are well struck. Avoid problem pieces with corroded surfaces or with aggressive cleaning. Most coin albums label a hole for this coin, so demand is moderately strong.

Collecting Mint State Pieces: The optimal collecting grade for Mint State coins is MS-63RB. These are very scarce, but the premium over the Open 3 style is lower due to weaker demand from date collectors. Most are found with streaky red-brown colors. Full red examples are very scarce. Beware of cleaned examples offered as gem full red.

Collecting Proof Issues: Proofs were struck in Closed 3 style only. These are moderately scarce, though much more common than the Mint State format. The dies seem to have been heavily polished prior to use. None are known from what numismatists call an early die state. Mirrors are usually medium. Cameo examples are rare.

1873, Closed 3: Circulation Strike

GSID	VG-8	F-12	VF-20	EF-40	AU-50	AU-58	MS-60	MS-63	MS-65
1329 (Brown)	$60	$85	$105	$210	$285	$390	$420	$550	$1,200
1330 (Red-Brown)	—	—	—	—	—	—	—	775	1,700
1331 (Red)	—	—	—	—	—	—	—	1,400	7,000

1873, Closed 3: Proof Strike

GSID	PF-63	PF-64	PF-65
1533 (Brown)	$365	$550	$850
1534 (Red-Brown)	440	650	1,000
1535 (Red)	775	1,150	2,750

Varieties

The main variety for this year is the Doubled LIBERTY, Snow-1 (see next entry). This variety is very popular. There is a second, less dramatic doubled LIBERTY, S-2. It has doubling on just the BERTY of LIBERTY. All known examples are struck with the Bold N reverse. A Shallow N reverse may exist on the S-2 as well as others, but none have been authenticated yet.

1873, Doubled LIBERTY

Circulation-Strike Mintage:
100,000 (estimated, out of 11,676,500 total)

1873, Doubled LIBERTY, Snow-1

1873, Doubled LIBERTY, Cent Production: This is the boldest doubled die in the series. It is commonly referred to as the *Doubled LIBERTY*, classified as Snow-1. The doubling is boldest on the headband and feathers. There is little or no doubling on the legend UNITED STATES OF AMERICA. This is due to the nature of the die-making process at the time. A blank die is given a shallow conical head when first turned down. The first impression of the hub into the die did not impress the entire design, only the central portion. The next impression of the hub filled out the design, but at a slightly rotated position. Thus, only the central portion of the design got doubled impressions. The date did not get doubled because it was added to the die after the portrait and legend.

Survivability: Walter Breen first described this variety in 1953. (At the time there was little knowledge regarding doubled dies. Collector interest in doubled dies grew after the discovery of the 1955 doubled-die Lincoln cent.) Few have turned up over the years. In Breen's 1988 *Complete Encyclopedia of U.S. and Colonial Coins* he proclaimed the possible finest known to be an MS-60 cleaned piece in the 1983 Roy Harte III sale. Today, about 150 examples of the Doubled LIBERTY are known, about 20 of which are in Mint State.

Collecting Challenges: These are highly sought after. It is very rare to find one unattributed, although it still happens. One of the greatest cherrypicks on record involved this coin. In 2000, a collection of Mint State Indian Head cents was offered to Indian Head cent collector Dr. Tom Turissini by a local dealer. The set contained many beautiful high-grade coins in an old-time holder. The 1873 cent was an unattributed example of the famed Doubled LIBERTY. It later was graded MS-64RD by PCGS, and sold for nearly double the record price for the variety at the time. Later still, it surfaced in the Stewart Blay Collection (the example pictured on page 123); this is still the only example graded full red.

The finest graded piece, a nearly full red MS-65RB graded by PCGS, was initially bought as a generic "BU" (Brilliant Uncirculated) from a seller on the Internet for $5,000 in 1996. It later sold at auction for $69,000 in 2005.

At the 1990 ANA show in Seattle, Brian Wagner walked into the show, and at the first table he stopped at, bought an 1873 cent in About Uncirculated for $60. It was not even labeled as a Closed 3, let alone the Doubled LIBERTY. He sold it right away for $1,800. He probably should have held on to the coin, as it has advanced considerably in value since then. The coin was featured on the cover of the premier issue of *Longacre's Ledger* in 1990.

Buying an already attributed Doubled LIBERTY is the route most collectors have to go to get this famous coin. Most examples will have problems such as heavy or numerous marks. The high-quality pieces usually do not have to wait too long to find ready buyers, unless grossly overpriced.

Collecting Circulated Pieces: The optimal collecting grade for these is VF-20 or F-12, below which the details of interest will be worn away. On Very Good and lower examples, the doubling is visible on the nose and the ES of STATES. Problems such as scratches and nicks may be acceptable if they are reflected in the price. There usually are large price jumps between grades, so be careful about overgraded pieces.

Collecting Mint State Pieces: Mint State examples are very rare and as such, very expensive. Most are dark red-brown or brown. Presently only one full red example is known. Only about 20 other Mint State examples exist. Most are well struck. One example has a machine oil strike-through on the ERTY, leaving only the feathers and LIB showing doubling—an unfortunate situation.

One famous example of this coin is an MS-65RB example, which was featured on the cover of my book *Flying Eagle and Indian Cents* (1992). This coin was graded MS-65RB by NGC in 1993, after being photographed for the book; however, NGC failed to designate its Doubled LIBERTY status on the holder. Elliott Goldman, proprietor of Allstate Coin Co. of Tucson, Arizona, owned the coin. Elliott sent the coin back to NGC and it was stolen en route. Although it was insured, it was a loss to the numismatic community. Since this was the cover plate coin on my book as well as being the first 1873 Doubled LIBERTY cent to receive the MS-65RB grade, it was very difficult for the insurance company to figure out what it was worth. Eventually a $35,000 settlement was arrived at.

In 1998, this coin surfaced. A dealer member of the Professional Numismatists Guild was offered the coin. He held it until the rightful owner could be found. Elliott Goldman had passed away in 1995, and the insurance case was difficult to track down. Finally, after much research and legal wrangling, the coin was returned to the insurance company and sold back to the numismatic community. As it turned out, the thief did not know what he had, as it was unattributed in its NGC holder. He sold the coin soon after the theft for $200, to the person who later tried to sell it in 1998. The buyer forfeited ownership when he discovered it was stolen. There were no prosecutions in the case.

1873, Doubled LIBERTY: Circulation Strike

GSID	VG-8	F-12	VF-20	EF-40	AU-50	AU-58	MS-60	MS-63	MS-65
1332 (Brown)	$360	$650	$1,200	$2,750	$3,450	$4,550	$4,750	$7,750	$18,000
1333 (Red-Brown)	—	—	—	—	—	—	—	8,250	50,500
1334 (Red)	—	—	—	—	—	—	—	15,000	—

1873, Open 3

Circulation-Strike Mintage:
9,000,000 (estimated, out of 11,676,500 total)

1873, Open 3, Cent Production: The new dies with the Open 3 were made as soon as it was practicable. It seems that the Closed 3 digit punch was reworked to make the balls of the 3 smaller. Coins from these new dies were apparently struck alongside those of the Closed 3 dies.

1873, Open 3

1873, Closed 3

Survivability: Although this date is scarce, examples survived the 1870's recoinage a bit better than earlier dates. A little more than six million coins, mostly early cents, were redeemed during the 1873 and 1874 fiscal years. After 1874, coins were no longer melted unless they were unfit for circulation. This saved many coins from this date onward from the melting pot. This date is mostly found in very low grades.

Collecting Challenges: This date is more readily available than earlier dates, but is still scarce enough to be difficult to find problem free.

Collecting Circulated Pieces: The optimal collecting grade for circulated coins is EF-40. As with most issues of this era, finding problem-free examples is very difficult.

Collecting Mint State Pieces: The optimal collecting grade for Mint State coins is MS-64RB. This coin is much more readily available than the Closed 3 digit style. It is similar in rarity to the 1874 and 1875 issues. Most examples have streaky red-brown toning, as the source of the metal for this issue was a mixture of melted-down bronze cents and virgin metal. Full red examples are scarce.

1873, Open 3: Circulation Strike

GSID	VG-8	F-12	VF-20	EF-40	AU-50	AU-58	MS-60	MS-63	MS-65
1326 (Brown)	$49	$75	$95	$180	$235	$300	$325	$470	$1,150
1327 (Red-Brown)	—	—	—	—	—	—	—	625	1,300
1328 (Red)	—	—	—	—	—	—	—	1,000	3,750

Varieties

A minor doubled die exists with doubling only on the L in LIBERTY. More interesting is a bold repunched date, Snow-1, which looks like a Closed 3 date style due to the multiple threes.

1874

Circulation-Strike Mintage:
14,187,500

Proof Mintage:
700+ (estimated)

1874 Cent Production: Obviously, with mintages climbing slightly this year, this date is more readily available than the earlier dates in the 1870's.

Survivability: Beginning this year, the Mint began to reissue cents redeemed under the provisions set in the Mint Act of 1871. The Mint was required to buy base-metal coins in quantities no smaller than $20 and melt them down only if there were too many in circulation. Of the four million older bronze cents redeemed this year, 372,500 were released back into circulation. The 1874 cent is available in most grades, but it is not common by any comparison.

Collecting Challenges: These come well struck. The planchets tend to be rather streaky, due to a variable alloy mix. Many have been cleaned over the years. As with other dates, search for problem-free examples.

Collecting Circulated Pieces: The optimal collecting grade for circulated coins is EF-40. These should not be very difficult to find, though problem-free examples are elusive.

Collecting Mint State Pieces: The optimal collecting grade for Mint State coins is MS-64RB. It is difficult to find evenly colored red-brown examples. Most have streaky colorations. This issue is typically found well struck.

Collecting Proof Issues: All examples are from a single die pair with a defect on the date numeral 4, which has in the past been erroneously described as a repunched date. The reverse die used is the same die as is found on the 1872 and 1873 Proof issues, with a bulging right pennant on the T in CENT.

These typically have streaky red-brown toning. As the mintage suggests, they are a bit scarcer than 1873 Proofs. Mirrors are usually medium, but deeply mirrored examples do exist. Full red examples are rare, as are cameo examples.

1874: Circulation Strike

GSID	VG-8	F-12	VF-20	EF-40	AU-50	AU-58	MS-60	MS-63	MS-65
1335 (Brown)	$40	$70	$75	$100	$135	$190	$200	$275	$625
1336 (Red-Brown)	—	—	—	—	—	—	—	360	850
1337 (Red)	—	—	—	—	—	—	—	625	2,300

1874: Proof Strike

GSID	PF-63	PF-64	PF-65
1538 (Brown)	$415	$625	$850
1539 (Red-Brown)	470	700	1,150
1540 (Red)	575	1,150	3,250

Varieties

A minor, but elusive doubled die is known, Snow-1. A few repunched dates are known, but these are all minor.

1875

Circulation-Strike Mintage:
13,528,000

Proof Mintage:
700+ (estimated)

1875 Cent Production: The mintage is moderately low, similar to those of 1873 and 1874. The Mint Act of 1871 required the Mint to melt down old base-metal coins if they were redundant in circulation. Apparently, the cent backlog in commerce was easing, as the Mint released back to circulation the nearly four million bronze cents it took in this year. Thus, the Mint actually sent out more than 17 million cents in 1875. During the early 1870's much of the bronze used for cents came from the melting of redeemed cents and two-cent pieces of earlier years. Now, most of the bronze used was produced from new copper.

Survivability: This issue is scarce overall, about on the same level as the 1874. These coins stayed in circulation for a long time and are available in lower grades.

Collecting Challenges: These come rather well struck, so it should not be difficult to find well-struck examples. Many are struck on streaky planchets. This is due to improperly mixed tin and zinc in the bronze.

Collecting Circulated Pieces: The optimal collecting grade for circulated coins is EF-40. Search out even-colored examples. In circulated grades naturally colored cents should be a chocolate brown. Corroded coins tend to be dark, close to black. Cleaned coins tend to be bright. There are fewer variations for original coins, so if you know what an original coin looks like, you should have little trouble determining which coins have been cleaned.

Collecting Mint State Pieces: The optimal collecting grade for Mint State coins is MS-64RB. Search out attractive coins without problems. Many have a woodgrain type of toning, which may be acceptable; personal preference plays a part here. This type of toning will hinder a coin's ability to stay full red, but does not effect the desirability of coins graded red-brown.

Collecting Proof Issues: For some reason, the Proofs of this year were made fairly carelessly. This applies not only to cents but to all denominations. As a result, high-grade examples are very difficult to find. Many have streaky red-brown toning. Full red examples are rare. Cameo examples are prohibitively rare.

Some of the Proofs were struck with the 1872 reverse die, with the bulging right pennant of the T.

1875: Circulation Strike

GSID	VG-8	F-12	VF-20	EF-40	AU-50	AU-58	MS-60	MS-63	MS-65
1338 (Brown)	$40	$70	$75	$130	$175	$230	$240	$305	$775
1339 (Red-Brown)	—	—	—	—	—	—	—	405	1,000
1340 (Red)	—	—	—	—	—	—	—	430	3,100

1875: Proof Strike

GSID	PF-63	PF-64	PF-65
1543 (Brown)	$420	$625	$950
1544 (Red-Brown)	500	700	1,600
1545 (Red)	650	1,300	5,500

VARIETIES

A few repunched dates are known for this year. None are particularly scarce and none gain a substantial premium. Most examples show deterioration on the top of the D in UNITED. This was caused by hub deterioration progressing over the 1873 to 1875 years. The hub is an exact image of the coin, without the date, on a steel die. It is used to impress the design into any number of coinage dies over a period of years.

1876

Circulation-Strike Mintage:
7,944,000

Proof Mintage:
1,150+ (estimated)

1876 Cent Production: Cent mintage dipped quite a bit in 1876. This was not due to lack of demand. On the contrary, the issuance of cents from the Mint was more than 13 million pieces. In addition to the nearly eight million *new* cents produced, 5,599,500 older cents were released back into circulation. The older coins had been redeemed under the Mint Act of 1871.

Survivability: 1876 cents stayed in circulation and are usually found well worn. This is a popular date with collectors and is one of the tougher dates to find in most grades.

Collecting Challenges: These are very scarce and desirable. It is difficult to locate problem-free examples. Coins of this era are frequently found with oil or water strike-throughs, resulting in missing detail on otherwise well-struck coins, or depressions in the field.

Collecting Circulated Pieces: The optimal collecting grade for circulated coins is VF-20. Problem-free examples are very difficult to locate. Most are in very low grades. Search out coins with smooth, chocolate-brown-colored surfaces.

Collecting Mint State Pieces: The optimal collecting grade for Mint State coins is MS-64RB. Many of these have average strikes. It might be a challenge to locate an example with all the qualities you desire. Full red examples are more readily available than might be expected. Many come from an original roll that surfaced in the 1970's.

Collecting Proof Issues: This issue is more readily available than the scarce 1875, about equal to the 1873 Proof. A small percentage of these are one-sided Proofs. These are similar to other Proofs in their striking qualities and obverse surface quality. However, the reverse die was roughly polished, leaving numerous heavy die striations in the field. Overall, the quality of this issue is quite good. Gems are easily found, as are full red examples. Cameo gems are very scarce.

1876: Circulation Strike

GSID	VG-8	F-12	VF-20	EF-40	AU-50	AU-58	MS-60	MS-63	MS-65
1341 (Brown)	$50	$90	$145	$200	$275	$325	$330	$365	$775
1342 (Red-Brown)	—	—	—	—	—	—	—	455	1,100
1343 (Red)	—	—	—	—	—	—	—	900	2,750

1876: Proof Strike

GSID	PF-63	PF-64	PF-65
1548 (Brown)	$420	$550	$850
1549 (Red-Brown)	525	775	1,150
1550 (Red)	625	1,100	2,050

Varieties

There are no varieties known for this year. A Shallow N example was reported but has been verified to be counterfeit (see page 198).

1877

Circulation-Strike Mintage:
852,500

Proof Mintage:
900+ (estimated)

1877 Cent Production: This is the rarest date in the Indian Head cent series. The low mintage of 852,500 accounts for its relative rarity, but the real reason for its scarcity is tied to the economy of the time and its effects on the redemption program called for in the Mint Act of 1871.

Since 1873 the country had been suffering from a severe depression. By 1877, 27% of the working population was jobless, and those who did have jobs saw their wages cut, in many cases nearly in half.

Other major events made this one of the toughest years, economically, since the Civil War. The reconstruction of the South was terminated as a bargaining chip in the controversial election of Rutherford B. Hayes. A nationwide railroad strike crippled the economy further and brought with it the birth of the modern labor movement.

This had a very important impact on the redemption of the minor coinage. Huge amounts of these coins flooded back to the Mint. Enough nickel three-cent and five-cent pieces were turned in that, except for Proofs, the Mint stopped production of those denominations. Nearly ten million cents were turned in to the Mint this year, of which 9,821,500 were reissued (see further discussion under 1871). In addition to the reissues, the number of cents minted was the smallest since 1823.

Survivability: Even with a mintage close to one million pieces, the number of surviving 1877 cents is unusually low. Only two obverse dies and a single reverse die are known on circulation-strike examples. The single reverse die is of the Shallow N style last used in 1872. It suffered only a minor die clash, and no die cracks, over its lifetime striking of 1877 cents. The average die life during this era has been calculated to be 150,000 to 250,000 pieces. This "miracle die" could not possibly have struck all the cents minted this year without totally deteriorating or busting into pieces. There might have been more than one reverse die used but presently no others are known. The 1878 Mint report says that three obverse and six reverse dies were in stock for coinage of cents, but then says that only two reverse dies were used, and the four remaining dies were used in 1878. This additional die may be one of the Proof dies.

There are a few possibilities for the missing coins, including:

1. Perhaps the Mint record shows examples struck with 1876 dies early in 1877. This practice was common in the early 1800's but was not standard procedure in 1877.
2. Perhaps three-fourths of the original mintage was destroyed, leaving not one coin from additional die pairs as evidence of their existence.

The fact remains that the purported original mintage of this date appears to be way too high compared to the number of observed surviving examples. An upper estimate of

200,000 coins struck seems more accurate. Very few of these were saved at the time. Taken with the ten million reissued cents, this estimated mintage amounts to only 5% of the total released by the Mint this year. This coin was scarce from the day it was issued.

Collecting Challenges: This is the top coin on every Indian Head cent collector's list. Due to the high cost and difficulty in finding acceptable coins, many collectors reduce their standards and buy anything to fill the void. I suggest waiting until the right coin becomes available. Cost should be a secondary consideration. Attractive coins will serve their owners very well when it comes time to sell. This date is always expensive.

Collecting Circulated Pieces: The optimal collecting grade for circulated coins is F-12. It is very difficult to find accurately graded examples, especially in Extremely Fine or About Uncirculated grades. Dealers and grading services tend to grade this date liberally because of its rarity. Properly graded coins often carry a significant premium over pieces reported in pricing guides.

The diamond detail on the lower ribbon is usually shallow and is quickly worn down to only three diamonds. It is very difficult to find full-diamond examples in circulated condition. When found they command an added premium.

Problems such as rim dents, scratches, and unnatural color may be acceptable if the price reflects the problem. If fully priced, wait for a problem-free example. Many coins, actually Fine or Very Fine, have been wire-brushed to simulate mint luster. These are dangerous to buy, as they have a very low resale value.

Counterfeits: Counterfeits are numerous for this date. Luckily, there are only two obverse dies and one reverse die known on authentic pieces. If the diagnostics for these are known, the counterfeits will be easy to spot. Coins with altered dates are typically altered from 1879- or 1875-dated coins. Both these dates always have the Bold N reverse. False-die counterfeits are typically seen with a reverse die that was transferred from a common-date coin, also with the Bold N reverse. Even though the majority of counterfeits are found with the Bold N reverse, this should not condemn all 1877 cents found with this style reverse. The Proofs of this year all have the Bold N reverse, so it is possible that a circulated Proof might be mistaken for a fake. The best protection is to buy coins certified and authenticated by a major grading service. It is strongly recommended that you purchase this date from a reputable dealer who offers a guarantee, has a return policy, and is easy to locate. This will protect your investment.

Collecting Mint State Pieces: The optimal collecting grade for Mint State coins is MS-63RB. Look for well-struck examples with even coloration. Although the diamond detail for this issue is typically shallow, it is usually fully visible on well-struck Uncirculated coins. The best indicator for a full strike is full feather tips. Minor problems are acceptable if they are reflected in the price. Problem-free examples are highly sought after and will generally get higher premiums than expected.

Although the 1872 and 1871 cents are rarer in full red condition, this date is much pricier due to higher collector demand. Beware of cleaned examples. Because of the great difference between red-brown and full red examples, there is a temptation for unscrupulous individuals to lighten the color in an attempt to get a higher premium.

Perhaps the finest 1877 Indian Head cent is the example pictured on page 131 from the collection of Stewart Blay. This coin set a record price when it sold uncertified for $71,300 in Stack's Americana sale, January 1999. Today it is graded MS-66RD by PCGS. Stewart Blay can easily boast of having the finest collection of small cents (Flying Eagle, Indian Head, and Lincoln) ever assembled.

Collecting Proof Issues: All Proofs of this year are struck with Bold N reverse dies. Three obverse dies were used along with three reverse dies. One of the reverse dies has a bulging right pennant of the T in CENT. This is a die first used in 1872 and is found on some examples from all dates from that year until 1878.

The actual mintage of Proof cents for this year (and all years prior to 1878, for that matter) is unknown. Walter Breen in his 1977 *Complete Encyclopedia of U.S. and Colonial Proof Coins* gave a figure of 510+ coins as the mintage. Research by R.W. Julian revised the estimate to 900. The 510 figure is the quantity of complete sets sold, not including gold issues. At least 400 smaller sets of only the nickel and copper coins were also distributed. These numbers represent coins sold, not produced. It is likely that at least 1,500 coins were produced, with the remaining unsold pieces being destroyed or released into circulation. The quantity of survivors in population reports is similar to the 1876 issue.

Examples are usually readily available, and these are priced much higher than other Proof issues of similar rarity due to date-collector demand. However, prices are much lower than the Mint State circulation-strike issue. Some collectors will substitute a Proof 1877 for a circulation strike if the price differential is too great.

The issue is typically found with slightly subdued mirrors. One of the die pairings is weak on the right side. Some are found singly struck; these will have rounded edges. (Proofs are normally double struck, giving them very sharp edges.) Enough coins are usually available for collectors to be able to find a suitable example, without problems. Gems are also available, but cameo examples are quite scarce.

1877: Circulation Strike

GSID	VG-8	F-12	VF-20	EF-40	AU-50	AU-58	MS-60	MS-63	MS-65
1344 (Brown)	$950	$1,150	$1,550	$2,600	$3,000	$4,500	$4,750	$6,250	$12,000
1345 (Red-Brown)	—	—	—	—	—	—	—	7,250	14,500
1346 (Red)	—	—	—	—	—	—	—	9,750	29,000

1877: Proof Strike

GSID	PF-63	PF-64	PF-65
1553 (Brown)	$4,500	$5,000	$6,000
1554 (Red-Brown)	5,000	5,500	7,000
1555 (Red)	4,750	5,750	11,500

Varieties

There are no varieties known for this year. Collectors might want to acquire both the Proof and circulation-strike issue as an example of the Bold N and Shallow N reverse-design styles.

An example is known struck on a copper-nickel one-centavo piece from Venezuela. It is graded MS-61 by NGC. In 1876, ten million one-centavo coins were struck for the Venezuelan government at the Philadelphia Mint.

1878

Circulation-Strike Mintage:
5,797,500

Proof Mintage:
2,350

1878 Cent Production: The quality of cents improved in 1878. Since 1864, the Mint had been purchasing all its copper planchets from private businesses (usually Scovill Manufacturing in Waterbury, Connecticut, although they were not the sole provider). Yearly bids were asked for the planchet contract. Competition came from Benedict & Burnham Brass & Copper Co., also of Waterbury. This year more than eight million older cents were redeemed and issued alongside the nearly six million new cents.

Survivability: This is a very difficult date to locate in the upper circulated grades. Apparently the coins were released into circulation and stayed there well into the 20th century. However, enough of the coins escaped circulation that finding this date in Mint State is relatively easy.

Collecting Challenges: This is one of the last dates many collectors locate for their Extremely Fine and About Uncirculated sets. Collectors need to target this date to ensure finding a problem-free example.

Collecting Circulated Pieces: The optimal collecting grade for circulated coins is EF-40, with full diamond detail on the lower ribbon. Examples in grades below Fine are easy to locate; however, finding examples in About Uncirculated is very difficult.

Collecting Mint State Pieces: The optimal collecting grade for Mint State coins is MS-64RB. These are usually available in all grades and are well struck. Search for examples with attractive eye appeal.

Collecting Proof Issues: The typical Proof from this year is well made; this is one of the more readily available dates in gem full red. Cameo examples are easier to find for 1878 than for most other dates.

From this date on, mintage figures are of actual coins produced as accounted in the report of the director of the Mint. Earlier, mintages of Proof minor coins were calculated from sales records of minor coin sets plus the production of silver sets (which had been recorded since 1859), or simply guessed at.

Starting about 1878, coin dealer David U. Proskey began a practice of purchasing the unsold cent, nickel three-cent, and five-cent Proof coinage from the Mint. This eventually grew into a vast hoard, which probably contained hundreds of each date of Proof cents from 1878 onward. In the 1920's these were sold to F.C.C. Boyd, who later sold them to Howard MacIntosh of Tatham Coin Co. in Springfield, Massachusetts. By this time many of the coins had toned to vivid iridescent blue colors. Apparently the coins were kept in original Mint paper wrappers, which imparted this unusual tone. The Tatham Coin Co. marketed these in their advertisements as iridescent Proofs. These coins are encountered occasionally today and are very hotly contested when they are found.

1878: Circulation Strike

GSID	VG-8	F-12	VF-20	EF-40	AU-50	AU-58	MS-60	MS-63	MS-65
1347 (Brown)	$43	$80	$160	$200	$275	$345	$350	$390	$650
1348 (Red-Brown)	—	—	—	—	—	—	—	490	950
1349 (Red)	—	—	—	—	—	—	—	775	1,500

1878: Proof Strike

GSID	PF-63	PF-64	PF-65
1558 (Brown)	$285	$365	$525
1559 (Red-Brown)	340	525	900
1560 (Red)	470	950	1,300

Varieties

The three varieties known include a repunched date (Snow-1), misplaced date (Snow-2), and reverse doubled die (Snow-3). None of these are under any great collector demand.

1879

Circulation-Strike Mintage:
16,228,000

Proof Mintage:
3,200

1879 Cent Production: The mintage during this period increased significantly. In addition, more than three million redeemed coins were reissued alongside the new coins. Starting this year, the Mint cut back on the production of all coinage except cents, silver dollars, and gold issues. The coinage crisis from the Civil War was over. The paper greenback was now fully redeemable in gold. The massive amounts of silver coinage struck the previous five years, together with large quantities of coins struck between 1853 and 1860, were now available in excessive quantities in commerce. After December 17, 1878, gold coinage circulated for the first time since 1861.

Survivability: 1879 is the first of the semi-common dates in the series. Examples are widely available in all grades, as are all dates from here on, with the exception of the San Francisco Mint coinage at the end of the series.

Collecting Challenges: Coins are readily available with minimal searching. These are typically well struck. Finding attractive coins with minimal problems should be the goal here.

Collecting Circulated Pieces: The optimal collecting grade for circulated coins is AU-50. Problem-free examples can be difficult to locate, as dealers can find them very easy to sell, leaving only the "second tier" of quality coins to choose from. Waiting for the right coin is advised.

Collecting Mint State Pieces: The optimal collecting grade for Mint State coins is MS-65RB. These are quite easy to locate in all grades. When buying certified coins, select coins with good eye appeal and few problems. Uncertified coins above MS-63 should be carefully inspected for original color.

Collecting Proof Issues: Mintage figures escalated during this period. This issue is the highest-mintage Proof up until this date; this and many of the dates in the next decade are the common dates in the Proof series. Full red gem 1879 Indian Head cents are about as common as any date in the series.

Two of the three known Proof dies show repunching on the date. One of these, with wide repunching on the 8 and 9 to the right, is also found on regular-production coins (Snow-1). It was not unusual for Proof dies of this era to later be put into use for regular-production coins. After a very short time at the regular-production speed the dies lost their mirrored finish and produced coins that look like normal Mint State pieces.

1879: Circulation Strike

GSID	VG-8	F-12	VF-20	EF-40	AU-50	AU-58	MS-60	MS-63	MS-65
1350 (Brown)	$11	$20	$40	$70	$80	$90	$95	$170	$360
1351 (Red-Brown)	—	—	—	—	—	—	135	235	575
1352 (Red)	—	—	—	—	—	—	—	420	1,750

1879: Proof Strike

GSID	PF-63	PF-64	PF-65
1563 (Brown)	$285	$365	$525
1564 (Red-Brown)	340	500	775
1565 (Red)	390	600	1,100

Varieties

There are three repunched dates known for this date. Snow-1 is struck from dies earlier used on Proof issues.

1880

Circulation-Strike Mintage:
38,961,000

Proof Mintage:
3,955

1880 Cent Production: The mintage of cents for 1880 more than doubled compared to the previous year. This was the highest-production year since 1863. Quality was very high, for the most part. Many of the date punches used had broken elements that imparted digits with missing sections; the majority of these were later corrected.

Survivability: Although one of the largest production years of the 1880's, this issue circulated widely. The vast majority of coins wore down to low grades before being withdrawn from circulation and melted during the early 1900's; however, enough pieces survived to satisfy collector needs in all grades.

Collecting Challenges: Search out problem-free coins regardless of the grade level desired.

Collecting Circulated Pieces: The optimal collecting grade for circulated coins is AU-50. Select pieces with a full strike and even, natural color.

Collecting Mint State Pieces: The optimal collecting grade for Mint State coins is MS-65RB. Find an example with exceptional eye appeal. Examples with vibrant luster and a high percentage of red color are usually in high demand.

Collecting Proof Issues: As one of the higher mintages of the series, this issue should be classified and priced at the common "type" price. Vividly toned examples are in high demand and sometimes garner exceptional prices. These are usually a deep cobalt blue or purple. Although these coins are typically graded with a BN (for *brown*) designation, they trade at RB to RD price levels or even greater if the toning is exceptional.

The 1880 Proof Indian Head cent is occasionally available with a cameo contrast. Such pieces are highly sought after and usually get good premiums over non-cameo examples.

1880: Circulation Strike

GSID	VG-8	F-12	VF-20	EF-40	AU-50	AU-58	MS-60	MS-63	MS-65
1353 (Brown)	$4	$8	$13	$31	$49	$55	$70	$100	$340
1354 (Red-Brown)	—	—	—	—	—	—	—	180	550
1355 (Red)	—	—	—	—	—	—	—	575	3,500

1880: Proof Strike

GSID	PF-63	PF-64	PF-65
1568 (Brown)	$285	$365	$525
1569 (Red-Brown)	340	500	725
1570 (Red)	390	600	1,100

VARIETIES

The Snow-1 variety has a very wide off-center clash mark on the reverse. A semi-circular impression from an obverse die is seen curving from the N in CENT through the E in ONE, towards the upper-right wreath. Apparently, this interesting and rare variety was caused by an obverse die that possibly fell out of the hammer position of the press onto the face of the reverse die. This variety also features a slight doubled LIBERTY on the obverse. This is one of the most interesting and popular varieties of the Indian Head cent series.

1880, Off-Center Clash, Snow-1

1881

Circulation-Strike Mintage:
39,208,000

Proof Mintage:
3,575

1881 Cent Production: The 1881 issue is very similar in mintage quantity and production quality to the 1880 issue. The date shape seemed to be in a transition phase this year. Between 1872 and 1880 the date punch had a straight base, but after 1881 the dates were curved. In 1881 only, the date punch had the first pair of digits straight and horizontal while the second pair of digits were straight but at an angle to the horizontal digits.

Survivability: This issue was placed into circulation and stayed there for many years. Most examples that survived are in very low grades. The odd original roll or long-time accumulation (yes, they had "penny jars" back then) is the main source of high-grade examples today.

Collecting Challenges: Selecting a problem-free and eye-appealing example is the main goal of collectors. The 1881 cent is normally well struck, but many pieces have mushy details. This is caused by extreme die wear. Die wear results as the dies strike thousands of coins. The friction of the planchets against the face of the die causes the surface to abrade. This constant abrasion causes minute radial grooves called *flow lines*, which create a cartwheel effect when the coin is slowly turned in a strong light source. This is desirable, as it contributes to the eye appeal of the coin, but too much die wear will cause design elements to disappear. For many collectors, die state is as important as strike and condition.

Collecting Circulated Pieces: The optimal collecting grade for circulated coins is AU-50. Select problem-free examples. Collectors tend to discount problems (such as corrosion, large hits, and scratches) much less than dealers do. As a result, a "bargain"-priced coin with corrosion might in fact be priced much higher than one can ever hope of recovering when the time comes to sell.

Collecting Mint State Pieces: The optimal collecting grade for Mint State coins is MS-65RB. As with other dates in the early 1880's, it is possible (with patience) to find attractive eye-appealing coins without too much trouble.

Collecting Proof Issues: 1881 was another high-mintage year. This is a common date and is typically priced with no premium. It makes an affordable date for type collectors who want only one example to show off the design. Examples are usually attractive, with above-average mirrors. Cameos are a bit tougher to find than in earlier dates. Spots are a problem with this issue, as many 1881 cents were not stored carefully over the years. This applies in general to many of the Proofs of this era. Vivid toning is occasionally seen and is worth a substantial premium.

1881: Circulation Strike

GSID	VG-8	F-12	VF-20	EF-40	AU-50	AU-58	MS-60	MS-63	MS-65
1356 (Brown)	$4	$8	$10	$27	$38	$49	$60	$105	$340
1357 (Red-Brown)	—	—	—	—	—	—	—	195	650
1358 (Red)	—	—	—	—	—	—	—	430	950

1881: Proof Strike

GSID	PF-63	PF-64	PF-65
1573 (Brown)	$285	$365	$525
1574 (Red-Brown)	340	500	725
1575 (Red)	390	675	1,250

Varieties

Only seven minor repunched dates are known for this year. No major varieties exist.

1882

Circulation-Strike Mintage:
38,578,000

Proof Mintage:
3,100

1882 Cent Production: This is another high-mintage date of the 1880's; the quality of these coins is usually high.

By this time new issues from the last few years dominated the cents in circulation. The redemption program started in 1871 was essentially ended. Many of the older bronze cents had been redeemed and melted or reissued. Now only spoiled cents were being turned in. Copper-nickel cents still in circulation continued to be redeemed and melted.

Survivability: Much of this issue went into circulation and remained there. Most wore down to low grades before being removed from commerce. The few that survived by chance are typically above average for this era.

Collecting Challenges: Seek out problem-free and attractive examples.

Collecting Circulated Pieces: The optimal collecting grade for circulated coins is AU-50. This date should easily be found in most grades. Most are well struck. Finding problem-free examples should be the main concern.

Collecting Mint State Pieces: The optimal collecting grade for Mint State coins is MS-65RB. This issue can easily be found in most grades. Full red examples may be difficult to find without spots or detracting problems. True gems are very tough to locate. Prices for this date in all grades are similar to those of the 1880 through 1883 issues.

Collecting Proof Issues: 1882 is another high-mintage Proof issue, one of the easiest dates to find. However, examples graded PF-65RD and higher are very difficult to find. On the other hand, this is the most available date with vivid blue toning. Perhaps a larger percentage of this date remained in the Proskey hoard compared to other dates. (See 1878 for details on this hoard.)

1882: Circulation Strike

GSID	VG-8	F-12	VF-20	EF-40	AU-50	AU-58	MS-60	MS-63	MS-65
1359 (Brown)	$4	$8	$11	$27	$38	$49	$60	$115	$290
1360 (Red-Brown)	—	—	—	—	—	—	—	180	550
1361 (Red)	—	—	—	—	—	—	—	440	1,400

1882: Proof Strike

GSID	PF-63	PF-64	PF-65
1578 (Brown)	$285	$365	$525
1579 (Red-Brown)	340	500	725
1580 (Red)	390	775	1,100

Varieties

Snow-6 is a very popular and rare variety, with the bases of numerous 1 digits in the neck and pearl necklace. Of all the major varieties, this is one of the most elusive.

1883

Circulation-Strike Mintage:
45,591,500

Proof Mintage:
6,609

1883 Cent Production: This is the highest-mintage date of the 1880's for both Proof and circulation-strike formats. The circulation-strike production continued the record mintages of the previous three years. The high Proof production was due to the increased sales of minor coinage sets. These sets included, along with the cent and nickel three-cent piece, one of three types of five-cent nickel designs. Collectors who ordered their sets early in the year got a four-piece minor Proof set with both the old Shield design and the new Liberty Head design. The new nickel lacked the word CENTS, which was added to a revised design included in the Proof sets by June. Collectors who ordered early had to reapply to get the five-piece set containing the nickel with the word CENTS. A number of dealers speculated on the popularity of the nickel five-cent pieces and bought many coins of this issue.

Survivability: 1883 Indian Head cents mostly went into circulation and stayed there. Most of the remaining examples are in very low grades. Mint State survivors are plentiful, but many were not cared for properly over the years. Gem survivors are difficult to find.

Collecting Challenges: Search out attractive problem-free examples. Many of these will have mushy details due to extended die wear. Examples with crisp details are always preferred.

Collecting Circulated Pieces: The optimal collecting grade for circulated coins is AU-50. While the large mintage ensures plenty of examples in all grades, finding attractive examples in Extremely Fine and About Uncirculated is rather difficult.

Collecting Mint State Pieces: The optimal collecting grade for Mint State coins is MS-65RB. The 1883 issue is similar in rarity to the 1880 to 1882 dates. On all high-grade examples of this era, beware of uncertified coins offered at premium prices. The practice of artificially lightening the color of a coin to full red is seen more and more often as the values escalate.

Collecting Proof Issues: As the high-mintage date of the 1880's, 1883 holds the banner as being the common coin. However, survivability of the cents is quite low, as many buyers of the day were more interested in the nickel five-cent coinage. Dealers who had bought large quantities of the minor sets for the nickel five-cent pieces had quantities of the cent for decades. Many of these were stored in envelopes or mint wrappers, and over the years the coins toned to red-brown or brown. Some of these toned to the highly desirable wild iridescent-blue. Examples in full red are quite difficult to find. Due to the higher mintage, early-die-state examples with cameo contrast form a smaller percentage and are a bit harder to find.

1883: Circulation Strike

GSID	VG-8	F-12	VF-20	EF-40	AU-50	AU-58	MS-60	MS-63	MS-65
1362 (Brown)	$4	$7	$10	$23	$34	$49	$60	$120	$340
1363 (Red-Brown)	—	—	—	—	—	—	—	160	525
1364 (Red)	—	—	—	—	—	—	—	325	1,100

1883: Proof Strike

GSID	PF-63	PF-64	PF-65
1583 (Brown)	$285	$365	$525
1584 (Red-Brown)	340	500	725
1585 (Red)	390	600	1,100

Varieties

The best variety of this year is the Snow-1, which shows the base of a numeral 1 sticking out of the neck, below the first pearl. On a few other dies, a defective digit punch shows a bit of an extra 3 above the digit. Since this defective digit punch was pressed into a number of dies, it is not considered an important variety.

1884

Circulation-Strike Mintage:
23,257,800

Proof Mintage:
3,942

1884 Cent Production: For four years the Mint had pumped out record numbers of cents. Now it slowed production to about half the previous year's emission.

Survivability: These coins were mostly placed in circulation, and stayed there for long periods. Most are lower-grade circulated pieces. Examples that escaped circulation or destruction are slightly scarce in comparison to the earlier four years. In fact, the percentage of Mint State survivors of any date of the 1880's is very small compared to the number of coins minted.

Collecting Challenges: Search for attractive examples with sharp details. Avoid problems such as corrosion and heavy spots. Toning should be even and attractive.

Collecting Circulated Pieces: The optimal collecting grade for circulated coins is AU-50. Search out attractive, problem-free examples. Avoid cleaned coins at full price. Many collectors attempt to color-match their sets—striving to get all the coins in a chocolate brown color, for instance. A cleaned coin will usually not blend in well with original coins.

Collecting Mint State Pieces: The optimal collecting grade for Mint State coins is MS-65RB. Choose attractive coins with even coloration. These will usually come well struck, so the main problem is selecting the right eye appeal. Although a tougher date to find than those of 1880 to 1883, the survivors are nearly as plentiful as those dates. The rarity of these coins in high grades depends more on the chance survival of even as small a quantity as a few rolls.

Collecting Proof Issues: This is another high-mintage date. It is one of the easiest dates to locate in PF-63RB to PF-65RD. Full red gems are plentiful. Cameo examples may be a bit difficult to find but not prohibitively so. Carbon spotting plagues many coins from this decade. The size and placement of spots is usually the determining factor between one that is attractive or unattractive. Copper is a highly reactive metal and care should always be taken to handle these coins very carefully. Prior to modern plastic encapsulation these coins could easily develop spots by careless collectors talking over their exposed collections.

1884: Circulation Strike

GSID	VG-8	F-12	VF-20	EF-40	AU-50	AU-58	MS-60	MS-63	MS-65
1365 (Brown)	$8	$8	$18	$35	$49	$75	$80	$130	$360
1366 (Red-Brown)	—	—	—	—	—	—	—	170	575
1367 (Red)	—	—	—	—	—	—	—	575	1,500

1884: Proof Strike

GSID	PF-63	PF-64	PF-65
1588 (Brown)	$285	$365	$525
1589 (Red-Brown)	340	500	725
1590 (Red)	390	675	1,100

Varieties

There are only a few minor varieties known for this year: one misplaced date and two repunched dates.

1885

Circulation-Strike Mintage:
11,761,594

Proof Mintage:
3,790

1885 Cent Production: Planchets this year were ordered from the firm of James Watson & Son. Their last shipment arrived on February 20; no new planchet deliveries were made until 1887. Coinage for both the cent and five-cent denominations was halted on February 16 and did not resume until late 1886. As a result it is probable that the planchets on hand were used for two years of cent production. Mintages for 1885 and 1886 fell to roughly half the normal amount, a low for the decade.

Survivability: Although today 1885 is recognized as a relatively scarcer date, this was not recognized until the coins were in circulation for many years. Most cents of this year are well worn. Any examples that survived extensive circulation were likely originally saved by happenstance. Numerous treasures could be found in the bottom of a 50-year-old "penny jar." Most of the Uncirculated pieces are from random accumulations.

Collecting Challenges: Since the 1885 date will be slightly more difficult to locate than others of the era, you should target it early in your search. These usually come well struck, so avoid weak and problem pieces.

Collecting Circulated Pieces: The optimal collecting grade for circulated coins is AU-50. Search for well-struck, problem-free pieces. Due to its higher demand, some dealers may find it easy to push their grading on this date. Make sure you don't get overexcited about finding a bargain-priced coin of this date. Chances are it is not as great a deal as you may think. An overgraded coin is likely an overpriced coin.

Collecting Mint State Pieces: The optimal collecting grade for Mint State coins is MS-64RB. Full red gems are very hard to locate. It is not the most difficult date of the decade to find—that honor goes to 1888 and 1889. Many 1885 cents come with vibrant luster and a sharp strike. Most examples are red-brown.

Collecting Proof Issues: Although this is another high-mintage date, they have not survived the decades very well. Most collectors of the time sought the Proof issues only to satisfy their date collections. Many old-time collections with intact Proof sets may have vibrant gems in all other denominations, but the cent will have toned dark brown. In fact, the majority of this issue is found with a deep, even, brown color (sometimes with vivid blue toning). It is very difficult to find full red examples, and examples with deep cameo contrast are very tough to find.

1885: Circulation Strike

GSID	VG-8	F-12	VF-20	EF-40	AU-50	AU-58	MS-60	MS-63	MS-65
1368 (Brown)	$14	$16	$34	$75	$95	$130	$130	$180	$495
1369 (Red-Brown)	—	—	—	—	—	—	—	245	875
1370 (Red)	—	—	—	—	—	—	—	455	1,400

1885: Proof Strike

GSID	PF-63	PF-64	PF-65
1593 (Brown)	$285	$365	$525
1594 (Red-Brown)	340	500	725
1595 (Red)	390	675	1,100

Varieties

Only a few minor varieties are known.

1886, Variety 1

Circulation-Strike Mintage:
14,000,000 (estimated, out of 17,650,000 total)

Proof Mintage:
2,500 (estimated, out of 4,290 total)

Variety 1 and Variety 2 Identification: The change in the design this year was not noticed by collectors until 1954. The redesign by Charles Barber only slightly altered the shape of the portrait, and slightly lowered the relief. The reason for the change may have been the elimination of the extra outlines found on Longacre's master die since the 1864 With L design was introduced. Extra outlines are found on many of Longacre's designs. They are light shelves around the devices and letters. As a master die artifact, these were transferred to each hub that was made. The dies made from these hubs did not always have this detail. It depended on whether the dies were sunk deep enough to show it clearly.

Extra Outlines

Collectors often call the different styles *Type I* (or *Type 1*) and *Type II* (or *Type 2*). The use of the Roman numeral rather than the Arabic numeral is more custom than convention. A seldom used, but more accurate, way to describe the difference would be *Type of 1885* and *Type of 1887*. Some grading services and collector-album makers use *Variety 1* and *Variety 2*, as does the *Red Book*. In my opinion this might confuse collectors, as the difference is considered to be not an individual *die* variety, but a minor design change. This book follows the *Red Book* convention.

The easiest way to determine the difference is the placement of the last feather in relation to the ICA in AMERICA. On a Variety 1 coin, the feather points between I and C. On a Variety 2 coin, the feather points between C and A. While these differences are well known, many collectors have trouble remembering which definition fits which design. I would recommend thinking of the feather as a clock hand, with the Variety 1 being an earlier "time" than the Variety 2. Comparison with earlier and later dates will also help.

1886, Variety 1, Cent Production: Overall this is a scarcer date in the context of the decade. The further division of this date between the two design styles raises their scarcity even more. The estimated division of the mintage is based on the survivor ratio rather than actual pieces produced.

Although coin production ceased in early 1885, die production did not. Records show 44 dies being made in 1885, and 45 dies in 1886. It is likely that about 75 undated Variety 1 dies were made in early 1885, with only 44 dated 1885. The remaining 30 or so undated dies would then have been dated and used when production started up again in late 1886. Then, to satisfy the demand from the coining department, the Mint made 15 or so more dies of the new design. Both designs could have been struck at the same time.

Survivability: These cents have survived as well as any other date of the 1880's. There was no added collector demand for the date until many years after they were mostly all worn down. Any survivors exist strictly by chance.

Collecting Challenges: These are slightly scarcer than the 1885 issue. Most are well struck. Search for problem-free examples with good eye appeal. Extra effort should be placed in searching for the Variety 1. Typically, the higher value for the Variety 2 will bring more examples on the market than Variety 1 pieces.

Collecting Circulated Pieces: The optimal collecting grade for circulated coins is AU-50. Beware of cleaned and corroded coins. Choice chocolate-brown coins are very difficult to find.

Collecting Mint State Pieces: The optimal collecting grade for Mint State coins is MS-64RB. These are only slightly scarcer than the 1885 issue. Survivors mainly come from the chance find, rather than old-time collector accumulations. Most are well struck with sharp dies. Full red gems are very difficult to find. These are usually similarly priced to the 1885, but in practice are slightly scarcer.

Collecting Proof Issues: The estimated breakdown of the mintage figures between the two types is not known from Mint records. The estimate is based on observed survivors rather than actual production. As one of the highest-mintage dates overall, it would be expected that these would be widely available. This is true only in red-brown grades. Full red examples are rare, with cameo examples very difficult. The planchets for some of this issue come a lighter tan-gold color.

1886, Variety 1: Circulation Strike

GSID	VG-8	F-12	VF-20	EF-40	AU-50	AU-58	MS-60	MS-63	MS-65
1371 (Brown)	$12	$22	$70	$170	$195	$215	$220	$280	$650
1372 (Red-Brown)	—	—	—	—	—	—	—	420	1,600
1373 (Red)	—	—	—	—	—	—	—	900	3,900

1886, Variety 1: Proof Strike

GSID	PF-63	PF-64	PF-65
1598 (Brown)	$330	$410	$575
1599 (Red-Brown)	385	550	775
1600 (Red)	575	850	1,750

Varieties

Some minor repunched dates are known. None are of any substantial interest. Listings of the Snow variety numbers include the design type as part of the variety identification (*1886, Variety 1, Snow-3*, for example).

1886, Variety 2

Circulation-Strike Mintage:
3,650,000 (estimated, out of 17,654,290 total)

Proof Mintage:
1,750 (estimated, out of 4,290 total)

1886, Variety 2, Cent Production: It is not known when the Mint produced the new obverse master die by Charles Barber, although it was probably made during the hiatus of cent and nickel production early in the year. If so, then the estimated 15 Variety 2 dies dated 1886 would have struck coins at the same time as older Variety 1 dies when coinage resumed. A larger number of coins from the Variety 2 dies show extreme die wear. Perhaps near the end of the year the Mint chose to stretch the life of the dies rather than make more. Dies used to strike Proofs were also put into service to strike regular issues.

1886, Variety 1. The last feather points between the I and C in AMERICA.

1886, Variety 2. The last feather points between the C and A.

Survivability: There was no special significance placed on the Variety 2 style early on, as it was a relatively minor alteration. It was only after 1954 that collectors started to collect these coins as separate entities. As a result, nearly the entire mintage went into circulation and stayed there until they were well worn. The survival of any examples is based on chance rather than from collector hoards. A roll of 50 coins from the same dies appeared in Superior Galleries' section of Auction '81, bringing $30,000. While the appearance of a roll like this greatly altered the relative rarity of this date, it did little to lower the prices. It just made more coins available to collectors.

Collecting Challenges: Quality is quite poor on most of the pieces encountered. Search out pieces struck from an early-die-state die. These will have crisp details and flat fields. Many have been chemically altered by dishonest people seeking to capture the high prices asked for high-grade pieces.

Collecting Circulated Pieces: The optimal collecting grade for circulated coins is EF-40. Select coins with attractive original surfaces. Target this date early on in your collecting, as it will take a while to find an attractive example.

Collecting Mint State Pieces: The optimal collecting grade for Mint State coins is MS-63RB. This is one of the tougher dates in all grades. However, as small groups have come to light its rarity has lessened slightly. It is believed that the 50 pieces that came from the Auction '81 roll were mostly full red and all from the same die. These were all later-die-state coins, which have a look likened to melted butterscotch. Another group of 32 1886 Variety 2 pieces was found in 1994 in a bottle buried in Connecticut. Later, they were placed in the Bowers & Merena "Boys Town" sale in March 1998 (lots 353 to 363) where they were graded MS-61RB to MS-64RB. Among these pieces, 18 were of the same variety, Snow-7.

Full red gems are still very rare. Prices for MS-64RD and MS-65RD certified coins have climbed to levels seen only for the top three or four dates in the series.

Collecting Proof Issues: The mintage is estimated from the quantity of known survivors. No official figures break down the division between the two types. The 1886 Variety 2 Proof is prohibitively rare in full red gem condition. Cameo examples are nearly impossible to find. Most available examples are red-brown or totally brown, sometimes with vivid blue toning. The limited quantity of full red coins is curious. Many original coins exhibit a tan-golden color which grading services may find unusual. Perhaps the majority of remaining Proofs at the end of the year were Variety 2 pieces. If so, they may have been purchased by dealers, as was most of the leftover Proof minor coinage. If this is the case, then these would have sat for extended periods in their Mint wrappers, slowly toning to purple or brown.

Some of the five known die pairs used for Proof production were later used on regular coinage.

1886, Variety 2: Circulation Strike

GSID	VG-8	F-12	VF-20	EF-40	AU-50	AU-58	MS-60	MS-63	MS-65
1374 (Brown)	$18	$38	$105	$195	$260	$280	$290	$525	$1,400
1375 (Red-Brown)	—	—	—	—	—	—	—	950	1,600
1376 (Red)	—	—	—	—	—	—	—	2,200	7,000

1886, Variety 2: Proof Strike

GSID	PF-63	PF-64	PF-65
1601 (Brown)	$455	$775	$1,250
1602 (Red-Brown)	625	1,000	1,800
1603 (Red)	1,250	2,250	10,500

Varieties

There are a few minor repunched dates. The Snow variety listings must show the design type as well as the variety number (*1886, Variety 2, Snow-3*, for example).

1887

Circulation-Strike Mintage:
45,223,523

Proof Mintage:
2,960

1887 Cent Production: Planchets this year and 1888 were supplied by Joseph Wharton's firm. With full-time production restored, the mintage for the year rivaled the record levels of the early 1880's.

Survivability: Cents of 1887 circulated widely and are usually found in medium circulated grades. They are more readily available than dates with similar mintages in the earlier 1880's. Perhaps as more and more cents were struck there was less reason to constantly empty the "penny jar." Regardless of the reason, many more of these later-date cents have survived.

Collecting Challenges: Search out problem-free examples. These tend to be well struck, but many were struck from later-die-state dies. These will be mushy with wavy fields. Die state is not typically a factor in setting the price of a coin, so searching for early-die-state pieces should only cost you extra time.

Collecting Circulated Pieces: The optimal collecting grade for circulated coins is AU-50. Select problem-free examples with original chocolate-brown color.

Collecting Mint State Pieces: The optimal collecting grade for Mint State coins is MS-65RB or MS-64RD, which are generally priced similarly. Avoid coins with blotchy or strange toning. Search for full strikes and early die states. Full gems in both red-brown and red are scarce. Full red coins sometimes have a pale tan-golden color (as do some 1886 pieces).

Collecting Proof Issues: The mintage dipped slightly this year, but this does little to change the rarity rating compared to other dates in the 1880's. Many 1887 cents are found with pale tan-golden planchets. Many others have toned to brown, sometimes with vivid iridescent blue toning, which is worth a significant premium. Perhaps many of the issue were left over at the end of the year and were purchased by dealers such as David Proskey, who had been accumulating leftover minor Proof coinage for later sale. Due to all these factors this date is difficult to find graded full red. Sometimes these are found singly struck, which may hinder the resulting coins from reaching the higher grades. This is one of the toughest dates for collectors of PF-65RD coins. Examples with cameo contrast are exceedingly rare.

1887: Circulation Strike

GSID	VG-8	F-12	VF-20	EF-40	AU-50	AU-58	MS-60	MS-63	MS-65
1377 (Brown)	$3	$5	$7	$23	$35	$55	$55	$115	$305
1378 (Red-Brown)	—	—	—	—	—	—	—	180	900
1379 (Red)	—	—	—	—	—	—	—	495	1,900

1887: Proof Strike

GSID	PF-63	PF-64	PF-65
1604 (Brown)	$285	$365	$525
1605 (Red-Brown)	340	500	725
1606 (Red)	525	1,200	3,100

Varieties

The Snow-1 doubled die is one of the top ten varieties of the series. This variety has significant doubling on the right obverse. The doubling is mostly on the central veins of the feathers and OF AMERICA.

1887, Doubled-Die Obverse, Snow-1

1888

Circulation-Strike Mintage:
37,489,832

Proof Mintage:
4,582

1888 Cent Production: Production remained steady this year. One of the dies had its date repunched over an 1887 die (see 1888, 8 Over 7).

Survivability: There was no incentive for collectors to save this date, so most of the issue went into circulation and remained there until well worn.

Collecting Challenges: This date comes with an average strike, so it would be beneficial to take extra time to find a well-struck example. As with all other later-date Indian Head cents, average-quality specimens are widely available. You should make the extra effort to locate an example with a superior strike.

Collecting Circulated Pieces: The optimal collecting grade for circulated coins is AU-50. Select problem-free examples with exceptional eye appeal.

Collecting Mint State Pieces: The optimal collecting grade for Mint State coins is MS-64RB. The rarity of higher-grade Indian Head cents of this era depends on the chance survival of small groups of choice coins. If no original rolls are found then the date becomes rarer in higher grades. Likely, that is what happened to this date. True gems are very tough to find, regardless of the color designation. Full red examples are, of course, even tougher. This date will require extra effort to find nice, high-grade coins.

Collecting Proof Issues: Although this is one of the higher-mintage Proof dates, it remains slightly elusive in high grades. This date is very tough in full red, especially in gem. Cameos are very rare. Some of these come with golden-tan planchets. Most pieces are mostly brown or totally brown. Occasionally, some of these coins graded with the BN (for brown) color designation have vivid blue and purple colors. These are highly desired by collectors. Prices vary widely for these vividly toned coins. Sometimes, in an auction setting, prices for outstanding specimens can skyrocket to many multiples of the prices the typical BN designation warrants.

Many coins of this year are singly struck. This causes the coins to be less than what we expect for Proof issues of the era. Sometimes the feather tips or some of the denticles may show weakness, and rough planchet marks might not get totally struck out. The edge, which is usually sharp, will be highly beveled on singly struck coins. Sometimes singly struck examples with medium mirrors might be mistaken for prooflike circulation-strike coins. Typically, Proofs are double struck at slower speeds to bring out the design to its fullest. This takes time, and one might not be too surprised if the Mint, when producing 4,000+ coins, introduced some time-saving measure at the expense of quality. Perhaps a Mint employee at the time asked himself, “Who would care; after all, they are only pennies!”

1888: Circulation Strike

GSID	VG-8	F-12	VF-20	EF-40	AU-50	AU-58	MS-60	MS-63	MS-65
1380 (Brown)	$4	$4	$9	$24	$27	$75	$85	$175	$550
1381 (Red-Brown)	—	—	—	—	—	—	—	220	850
1382 (Red)	—	—	—	—	—	—	—	440	1,500

1888: Proof Strike

GSID	PF-63	PF-64	PF-65
1609 (Brown)	$285	$365	$525
1610 (Red-Brown)	340	500	725
1611 (Red)	390	1,250	3,750

Varieties

Aside from the ultra-rare 1888/7 Snow-1, the top variety is the 1888 Snow-2, which is known to numismatists as 1888/7 Die #2, FF 010.7. Noted numismatic author Bill Fivaz discovered the variety in July 1990. It was confirmed at the time and included in my *Flying Eagle and Indian Cents* (1992) as 1888 Snow-2.

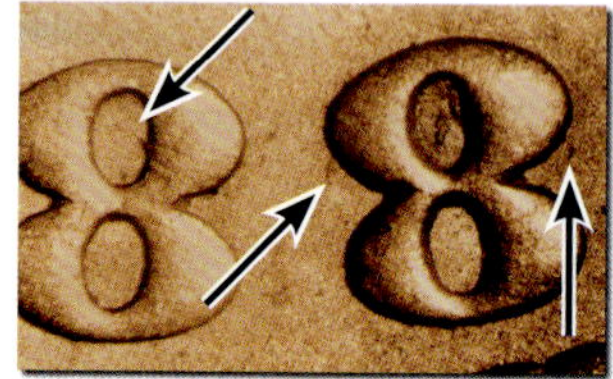

1888/888, Snow-2

Full-Date 1888, Snow-2

In 2000 the overdate status was questioned by one of the top collector-specialists, Dr. Tim Larson, in the pages of *Longacre's Ledger* (the publication of the Fly-In Club, the specialty club devoted to this series). Tim convincingly questioned the status of the overdate using overlay photos. It appears that the overdate is most likely just a repunched date: 1888/888. There is a vertical line in the upper loop of the 8 on this variety, and that did not match up to date overlays that Tim prepared. He suggested that the line was a die scratch. This is still a neat variety with a misplaced digit in the first pearl. Because overdates carry a much higher premium, the label should be placed only on varieties that can be certainly shown to be overdates. (See "1888/7 S2—Is it an Overdate?", Tim Larson, *Longacre's Ledger*, Vol. 10.2, June 2000.)

An example of the 1888 Snow-2 cent is known struck in copper-nickel! The coin is graded by PCGS as a nickel die trial. The coin showed up in 1997 during the ANA Summer Seminar, which I happened to be attending as an instructor. (This is a very worthwhile way to spend a week in the cool Colorado summer sun.) After finishing my class, I sat in with my good friends, J.P. Martin and Bob Campbell, who were teaching the Counterfeit Detection class. They were demonstrating the use of the scanning electron microscope to extract alloy information of coins using x-ray spectroscopy. One of the coins to be tested was an 1888 cent that looked like it was copper-nickel. Sure enough, it tested 25% nickel and 75% copper. After the test I examined the coin and discovered the variety. Everyone was thrilled—and so, I guess, was the owner. Unfortunately the ANA did not tell the owner about the variety. He discovered it independently later. I subsequently found out that East Coast dealer George Maroskos owned the coin. He offered it to me but I declined at the time. I asked to photograph it, and it was put on the cover of *Longacre's Ledger*, Vol. 9.3, August 1999.

The question remains: how did this coin come to be? The firm of Joseph Wharton sold both three-cent and five-cent nickel planchets to the Mint, along with cent planchets. Perhaps three-cent nickel stock was put in the cent blanking press and a few of these odd planchets found their way to the cent press just when the 1888 Snow-2 pieces were being struck. If this is the case, then perhaps there are other pieces yet to be discovered!

1888, 8 Over 7

Circulation-Strike Mintage: Unknown; fewer than 100 pieces are known to exist.

1888, 8 Over 7

1888, 8 Over 7, Cent Production: Apparently, one of the 1887 dies was repunched with an 1888 four-digit punch and put into service. The die developed a die break early on and possibly did not last too long, as specimens known from this die are extremely rare today.

Overdates garner much greater collector interest more than other varieties because they are generally collected as part of the regular date series. James F. Ruddy announced the discovered of this variety in the February 11, 1970, issue of *Coin World*. Two examples of the new variety, both Uncirculated, turned up in a small group of Indian Head cents in the attic of a mansion in Virginia. The obvious blob under the last 8 was determined to be the remnant of a 7, and a private search was launched for additional examples. After a few months, the discovery of this variety was announced in the hobby press since no one came forth with additional examples. The editors of *The Numismatist* billed the find as the one of the most important numismatic discoveries of the decade (April 1970, p. 531).

The extensive publicity brought out only one more example (graded Good) within the following year. Confident that this was a very rare variety, the two discovery pieces were offered for $4,950 each in 1971. This was an enormous premium at the time. By comparison, Bowers & Ruddy Galleries offered an 1885 Proof $20 double eagle (worth at least $50,000 today) in the same price list as the 1888/7 cents for $4,295. Eventually dealer Julian Leidman and collector Robert Marks purchased the two discovery pieces.

Survivability: Presently, fewer than 100 examples are known, mostly in low grades. This remains the most coveted variety in the Indian Head cent series and one of the hottest "cherrypicks" for collectors to find in unchecked accumulations.

Collecting Challenges: Obviously this is a rare coin. Only a few collectors are lucky enough to include a decent-grade example in their collection. One must decide if a medium-grade coin is worth the acquisition cost, even if an example becomes available. Due to its rarity, most collectors will have to omit the coin from their collection.

Collecting Circulated Pieces: Examples in Good or Very Good are occasionally available. Be certain the coin is genuine. Many worn 1888 cents with crud on the date look like a phantom 1888, 8 Over 7. See the attribution information below.

Collecting Mint State Pieces: These are seldom available.

Attribution: Most, but not all, 1888/7 cents show a cud (an unstruck area of the coin, where part of the die broke away) in the denticles, about the size of three denticles, at the 9 o'clock position on the obverse. This can be diagnostic and makes for quick attribution at arm's length—very important for cherrypickers to know. Most dealers will get slightly upset if you go through all their 1888 coins with a magnifying glass (they might get even more upset if they find you cherrypicked them!).

One example graded G-4 by PCGS is not the overdate. This is the plate coin in my *Flying Eagle and Indian Cents* (1992), as Snow-3. It was questionable then and has been delisted since. (See "The Continuing Story of the Mis-attributed 1888/7," Richard Snow, *Longacre's Ledger*, Vol. 11.4, December 2001.)

1888, 8 Over 7, Snow-1

1888, 8 Over 7, Snow-1, detail

1888, 8 Over 7, Snow-1, cud at 9 o'clock

1888, 8 Over 7: Circulation Strike

GSID	VG-8	F-12	VF-20	EF-40	AU-50	AU-58	MS-60	MS-63	MS-65
1458 (Brown)	$2,000	$3,600	$5,250	$7,750	$12,000	$27,000	$34,000	$45,500	—
1459 (Red-Brown)	—	—	—	—	—	—	—	53,000	—
1460 (Red)	—	—	—	—	—	—	—	90,000	—

1889

Circulation-Strike Mintage:
48,866,025

Proof Mintage:
3,336

1889 Cent Production: Mintages start to climb during this era. Planchets this year were purchased from Merchant & Company of Philadelphia. Merchant won the contract with a bid of 26¢ per pound. A slight difference is noticeable in the color of full red examples, which tend to be a bit paler than those of other years.

Survivability: As with the other dates of this era, these were workhorse coins that stayed in circulation long after the design was changed in 1909. High-grade examples survived only by chance.

Collecting Challenges: Select eye-appealing examples without problems, compared to ordinary coins. These mostly come well struck, but with odd or uneven toning.

Collecting Circulated Pieces: The optimal collecting grade for circulated coins is AU-50. Select problem-free examples with exceptional eye appeal. Many collections of circulated Indian Head cents start off from an accumulation, possibly plucked from circulation generations ago. Collections like these tend to start as a hole-filling exercise, which is fun as the set becomes complete. However, a much more rewarding collecting experience comes when a collection is upgraded from average circulated coins to choice circulated examples in the Extremely Fine to About Uncirculated grade range. The object is to search out the ideal coin for each date, taking into account color, strike, and overall quality in addition to the technical grade. In most cases, money spent on carefully selected coins will not be money lost.

Collecting Mint State Pieces: The optimal collecting grade for Mint State coins is MS-65RB or MS-64RD. Full reds are scarce, so a 64RD will likely cost more than a 65RB. Gem MS-65RD examples are quite rare. Most have a pale color. Woodgrain toning is prevalent for this issue—a type of toning caused by improperly mixed alloy. (When the planchet strip is rolled out to the correct thickness the pockets of tin and zinc alloy become stretched into streaks.) It will be harder for coins struck from these types of planchets to retain their full red color, so these are usually given a red-brown color designation.

Collecting Proof Issues: These are of average quality, with full red examples very difficult to find. Full red coins are sometimes found with a pale gold color. Full cameo examples are very rare. Curiously, one of the two known die pairs has clashed dies. Clashed dies are caused when the obverse and reverse dies make contact and impart the outline of their designs on each other. Although clashed dies do not alter the desirability of the resulting coins, it is unusual to find them on Proof coins. Many 1889 Proof cents are singly struck. Perhaps quality control was lacking at the Mint this year.

1889: Circulation Strike

GSID	VG-8	F-12	VF-20	EF-40	AU-50	AU-58	MS-60	MS-63	MS-65
1383 (Brown)	$3	$3	$6	$14	$27	$42	$55	$105	$340
1384 (Red-Brown)	—	—	—	—	—	—	120	155	550
1385 (Red)	—	—	—	—	—	—	—	340	1,450

1889: Proof Strike

GSID	PF-63	PF-64	PF-65
1614 (Brown)	$285	$365	$525
1615 (Red-Brown)	340	500	725
1616 (Red)	525	1,000	2,400

Varieties

Presently 33 different die varieties of interest are known. The best is Snow-1, which has a bold doubled die visible on the right wreath and shield on the reverse. Snow-31 has multiple off-center die clash marks. These show up as a series of dashes (transferred from the denticles of another die) through the O in ONE and C in CENT. Another series of dashes is visible to the left of the E in ONE. The remaining varieties are mostly repunched dates.

1890

Circulation-Strike Mintage:
57,180,114
Proof Mintage:
2,740

1890 Cent Production: Scovill Manufacturing Company of Waterbury, Connecticut, supplied planchets to the Mint this year. Scovill won the contract with a 20¢-per-pound bid for 500,000 pounds of planchets, which was much lower than the amount that won the contract the year before. One hundred cent blanks weigh one pound, so the contract supplied blanks for about 50 million cents.

Survivability: These coins saw extensive circulation, but enough survived that examples are plentiful in all grades.

Collecting Challenges: Select attractive, problem-free examples. This issue is usually missing some details on the first three feather tips. Otherwise, they are well struck.

Collecting Circulated Pieces: The optimal collecting grade for circulated coins is AU-50. Usually, collectors try to match the color throughout their set. Chocolate brown is the preferred color of circulated coins. In the later years it is easier to find choice-quality coins. Many of these may have a red-brown color. Many collectors include Mint State coins as well.

Collecting Mint State Pieces: The optimal collecting grade for Mint State coins is MS-65RB or MS-64RD. Select eye-appealing coins with few problems. Many coins have toned unevenly or were once cleaned.

Collecting Proof Issues: This date is readily available in most grades except in full red. The number of Proofs minted during the 1890's slides to new lows. Collectors mistakenly equate the more common dates struck for circulation as being common in Proof as well. The truth is that many of the dates in the 1890's and 1900's are very tough to find in gem Proof.

1890: Circulation Strike

GSID	VG-8	F-12	VF-20	EF-40	AU-50	AU-58	MS-60	MS-63	MS-65
1386 (Brown)	$3	$3	$4	$11	$32	$65	$75	$110	$495
1387 (Red-Brown)	—	—	—	—	—	—	—	195	725
1388 (Red)	—	—	—	—	—	—	—	235	1,250

1890: Proof Strike

GSID	PF-63	PF-64	PF-65
1619 (Brown)	$285	$365	$525
1620 (Red-Brown)	340	500	725
1621 (Red)	390	600	1,100

Varieties

Snow-1 is an interesting variety and is described as a *quadrupled die*. It shows four distinct outlines on the outer edges of the legend. The Snow-3 has the base of a numeral 1 sticking out of the neck just above the necklace. A total of 16 varieties of interest are presently known, mostly repunched dates.

1891

Circulation-Strike Mintage:
47,070,000

Proof Mintage:
2,350

1891 Cent Production: As the mintage indicates, these were produced in lower quantities than cents of 1890.

Survivability: The dates 1889 to 1893 are all of the same basic rarity. These coins circulated extensively for decades, and higher-grade survivors exist mainly by chance. Still, they are fairly common. In Uncirculated grades, the survival of a small hoard of, say, 50 coins (original roll quantity) can alter the availability significantly for a while. Prices usually do not go *down* with the discovery of an original roll, as collector demand will eventually absorb the coins. Many darkly toned coins of this date in MS-63 and MS-64 grades came from a hoard that entered the market in the early 1990's. They seemed to be everywhere for a while, but today the general rarity of this date is still on par with other dates.

Collecting Challenges: Select eye-appealing coins with attractive luster. The percentage of red found on Mint State coins may also be a factor, if it fits your goal.

Collecting Circulated Pieces: The optimal collecting grade for circulated coins is AU-50 to MS-63RB. Usually the availability and lower cost of Mint State pieces attract demand from collectors of circulated coins.

Collecting Mint State Pieces: The optimal collecting grade for Mint State coins is MS-65RB or MS-64RD. This date is widely available in most grades, including gem full red. Most have an average strike; look for full feather tips.

Collecting Proof Issues: This issue is slightly scarce in high grades. Full red gems are very tough to locate. Many come singly struck with beveled edges. Many come darkly toned with a small percentage of these having vivid purple toning, which is highly desired. Cameo gems are rare.

1891: Circulation Strike

GSID	VG-8	F-12	VF-20	EF-40	AU-50	AU-58	MS-60	MS-63	MS-65
1389 (Brown)	$3	$3	$4	$12	$27	$49	$60	$110	$220
1390 (Red-Brown)	—	—	—	—	—	—	—	150	850
1391 (Red)	—	—	—	—	—	—	—	310	1,200

1891: Proof Strike

GSID	PF-63	PF-64	PF-65
1624 (Brown)	$285	$365	$525
1625 (Red-Brown)	340	500	725
1626 (Red)	390	600	1,600

Varieties

The best variety of this year is the Snow-1 doubled die with strong doubling on the OF and LIBERTY. This variety was discovered in 1990, and very few have been discovered since. Twenty or so other varieties are known, mostly repunched dates, but there are a few doubled-die reverses known. These typically show doubling on the central veins of the wreath, not on the outside edges of the wreath.

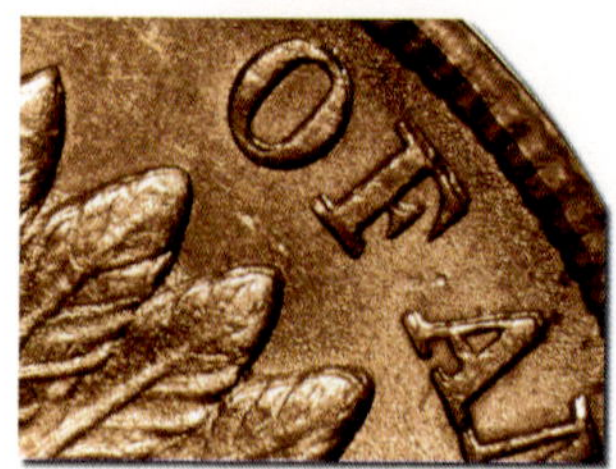

1891, Doubled-Die Obverse, Snow-1

1892

Circulation-Strike Mintage:
37,647,087

Proof Mintage:
2,745

1892 Cent Production: The slightly lower mintage this year is due to a problem in planchet procurement. Earlier, the winning low bid from planchet suppliers was around 20¢ per pound. This year's bids were significantly higher. Scovill Manufacturing was low bidder with a price just under 28¢. Two other bids received were slightly more than 28¢. Mint Director Edward Leach recognized that it was "a put up job" and recommended that all bids be rejected. The Mint struck cents from planchets that were on hand, with additional bronze coming from the melting of older cents and two-cent pieces. Director Leach also recommended that the Mint should start making its own planchets for minor coins.

Survivability: Coins this year survived in roughly the same quantities as those of the previous few years. True gem examples are quite tough to find.

Collecting Challenges: This date comes fairly well struck. Select coins with even color and attractive eye appeal.

Collecting Circulated Pieces: The optimal collecting grade for circulated coins is AU-50 to MS-63RB. Avoid problem coins.

Collecting Mint State Pieces: The optimal collecting grade for Mint State coins is MS-65RB to MS-64RD, which should be similarly priced. Certified populations for MS-65RB examples are very low, currently far under the quantity of MS-65RD pieces graded. Perhaps this shows that the source of most high-quality Mint State pieces is perhaps from the chance discovery of one or two original rolls rather than from average accumulations, such as generation-old "penny jars."

Collecting Proof Issues: This date is much more readily available than other dates of the era. Perhaps a select quantity was saved in gem condition, whereas in other years they toned down to brown. We can only guess why. Cameo examples are more readily available than other years, although still scarce.

1892: Circulation Strike

GSID	VG-8	F-12	VF-20	EF-40	AU-50	AU-58	MS-60	MS-63	MS-65
1392 (Brown)	$3	$4	$6	$14	$27	$49	$60	$130	$280
1393 (Red-Brown)	—	—	—	—	—	—	—	150	650
1394 (Red)	—	—	—	—	—	—	—	415	2,000

1892: Proof Strike

GSID	PF-63	PF-64	PF-65
1629 (Brown)	$285	$365	$525
1630 (Red-Brown)	340	500	725
1631 (Red)	390	600	1,100

Varieties

Most of the 13 or so known varieties are fairly minor repunched dates. A few minor reverse doubled dies are known.

1893

Circulation-Strike Mintage:
46,640,000

Proof Mintage:
2,195

1893 Cent Production: These were made from recoined cents and two-cent pieces. Their quality is average. Many are seen with strike-through depressions caused by some substance on the planchets at the time of striking. Strike-through depressions caused by machine oil or water will leave differing types of depressions, depending on the location of the design elements. A liquid strike-through on the field leaves a small, bright, circular area. If it is on the portrait then the liquid can migrate to the extremities of the design, like the bust point or feather tips. This will show up as weakness with bright luster, but will not be weakly struck, per se.

Survivability: These are about as plentiful as other dates in the era. There was no special reason to save these for many generations after they were struck.

Collecting Challenges: Select problem-free examples with superior eye appeal.

Collecting Circulated Pieces: The optimal collecting grade for circulated coins is AU-50 to MS-63RB. These are plentiful enough that finding a problem-free example should be no problem.

Collecting Mint State Pieces: These are widely available in MS-64RB but much more difficult in MS-65RB, at least for certified examples. A few original rolls turned up in the early 1990's. The average quality of these rolls was MS-64RD, and they tended to have lots of liquid strike-though depressions (see Production notes, above).

Collecting Proof Issues: These are a little scarcer than the common dates, but presently are priced as if they were the commonest date. Gem full red pieces are scarce, as are cameo examples. Vivid purple-toned examples exist and are highly desired by collectors even though they typically are graded "brown."

1893: Circulation Strike

GSID	VG-8	F-12	VF-20	EF-40	AU-50	AU-58	MS-60	MS-63	MS-65
1395 (Brown)	$3	$3	$5	$11	$27	$46	$60	$120	$290
1396 (Red-Brown)	—	—	—	—	—	—	—	130	525
1397 (Red)	—	—	—	—	—	—	—	365	1,000

1893: Proof Strike

GSID	PF-63	PF-64	PF-65
1634 (Brown)	$285	$365	$525
1635 (Red-Brown)	340	500	725
1636 (Red)	390	600	1,100

Varieties

17 varieties are known, but are mostly minor repunched dates.

1894

Circulation-Strike Mintage:
16,749,500

Proof Mintage:
2,632

1894 Cent Production: Mintage levels dropped this year to a low for the decade. In 1893 and 1894 an economic depression caused many coins from previous years to be brought out of hiding and into circulation. This caused a glut of cents and nickel five-cent pieces. As a result, coining operations for these denominations ceased in April and did not resume for many months.

Survivability: As the low-mintage date for the 1890's, these are more coveted by collectors, but in reality are not much scarcer than other dates of the era, except in very low grade. Most of the coins of this era stayed in circulation and were saved in higher grades by accident in the same average amounts each year.

Collecting Challenges: Search out problem-free examples with attractive eye appeal. These usually come well struck.

Collecting Circulated Pieces: The optimal collecting grade for circulated coins is AU-50 to MS-63RB. These are popular as a lower-mintage date. This may be a bit tougher date to find for lower-grade Good to VG collections. Check each example for the Snow-1 repunched date (see next page).

Collecting Mint State Pieces: The optimal collecting grade for Mint State coins is MS-65RB or MS-64RD. This is a popular date, and it brings a slight premium above other dates of the era. Most are moderate grades, MS-64RB being widely available, though no more than any other date of this era. Full red examples tend to be an orange-gold. Gems are available and are no rarer than other years of the decade.

Collecting Proof Issues: These come with good mirrors and usually have a good amount of red. Vivid purple-toned examples are slightly tougher to locate than in other dates. Gems are available, and are quite rare with cameo contrast.

1894: Circulation Strike

GSID	VG-8	F-12	VF-20	EF-40	AU-50	AU-58	MS-60	MS-63	MS-65
1398 (Brown)	$8	$16	$22	$50	$70	$90	$100	$155	$325
1399 (Red-Brown)	—	—	—	—	—	—	—	180	850
1400 (Red)	—	—	—	—	—	—	—	260	1,300

1894: Proof Strike

GSID	PF-63	PF-64	PF-65
1639 (Brown)	$285	$365	$525
1640 (Red-Brown)	340	500	725
1641 (Red)	390	600	1,100

Varieties

The Snow-1 repunched date (1894/1894) is one of the top varieties of the Indian Head cent series. Many advanced collectors collect it as part of the regular date set, an honor only given to only a few varieties (the 1867, 67 Over 67; 1869, 69 Over 69; and 1873, Doubled LIBERTY being other examples). This variety is an easily seen repunched date, so examples are easily discovered in low grades. These are usually well struck. A half-roll quantity came on the market in the early 1990's. Most of these pieces were of high quality although they may have numerous little carbon spots.

1894, Doubled Date, Snow-1

1894, Doubled Date: Circulation Strike

GSID	VG-8	F-12	VF-20	EF-40	AU-50	AU-58	MS-60	MS-63	MS-65
1401 (Brown)	$100	$130	$195	$455	$1,000	$1,350	$1,500	$2,400	$4,000
1402 (Red-Brown)	—	—	—	—	—	—	—	2,500	5,250
1403 (Red)	—	—	—	—	—	—	—	—	6,000

1895

Circulation-Strike Mintage:
38,341,574

Proof Mintage:
2,062

1895 Cent Production: Mintages rose this year, and would remain high until the last year of Indian Head cent coinage in 1909.

Survivability: Cents of this year are widely available. As the series drew to a close in the next 14 years, the coins saved from circulation tend to be of a higher quality.

Collecting Challenges: These come well struck and are easily located in most grades.

Collecting Circulated Pieces: The optimal collecting grade for circulated coins is AU-50 to MS-63RB. These are easily found in all grades. Search out a problem-free example. A common problem with all Indian Head cents is cleaning. In years past, when "Brilliant Uncirculated" meant "bright red," many examples were harshly cleaned to meet the expectations of beginner collectors. A quality-conscious collector should get a feel for how an original Uncirculated coin looks—and avoid harshly cleaned pieces, which have little resale value.

Collecting Mint State Pieces: The optimal collecting grade for Mint State coins is MS-64RD or MS-65RB. This date is widely available in low grades. Collectors should be cautioned that small imperfections on high-grade coins could hurt their desirability. Collectors impatient to search for high-quality coins should perhaps stick with MS-64RB graded coins.

Collecting Proof Issues: This is a relatively common date even though the mintage is much lower than those of earlier dates. These come with attractive eye appeal more often than other dates. Full red gems are as readily available as those of most other dates, but cameo examples are quite scarce. Of the five Proof die pairs of this year, three of them have repunched dates of varying boldness. Proof collectors tend to be interested strictly in date sets, not varieties, so these do not tend to bring much of a premium.

1895: Circulation Strike

GSID	VG-8	F-12	VF-20	EF-40	AU-50	AU-58	MS-60	MS-63	MS-65
1404 (Brown)	$2	$3	$4	$8	$30	$42	$55	$115	$215
1405 (Red-Brown)	—	—	—	—	—	—	—	125	420
1406 (Red)	—	—	—	—	—	—	—	290	1,000

1895: Proof Strike

GSID	PF-63	PF-64	PF-65
1644 (Brown)	$285	$365	$525
1645 (Red-Brown)	340	500	725
1646 (Red)	390	600	1,100

Varieties

Presently 30 varieties are known; most of these are repunched dates.

1896

Circulation-Strike Mintage:
39,055,431

Proof Mintage:
1,862

1896 Cent Production: As the country began to recover from the depression of 1893, businesses began to feel strong growth, justifying the need for more coins. The Mint experienced strong demand for cents and thus devoted much energy to increasing output this year and for the years to follow.

Survivability: The coins of this issue were put into circulation and stayed there for at least a generation.

Collecting Challenges: These are widely available in most all grades except in gem condition. Select eye-appealing coins with good strikes and no problems.

Collecting Circulated Pieces: The optimal collecting grade for circulated coins is AU-50 to MS-63RB. These should be easy to find without any problems.

Collecting Mint State Pieces: The optimal collecting grade for Mint State coins is MS-65RB or MS-64RD. These are a bit scarcer than other dates in the later 1890's, although this is not currently reflected in the price. Full red gems are surprisingly scarce. These tend to be a bit bright pale-gold, rather than the red-gold of other dates. Perhaps this makes them harder to be accepted as true gems.

Collecting Proof Issues: The mintage for this issue dips below the 2,000 mark for the first time since 1877. Mintages from here until the end of the series will remain at these lower levels. This date is very tough with full red color, especially in PF-65RD or higher grades. Many of the high-end examples will get the cameo designation.

1896: Circulation Strike

GSID	VG-8	F-12	VF-20	EF-40	AU-50	AU-58	MS-60	MS-63	MS-65
1407 (Brown)	$2	$3	$4	$8	$27	$42	$55	$110	$235
1408 (Red-Brown)	—	—	—	—	—	—	—	125	365
1409 (Red)	—	—	—	—	—	—	—	210	1,200

1896: Proof Strike

GSID	PF-63	PF-64	PF-65
1649 (Brown)	$285	$365	$525
1650 (Red-Brown)	340	500	725
1651 (Red)	575	875	1,250

Varieties

Presently 16 varieties are known, mostly minor repunched dates.

1897

Circulation-Strike Mintage:
50,464,392

Proof Mintage:
1,938

1897 Cent Production: This is a larger-mintage date. This and other dates of this era circulated extensively without any reason to be saved for 50 years. By the end of World War II they were curiosities of a distant age, saved by non-collectors (or future collectors) only because they were different.

Survivability: These are found in all grades easily, although most are worn down to Good condition.

Collecting Challenges: Select problem-free examples with attractive eye appeal.

Collecting Circulated Pieces: The optimal collecting grade in AU-50 to MS-63RB. Find problem-free examples. Avoid cleaned coins.

Collecting Mint State Pieces: The optimal collecting grade for Mint State coins is MS-65RB or MS-64RD. These are well struck and are easily found in most grades except for MS-65RD or higher. The lack of the survival of gem full red coins is quite interesting. The entire amount of all gem survivors of any date in the late 1890's could be the result of only two to five original rolls. The quality of these rolls will also dictate how rare the date will be in gem condition. Were they spotted, mildewed, water damaged? Or is the roll full of pristine gems of the highest order? These are the things that dictate the rarity of Indian Head cents in high grade.

Collecting Proof Issues: This is another lower-mintage issue, although they tend to be as readily available as other dates in the late 1890's. 1897 Proofs are a bit difficult to find in gem full red. However, some of the prettiest examples of Proof Indian Head cents are known for this year. Super-deep-mirror cameo gems are known for this date. The deep mirror cameo Proofs are the first coins made from new dies. In addition to a frosted design, these coins typically have a mirrored surface that is not smooth—it appears to be crystallized and is commonly referred to as *orange peel fields*. This happens because the die is initially polished while it is soft. During the hardening process the steel contacts slightly. This forces the fields to buckle slightly. Orange peel fields are highly desired by collectors.

1897: Circulation Strike

GSID	VG-8	F-12	VF-20	EF-40	AU-50	AU-58	MS-60	MS-63	MS-65
1410 (Brown)	$2	$3	$4	$8	$28	$46	$55	$100	$195
1411 (Red-Brown)	—	—	—	—	—	—	—	120	370
1412 (Red)	—	—	—	—	—	—	—	230	900

1897: Proof Strike

GSID	PF-63	PF-64	PF-65
1654 (Brown)	$285	$365	$525
1655 (Red-Brown)	340	500	725
1656 (Red)	390	600	1,400

Varieties

One of the most popular misplaced digit varieties of the series is the Snow-1 "1 in the Neck." It shows a bold base of a numeral 1 sticking out of the neck midway between the chin and pearls. It is a fairly scarce variety in high grades, but more readily available in low grades. This is due to the ease by which this variety can be seen in low grades—what is known as a *naked-eye variety*. These are surprisingly rare in gem and full red condition. Only an MS-63RD is presently known in full red and there are no MS-65RB pieces known. This variety is labeled on the holder by ANACS and PCGS, the authentication and certification attesting to it being a genuine variety, which, in turn, increases its desirability among collectors.

1897, Misplaced Digit, Snow-1, "1 in the Neck"

1897, 1 in Neck: Circulation Strike

GSID	VG-8	F-12	VF-20	EF-40	AU-50	AU-58	MS-60	MS-63	MS-65
1413 (Brown)	$75	$110	$160	$260	$325	$525	$725	$1,400	$3,100
1414 (Red-Brown)	—	—	—	—	—	—	—	2,000	4,500
1415 (Red)	—	—	—	—	—	—	—	3,100	—

1898

Circulation-Strike Mintage:
49,821,284

Proof Mintage:
1,795

1898 Cent Production: This issue is similar in mintage to the cent of 1897. The cent was by far the most abundant coin in the country. It was probably the most useful coin at the time to the average American. This was the era when the novelty games in penny arcades actually cost a cent.

Survivability: These coins circulated to a great extent and served the nation for at least 50 years. Examples are readily available in all grades except full red gem.

Collecting Challenges: Search out an attractive problem-free example.

Collecting Circulated Pieces: The optimal collecting grade for circulated coins is AU-50 to MS-63RB. The only challenge should be to find the best coin to match the other coins in your collection. The colors of bronze coins vary so much that matching a certain shade of red-brown, if desired, can be very difficult.

Collecting Mint State Pieces: The optimal collecting grade for Mint State coins is MS-65RD. Search out well-struck, problem-free examples. All gem full red Indian Head cents are scarce.

Collecting Proof Issues: Although this is another lower-mintage Proof issue, 1898 Proofs exist in average to higher-than-average quantities, so there should be little problem in finding an attractive specimen. Some of the prettiest gem cameo coins are found for this date; extra care must have been taken in their production. (In fact, all denominations of this year can be found with outstanding cameo contrast.)

1898: Circulation Strike

GSID	VG-8	F-12	VF-20	EF-40	AU-50	AU-58	MS-60	MS-63	MS-65
1416 (Brown)	$2	$3	$4	$8	$24	$35	$47	$100	$195
1417 (Red-Brown)	—	—	—	—	—	—	115	160	430
1418 (Red)	—	—	—	—	—	—	—	195	950

1898: Proof Strike

GSID	PF-63	PF-64	PF-65
1659 (Brown)	$285	$365	$525
1660 (Red-Brown)	340	500	725
1661 (Red)	390	600	1,200

Varieties

36 varieties of specialist interest are known for this year. These are mostly repunched dates, none of which are particularly dramatic.

1899

Circulation-Strike Mintage:
53,598,000

Proof Mintage:
2,031

1899 Cent Production: Mintages in the mid- to late 1890's crept up higher and higher each year.

Survivability: This date is a bit more common than most of the dates that follow. Perhaps more examples were saved over the years because of it being the last date in the 1800's (although it is not the last date in the 19th century).

Collecting Challenges: These are widely available and will be fairly easy to locate in all grades except full red gem.

Collecting Circulated Pieces: The optimal collecting grade for circulated coins is AU-50 to MS-63RB. Locate problem-free original coins with attractive eye appeal.

Collecting Mint State Pieces: The optimal collecting grade for Mint State coins is MS-65RD. These are widely available in all grades. MS-65RD and better pieces are a bit tougher, but such examples are among the easiest to find of the era (only 1909 is easier).

An example of this date, graded MS-68RD by PCGS, is the finest graded coin of the entire Indian Head cent series. It sold for an astounding $69,000 when it was auctioned as part of the Joseph P. Gorrell collection by Heritage at the Florida United Numismatists (FUN) show in January 2003. Earlier, it was in the Dr. Alan Epstein collection, which was the finest Indian Head cent collection ever assembled. When my firm, Eagle Eye Rare Coins, purchased the Dr. Epstein collection in 1996, this particular coin was so special to its previous owner that it was repurchased at the full asking price of $13,500. A bit later Dr. Epstein resold it though Eagle Eye into the Gorrell collection, for $14,500. Nobody could have guessed the astounding price it would command a few years later.

Collecting Proof Issues: Although this date has a lower Proof mintage than some others, examples seem to have survived a bit better than earlier years. Very high-quality examples are readily available. Beware of spotted coins, as the exquisite beauty of a gem Proof can be greatly diminished by the existence of an obvious dark spot.

1899: Circulation Strike

GSID	VG-8	F-12	VF-20	EF-40	AU-50	AU-58	MS-60	MS-63	MS-65
1419 (Brown)	$2	$3	$4	$8	$24	$35	$47	$95	$180
1420 (Red-Brown)	—	—	—	—	—	—	—	115	290
1421 (Red)	—	—	—	—	—	—	—	215	750

1899: Proof Strike

GSID	PF-63	PF-64	PF-65
1664 (Brown)	$285	$365	$525
1665 (Red-Brown)	340	525	750
1667 (Red)	390	600	1,100

Varieties

There are 22 varieties known for this date. Most are minor repunched dates. Snow-13 is a so-called "overdate" 1899/7. It was listed as such in *Walter Breen's Complete Encyclopedia of U.S. and Colonial Coins*, but what appears to be an overdate is nothing more than a die chip inside the last 9. This is still a popular variety, though.

1900

Circulation-Strike Mintage:
66,831,502

Proof Mintage:
2,262

1900 Cent Production: A record number of cents was produced this year, although this is one of the lower-mintage dates of the 1900's. Mint Director George E. Roberts began to call for the striking of Indian Head cents at the branch mints of San Francisco and New Orleans.

Survivability: These were not saved from circulation early on, and most examples are well circulated. Enough are available to satisfy collector demand in all grades except MS-65RD and higher.

Collecting Challenges: Select eye-appealing coins with few problems.

Collecting Circulated Pieces: The optimal collecting grade for circulated coins is AU-50 to MS-63RB. There is no particular difficulty in finding this date in an attractive grade.

Collecting Mint State Pieces: The optimal collecting grade for Mint State coins is MS-65RD. This date is very hard to find in gem condition, at least in relation to other dates in the 1900's.

Collecting Proof Issues: These are about as readily available as other dates in the era. This is a popular date to collect as part of a turn-of-the-century Proof set. Gem full red examples are scarce, but only in the context of some of the more common dates of the 1880's. Cameos are available, although few have graded as such.

1900: Circulation Strike

GSID	VG-8	F-12	VF-20	EF-40	AU-50	AU-58	MS-60	MS-63	MS-65
1422 (Brown)	$2	$3	$4	$8	$24	$35	$47	$95	$180
1423 (Red-Brown)	—	—	—	—	—	—	—	115	290
1424 (Red)	—	—	—	—	—	—	—	195	700

1900: Proof Strike

GSID	PF-63	PF-64	PF-65
1669 (Brown)	$285	$365	$525
1670 (Red-Brown)	340	500	725
1671 (Red)	390	600	1,100

Varieties

There are 23 collectible varieties. Most are minor repunched dates. Three examples of this date are known struck in gold, and at least one example in silver. The reason for the existence of these coins is a mystery. The gold examples weigh 4.26 to 4.35 grams, which is slightly more than the official 4.18-gram weight of a quarter eagle planchet, so they are probably not accidental off-metal errors. Both the silver and gold examples are struck from the same dies, with light roughness on the reverse die, probably from die rust. These were likely struck outside the knowledge of Mint officers. When they show up in auctions they always generate extremely high interest.

1901

Circulation-Strike Mintage:
79,609,158

Proof Mintage:
1,985

1901 Cent Production: In 1901 the Mint again set a production record, breaking the previous year's record. This is technically the first issue of the 20th century, but collectors prefer to group the 20th-century issues as all the coins dated "19—." The third Philadelphia Mint opened for production this year. The building had a classical Roman temple façade. Massive Ionic columns led to a lobby with vaulted ceilings that were bejeweled with seven Tiffany glass mosaics. Today the building houses Philadelphia Community College. This improved facility allowed for a much higher production of cents.

Survivability: Very few coins were saved at the time of issue. A popular souvenir item that sold at events such as the 1901 Pan American Exposition (in Buffalo, New York) were newly issued cents encased in aluminum advertising cards. These came in a variety of styles and sayings, such as "Keep me for good luck." These *encased coins* are collected quite actively today, and the encasements are worth much more with the original coins intact. Many times, though, the temptation to remove high-grade examples of Indian Head cents from these holders is too much for their owners. A coin, when removed from such a holder, is usually found to be slightly damaged from the encasing process. Part of an advertising design may be impressed into the rim of the coin, or it may be slightly bent.

Collecting Challenges: Search for problem-free examples. These are found with average to full strikes. Avoid coins damaged from being inserted in aluminum encasements.

Collecting Circulated Pieces: The optimal collecting grade for circulated coins is AU-50 to MS-63RB. These, like other issues of the 1900's, are widely available.

Collecting Mint State Pieces: Available in most grades, the optimal collecting grade for the 1901 cent is MS-65RD. However, finding a problem free MS-65RD example may require some patience.

Collecting Proof Issues: These are available with some searching. Full red gems are scarce, as with all Proofs of this era. Cameos are available, but are very tough to find.

Many early-die-state examples from this date onward until 1907 show fine die-polishing lines across the whole face of the die, including the portrait. When the coin is turned in the light it will appear as if the coin has been wiped with an abrasive rag. As the coin is turned further the lines disappear and the coin shows very deep mirror fields. These are actually lines on the die that are transferred to the coin, and are desirable as the earliest die state of the dies. Most cameos will show these lines.

1901: Circulation Strike

GSID	VG-8	F-12	VF-20	EF-40	AU-50	AU-58	MS-60	MS-63	MS-65
1425 (Brown)	$2	$3	$4	$8	$24	$35	$47	$95	$180
1426 (Red-Brown)	—	—	—	—	—	—	—	115	290
1427 (Red)	—	—	—	—	—	—	—	195	650

1901: Proof Strike

GSID	PF-63	PF-64	PF-65
1674 (Brown)	$285	$365	$525
1675 (Red-Brown)	340	500	725
1676 (Red)	390	600	1,200

Varieties

There are 20 varieties listed. Most are minor repunched dates.

1902

Circulation-Strike Mintage:
87,374,704

Proof Mintage:
2,018

1902 Cent Production: This was another record year of production. Possibly in an effort to extend the die life, the gap between the dies was set a bit wider. Cents of this date show weakness in the feather tips and bust point a bit more often than other dates. The shield and denticles are also typically weak. Some of the dies have the design sunk slightly deeper, which also contributed to the weakness encountered on this year's coinage.

Survivability: These circulated widely and were not plucked from circulation until the late 1940's.

Collecting Challenges: Choose problem-free examples with exceptional eye appeal.

Collecting Circulated Pieces: The optimal collecting grade for circulated coins is AU-50 to MS-63RB. This date is common in the context of the later Indian Head cents. Search for well-struck examples with full details on the shield.

Collecting Mint State Pieces: The optimal collecting grade for Mint State coins is MS-65RD. These are available in all grades. MS-65RD and higher grades are difficult to find. One roll, possibly two, showed up in the late 1990's, with many coins graded MS-65RD, but with numerous light carbon spots.

Collecting Proof Issues: The 1902 Proof comes very attractive and is one of the most common dates in the series in gem condition. This is due to the chance survival of a few exceptional coins, as the mintage is fairly low for the series. Early-die-state coins come with fine die-polishing lines. During this year, and the next two, a change in die preparation eliminated the cameo contrast on most denominations. Only the first couple of coins minted from a die will have any contrast between the devices and field. Coins of this date designated as cameos are very rare.

1902: Circulation Strike

GSID	VG-8	F-12	VF-20	EF-40	AU-50	AU-58	MS-60	MS-63	MS-65
1428 (Brown)	$2	$3	$4	$8	$24	$35	$47	$95	$180
1429 (Red-Brown)	—	—	—	—	—	—	—	115	290
1430 (Red)	—	—	—	—	—	—	—	195	650

1902: Proof Strike

GSID	PF-63	PF-64	PF-65
1679 (Brown)	$285	$365	$525
1680 (Red-Brown)	340	500	725
1681 (Red)	390	600	1,100

Varieties

14 varieties are presently known, mostly repunched dates. Snow-4 has a dramatic die gouge by the eye on the portrait. It is very similar to the 1890-CC "Tail Bar" Morgan silver dollar.

1903

Circulation-Strike Mintage:
85,092,703

Proof Mintage:
1,790

1903 Cent Production: 1903 is another high-mintage date.

Survivability: These circulated extensively and today are available in all grades.

Collecting Challenges: As with other dates, select problem-free original examples.

Collecting Circulated Pieces: The optimal collecting grade for circulated coins is AU-50 to MS-63RB. Beware of cleaned coins, as they have a limited resale value.

Collecting Mint State Pieces: The optimal collecting grade for Mint State coins is MS-65RD. These come well struck with good luster. Regardless that this date (as well as others of the 1900's) is considered common, collectors should exert the same amount of care as they would if they were buying a coin worth ten times as much. To many collectors, the thrill is in the chase and capture of the one prized example that "speaks" to them stronger than any other.

Collecting Proof Issues: Although this is a lower-mintage date, there tends to be enough high-grade examples available. PF-65RD examples and higher tend to be no rarer than most other dates in the late-date set, which traditionally covers 1879 to 1909. This date, as is seen in 1902, does not come with any appreciable cameo contrast. Most early-die-state examples have die polishing lines which appear when the coin is turned a certain way in the light, and then disappear when the coin is turned further. The die polishing lines may look like hairlines on the coin to the uninitiated. In the past, I have been able to buy superb uncertified gem Proofs of this date for PR-63 or lower prices from dealers who do not handle enough of these coins to know about the die polishing.

1903: Circulation Strike

GSID	VG-8	F-12	VF-20	EF-40	AU-50	AU-58	MS-60	MS-63	MS-65
1431 (Brown)	$2	$3	$4	$8	$24	$35	$47	$95	$180
1432 (Red-Brown)	—	—	—	—	—	—	—	115	290
1433 (Red)	—	—	—	—	—	—	—	195	700

1903: Proof Strike

GSID	PF-63	PF-64	PF-65
1684 (Brown)	$285	$365	$525
1685 (Red-Brown)	340	500	725
1686 (Red)	390	600	1,100

Varieties

There are 23 or so known varieties. These are mostly minor repunched dates.

1904

Circulation-Strike Mintage:
61,326,198

Proof Mintage:
1,817

1904 Cent Production: This is another higher-mintage date, although slightly fewer coins were minted compared to other dates of the 1900's.

Survivability: Although produced in lower quantities than most other dates of the era, there appears to be about the same number of surviving 1904 cents. This date is no more scarce than any other of the 1900's. The chance survival of only a few original rolls can alter the rarity of the high-end examples in the collector market. In the 1990's and beyond, the discovery of original rolls has been a very rare occurrence.

Collecting Challenges: Select problem-free examples with attractive eye appeal.

Collecting Circulated Pieces: The optimal collecting grade for circulated coins is AU-50 to MS-63RB. These tend to come well struck and attractive.

Collecting Mint State Pieces: The optimal collecting grade for Mint State coins is MS-65RD. Select eye-appealing coins with no problems. All brown and red-brown coins graded MS-65 or higher, and all red coins, should be purchased certified. Grade certification is not a cure-all, as the coins still need to be looked at for strike, problems, and eye appeal, but it is a good starting point. At least the *worst* cleaned and altered coins will be eliminated from the selection of contenders for your collection.

Collecting Proof Issues: This is a lower-mintage date in Proof. Early-die-state pieces hardly ever come with a cameo contrast, but do have the die-polishing lines seen on other issues from 1901 to 1907. True full red gems are very scarce and hotly contested. The prices for many later-date Proofs in gem condition are presently deceptively low compared to more common earlier dates. Collectors and price-guide writers both typically equate the scarcer Proof dates in the 1900's with the common circulation strikes.

1904: Circulation Strike

GSID	VG-8	F-12	VF-20	EF-40	AU-50	AU-58	MS-60	MS-63	MS-65
1434 (Brown)	$2	$3	$4	$8	$24	$35	$47	$95	$180
1435 (Red-Brown)	—	—	—	—	—	—	—	115	290
1436 (Red)	—	—	—	—	—	—	—	195	675

1904: Proof Strike

GSID	PF-63	PF-64	PF-65
1689 (Brown)	$285	$365	$525
1690 (Red-Brown)	340	500	725
1691 (Red)	390	725	1,400

Varieties

Only 12 varieties are known for this year. These are mostly minor repunched dates.

1905

Circulation-Strike Mintage:
80,717,011

Proof Mintage:
2,152

1905 Cent Production: Cent mintage climbed back up to a near-record level this year.

Survivability: A good estimate of the survivors in various grades might show the high degree of attrition these coins suffered over the years. Each year, between one million and five million cents of earlier years were deemed unfit for circulation, melted by the Mint, and recoined into new cents. My own estimate of surviving coins of this year breaks down roughly, by grade, as: Poor to Very Good, 2,000,000; Fine to About Uncirculated, 50,000; Mint State, Red-Brown, 15,000; Mint State, Full Red, 1,000.

Collecting Challenges: Find an eye-appealing example with a good strike and no problems. While strike is not a common problem with this date, it is worthwhile to search out the best coins you can find for whatever grade level you desire.

Collecting Circulated Pieces: The optimal collecting grade for circulated coins is AU-50 to MS-63RB. Buy only problem-free examples. The major problems to avoid are cleaning, scratches, rim hits, corrosion, and spotting.

Collecting Mint State Pieces: The optimal collecting grade for Mint State coins is MS-65RD. Cents of this date are easily found in all grades except MS-65RD and higher. Fully struck pieces are harder to find than weakly struck. The common weak area is the feather tips.

Collecting Proof Issues: 1905 was not a particularly low-mintage year. Many of the coins, especially early-die-state coins, come with the die-polishing lines commonly found on 1901 to 1907 issues. These do not affect the grade of the coin, or at least they shouldn't. It seems that many coins that warrant a PF-65 grade or higher are only graded PF-64 because of these die-polishing lines. Typically these coins were graded early in the history of the grading services. Today's more experienced grader knows not to equate the presence or lack of die-polishing lines into the grade.

1905: Circulation Strike

GSID	VG-8	F-12	VF-20	EF-40	AU-50	AU-58	MS-60	MS-63	MS-65
1437 (Brown)	$2	$3	$4	$8	$24	$35	$47	$95	$180
1438 (Red-Brown)	—	—	—	—	—	—	—	115	290
1439 (Red)	—	—	—	—	—	—	—	195	675

1905: Proof Strike

GSID	PF-63	PF-64	PF-65
1694 (Brown)	$285	$365	$525
1695 (Red-Brown)	340	500	725
2696 (Red)	470	700	1,250

Varieties

There presently are 27 varieties, mostly minor repunched dates. Three varieties are known with doubled-die reverses.

1906

Circulation-Strike Mintage:
96,020,530

Proof Mintage:
1,725

1906 Cent Production: The Mint produced a record number of cents this year.

Survivability: These coins circulated widely, and were not saved for numismatic purposes until the late 1940's. Original-roll quantities were occasionally discovered as late as the 1960's. Since the advent of third-party certification, any original roll that still exists does not stand much chance of staying intact. For protection purposes alone, certification offers many benefits. A gem full red Indian Head cent that has existed in a roll for 100 years will certainly stay that way even longer if nothing gets on its surface. The chance slip of a finger to the surface of a coin may leave skin oils that will turn into a fingerprint in the future. Also, someone coughing or speaking carelessly in the vicinity of an exposed coin may lead to ugly spotting over time.

Collecting Challenges: This date is usually found fully struck. Search out eye-appealing coins.

Collecting Circulated Pieces: The optimal collecting grade for circulated coins is AU-50 to MS-63RB. This is one of the most plentiful dates in average circulated grades.

Collecting Mint State Pieces: The optimal collecting grade for Mint State coins is MS-65RD. Select problem-free examples with attractive eye appeal.

Collecting Proof Issues: This is a lower-mintage date in the late-date series, 1879 to 1909. These coins are fairly difficult to locate in all grades except PF-64RB. Gem full red examples are difficult, but some exceptional pieces are seen from time to time. Cameos are available for this date more frequently than for previous dates.

1906: Circulation Strike

GSID	VG-8	F-12	VF-20	EF-40	AU-50	AU-58	MS-60	MS-63	MS-65
1440 (Brown)	$2	$3	$4	$8	$24	$35	$47	$95	$180
1441 (Red-Brown)	—	—	—	—	—	—	—	115	290
1442 (Red)	—	—	—	—	—	—	—	195	675

1906: Proof Strike

GSID	PF-63	PF-64	PF-65
1699 (Brown)	$285	$365	$525
1700 (Red-Brown)	340	500	725
1701 (Red)	390	625	1,250

Varieties

There are more than 40 varieties recorded for this date. Most are minor repunched dates. Three dies are known with minor doubled dies. An example struck on a gold quarter-eagle planchet is known. It is graded AU-58 by NGC. Unlike the 1900 gold Indian Head cent, this appears to be a true wrong-metal planchet error.

1907

Circulation-Strike Mintage:
108,137,143

Proof Mintage:
1,475

1907 Cent Production: This date holds the record for production of any coin minted by the United States up until this time. The Mint would break this production record again in 1909, but that year's mintage is divided between Indian Head cents and those of the new Lincoln design.

Late in 1907 the country saw a financial panic due to the failure of a few large businesses. Stock prices crashed and nearly started an economic meltdown. Financier J.P. Morgan and a group of bank executives temporarily supported the failing banks and restored stability to the market. The resulting inquiry resulted in the beginnings of what would become the Federal Reserve System.

Survivability: Cents of 1907 circulated widely and are the most commonly found in average circulated condition. Even if only 5% of the mintage were saved, which is likely, there would be enough coins to satisfy demand from collectors. Even so, examples in Good condition sell today for at least 100 times their face value! This is a testament to both the collector demand for Indian Head cents and the shrinking value printed on their face.

Collecting Challenges: Select problem-free coins. These are plentiful enough that a quality example should be easy to acquire.

Collecting Circulated Pieces: The optimal collecting grade for circulated coins is AU-50 to MS-63RB. Avoid problems and take extra care to find the coin that matches your set the best.

Collecting Mint State Pieces: The optimal collecting grade for Mint State coins is MS-65RD. Only in lower Mint State grades is this date the most common. In gem condition a 1907 cent is slightly more difficult to find than many other dates. The issue of quality over technical grade is an important concern here. Many 1907 cents do not come with the great eye appeal found on other dates. This is purely a factor of chance survival of a few lesser-quality rolls than anything else. Take extra time to find the real attractive pieces.

Collecting Proof Issues: This is the low-mintage date of the later dates, 1879 to 1909, in Proof format. This is surprising to newer collectors. The Mint did not produce Mint State coins for collectors, and they didn't want to make more Proof issues than they could sell. Coins this year come with die-polishing lines more often than do other dates. True gems are very scarce and command a good premium over other dates. Full cameo examples exist but are scarce.

1907: Circulation Strike

GSID	VG-8	F-12	VF-20	EF-40	AU-50	AU-58	MS-60	MS-63	MS-65
1443 (Brown)	$2	$3	$4	$8	$24	$35	$47	$95	$180
1444 (Red-Brown)	—	—	—	—	—	—	—	115	290
1445 (Red)	—	—	—	—	—	—	—	195	650

1907: Proof Strike

GSID	PF-63	PF-64	PF-65
1704 (Brown)	$285	$365	$525
1705 (Red-Brown)	340	500	725
1706 (Red)	390	725	1,500

Varieties

There are 47 varieties of this date currently recorded, more than any other date. Collecting these could be a daunting task. Collections assembled by early variety collectors Joe Haney and Al Mays Sr. were close to complete, and formed the basis of my *Flying Eagle and Indian Cent Attribution Guide, Volume 6, 1900–1909*. Today, at least, collectors have a referral list or attribution guide. Joe Haney had been collecting Indian Head cent varieties long before anyone else thought to look for them. Al Mays Sr. started collecting them in the late 1990's when I decided to add the known varieties to the book that was published in 1992. Al purchased many of the known varieties. The Al Mays collection was auctioned through Heritage Galleries in 2005. Today, collecting later-date Indian Head cents can be a fascinating excursion. There are certainly enough coins to look through. A collector on a modest budget can look through and buy many interesting repunched dates, misplaced dates, and even doubled dies, for small premiums.

1908

Circulation-Strike Mintage:
32,326,367

Proof Mintage:
1,620

1908 Cent Production: Mintage figures dropped dramatically this year.

Survivability: Although fewer coins were minted in 1908 compared to the previous year, this date is essentially no harder to locate today than any other, except perhaps in low grades.

Collecting Challenges: Examples in every grade are available. Select the most attractive and problem-free coin you can.

Collecting Circulated Pieces: The optimal collecting grade for circulated coins is AU-50 to MS-63RB. Avoid problem pieces. Examples with odd color have usually been cleaned and should be avoided as well. Collecting choice Extremely Fine and About Uncirculated Indian Head cents is a very difficult and challenging pursuit. Many collectors who are very active have said to me that they maintain multiple collections in varying grades. As they upgrade their top set, the duplicates go into secondary collections. Only when collectors need money for a very expensive date will they part with their lowest set.

Collecting Mint State Pieces: The optimal collecting grade for Mint State coins is MS-65RD. These come well struck with better-than-average luster. 1908 cents are not any scarcer than those of other dates, although the mintage might suggest otherwise. All Indian Head cents in gem full red condition are difficult to find. Additional effort should be taken to acquire pieces with no major problems such as spots.

Collecting Proof Issues: This is a lower-mintage date within the later-date Proofs. These tend to come with very good mirrors, although deep mirror cameo examples are quite scarce. The Mint's practice of leaving die-polishing lines on the dies seems to have ended, as this date is not usually found with them.

1908: Circulation Strike

GSID	VG-8	F-12	VF-20	EF-40	AU-50	AU-58	MS-60	MS-63	MS-65
1446 (Brown)	$2	$3	$4	$8	$24	$35	$47	$95	$180
1447 (Red-Brown)	—	—	—	—	—	—	—	115	290
1448 (Red)	—	—	—	—	—	—	—	195	675

1908: Proof Strike

GSID	PF-63	PF-64	PF-65
1708 (Brown)	$285	$365	$525
1709 (Red-Brown)	340	500	725
1710 (Red)	390	600	1,100

VARIETIES

26 varieties are known for this date. About half of these are repunched dates of moderate interest. The remaining varieties are misplaced dates, which are quite prevalent for this year. Misplaced dates are varieties wherein remnants from some of the digits are found in the denticles or areas of the portrait. (They could conceivably be anywhere on the design, but tend to be found in these two areas.) Prevailing opinion is that these digits were intentionally tapped into the dies, perhaps to test their hardness. The digits are usually found only on obverse dies. Collectors pay the highest premiums for the most prominent examples with the errant digit extending into the field area or in some other obvious place. Significant misplaced date varieties are listed in my *Flying Eagle and Indian Cent Attribution Guide, Volume 6, 1900–1909*. Additional examples are listed in *Two Dates are Better Than One, A Collectors Guide to Misplaced Dates*, by Kevin Flynn. One collector-researcher, Marvin Erickson, has assembled an enormous collection of misplaced dates. He began a search for these varieties long before they became well known to the general collecting public.

1908-S

Circulation-Strike Mintage:
1,115,000

1908-S Cent Production: This cent is important as being the first minor coinage struck at a branch mint. The San Francisco Mint, nicknamed *The Granite Lady*, was built in 1874 and had survived the great earthquake of the morning of April 18, 1906, with just slight damage. The fire that raged on all sides of the building later on that day blackened the stone and buckled the heavy iron shutters. The fire destroyed most of the city, but the mint was spared destruction because it had its own well that firefighters could tap into.

In years prior to the earthquake and subsequent economic hardships, gold and silver coins were the only coinage used in the Western states. Transactions were rounded to the nearest 5¢. Now, due to changes in the economy (brought on in part by the relative ease of railroad travel from the East), it was desirable to have the cent denomination available so that prices could be increased in smaller increments. The introduction of a sales tax alone necessitated the use of the cent. In addition, the streetcar fare was raised from 5¢ to 6¢.

The Mint delivered the entire mintage of coins on November 27. These were struck on presses used for silver coinage, as the two presses for cent production were not yet delivered. This is the third-lowest mintage of the Indian Head cent series. Planchet stock for this year was often improperly mixed, so the coins vary with either woodgrain toning or a bright golden color.

Survivability: The new cents were certainly a curiosity to the local population, and initially circulated widely. Later, by the time the new Lincoln design became dominant, the general public selectively removed the Indian Head cents from circulation. There seems to have been no initial interest in saving these coins before they entered circulation. Today, the coins are scarce in low grades, but available in mid-range grades, most being Fine to Very Fine. Mint State survivors are very scarce overall. The chance survival of a few roll quantities has made gem full red examples somewhat readily available. Many of these come from a roll that had a filled final A in AMERICA on the obverse.

Collecting Challenges: These cents are scarce and popular, so demand is high. Many come with weak feather tips. Search for fully struck examples.

Collecting Circulated Pieces: The optimal collecting grade for circulated coins is AU-50 to AU-58. There is not a great difference in prices between coins graded Good to Very Fine. For collectors on a budget it is worthwhile to buy the highest grade with the price jumping less than 50%. For example, a Fine coin lists for $85, a Very Fine at $100, and an Extremely Fine at $150. The extra $15 to buy the Very Fine will give you a lot more value for the money than would the extra $50 to buy the Extremely Fine. On the other hand, the best advice is always to buy the best coin you can afford that fits your collection.

Collecting Mint State Pieces: The optimal collecting grade for Mint State coins is MS-65RB or MS-64RD. It might be difficult to find coins with full feather tips. Take extra time to search these out. These come with woodgrain toning, which is acceptable for red-brown graded coins. Full red coins should be struck on evenly colored planchets. Many full red coins are of a lighter golden color. Some original coins might easily be mistaken as being cleaned if compared to their Philadelphia Mint contemporaries. Occasionally prooflike examples are available. These are highly desired and are worth an additional premium.

1908-S: Circulation Strike

GSID	VG-8	F-12	VF-20	EF-40	AU-50	AU-58	MS-60	MS-63	MS-65
1461 (Brown)	$95	$110	$130	$175	$220	$310	$325	$525	$1,200
1462 (Red-Brown)	—	—	—	—	—	—	410	700	1,700
1463 (Red)	—	—	—	—	—	—	—	1,150	2,400

Varieties

A repunched mintmark, Snow-1, is known for this date. The repunching is to the south and is visible in the upper part of the S. Many other repunched dates have been reported but all others have turned out to be caused by strike doubling. When the lower die (anvil die) is loose in the press it can move slightly when the coin is struck. This action leaves a microscopic outline on the design elements in one direction. (The clue to detecting strike doubling: the doubling is seen on the mintmark as well as on some of the surrounding design elements. Since the mintmark is added to the die separately from the design element, it cannot be a repunched mintmark.)

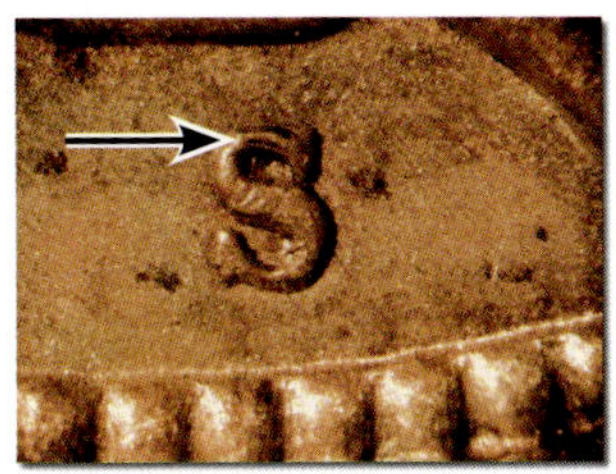
1908-S, S Over S, Snow-1

1909

Circulation-Strike Mintage:
14,368,470

Proof Mintage:
2,175

1909 Cent Production: The Mint changed its procedure for making cent dies this year. For this date only, and continuing on all Lincoln cents, the entire design with the date was sunk into the die at one time. Prior to this year the procedure was to add the date after the obverse die was sunk with the design and legend. This change eliminated the possibility of a repunched date. Every cent with doubling on the date from this year onward is called a *doubled die*, rather than a *repunched date*.

Up until this time, many of the planchets used were purchased by contract from manufacturing companies. This year the Mint crafted its own planchets for the entire mintage.

Coinage of Indian Head cents ceased mid-year, awaiting the new Lincoln design by Victor D. Brenner to be finished. The 1909 mintage is the lowest since 1885.

Survivability: As the last Indian Head cent, many people put away examples of this date. Many roll quantities existed, making this the most common date in gem full red condition. However, most of the 1909 cents put away were the new Lincoln design with the designer's initials V.D.B. on the reverse, which are today on the order of 100 times more common than the 1909 Indian Head cent. In lower grades the coin is as common as any other, although catalogers tend to price it a bit higher than earlier dates. Only in Good and Very Good is it slightly scarcer, but not enough to warrant paying more.

Collecting Challenges: Search out exceptional pieces. Try not to pay a large premium over other common dates.

Collecting Circulated Pieces: The optimal collecting grade for circulated coins is AU-50 to MS-63RB. These come well struck, so buy the most attractive coin available.

Collecting Mint State Pieces: The optimal collecting grade for Mint State coins is MS-65RD. This is the most readily available date in the series in high grade. Select eye-appealing examples.

Collecting Proof Issues: 1909 Proofs tend to be available with good eye appeal. Gem full red examples are difficult to find. Mirrors tend to be moderate, with cameo examples being fairly scarce. As a year with three designs (Indian Head, Lincoln with V.D.B., and Lincoln without V.D.B.), there is slightly higher demand for this date over others.

1909: Circulation Strike

GSID	VG-8	F-12	VF-20	EF-40	AU-50	AU-58	MS-60	MS-63	MS-65
1449 (Brown)	$8	$10	$12	$20	$32	$42	$47	$95	$180
1450 (Red-Brown)	—	—	—	—	—	—	—	115	290
1451 (Red)	—	—	—	—	—	—	—	195	650

1909: Proof Strike

GSID	PF-63	PF-64	PF-65
1713 (Brown)	$285	$365	$525
1714 (Red-Brown)	340	500	725
1715 (Red)	390	600	1,100

Varieties

No repunched dates are possible, as the date was added to the hub instead of to coinage dies starting this year. At least two dies are known with doubling on the designer's initial L. This is a minor doubled die and is relatively common.

1909-S

Circulation-Strike Mintage:
309,000

1909-S Mintmark

1909-S Cent Production: This is the lowest-mintage cent of the entire series. Its dies, produced in Philadelphia, were completely hubbed with the date incorporated. As a result, there are no positional variations for the date. The obverse dies always show slight weakness on the first feather tip. Collectors should rely on a full shield and bust point to confirm a full strike, as all 1909-S cents will show this feather-tip weakness. In fact, any example with full feather tips should be checked for an added mintmark. The mintmark is slightly larger than the one used for the new Lincoln design. Planchets tend to be a bit lighter than their Philadelphia Mint counterparts. They tend to be a straw-golden color.

Survivability: These coins were saved as the last of their issue. Non-collectors saved them as the last of the design, and numismatists pulled them quickly from circulation due to their known low mintage. The rarity is much lower than the low-mintage coins of earlier years because of this higher survival rate.

This date is very rare in low grades, so prices for grades below Very Fine tend to be very similar. Most examples grade Very Fine to About Uncirculated. In Mint State, the coins are fairly scarce. Full red examples are very difficult to locate.

Collecting Challenges: Avoid problem pieces. Don't expect to find any bargain-priced examples unless the coins are cleaned or have had some other indignity performed on them.

Collecting Circulated Pieces: The optimal collecting grade for circulated coins is EF-40. Overgrading is a problem because dealers believe there is not a big enough spread between grades to make their profit margin. I argue that the ease of selling these at present levels *should* equate to lower margins.

Collecting Mint State Pieces: The optimal collecting grade for Mint State coins is MS-64RB. The certified populations on this date are similar in most grades to many of the semi-common dates. This may be the case, but most 1909-S cents are submitted for certification and the more common dates of Indian Head cents are often not submitted. The 1909-S is a very popular cent and should be compared to another coin of similar mintage that is usually always submitted for certification, the 1909-S V.D.B. Lincoln cent. In MS-65RB and MS-65RD, the number of 1909-S V.D.B. coins graded by ANACS, NGC, and PCGS is ten times what is shown for the 1909-S Indian Head cent.

Counterfeits: Many counterfeits exist for this coin. Some are false-die counterfeits. These tend to have very sharp, flat edges, whereas the genuine 1909-S issue has a beveled edge. Most numerous are Philadelphia Mint 1909 cents with an added mintmark. These will usually have a very sharp first feather tip. Since all authentic 1909-S coins have a slight weakness on this point, a sharp feather tip might give away a suspicious offering. Certification and a written bill of sale from a reputable dealer will greatly decrease your chance of purchasing a counterfeit.

For more on counterfeit and altered cents, see appendix D.

1909-S: Circulation Strike

GSID	VG-8	F-12	VF-20	EF-40	AU-50	AU-58	MS-60	MS-63	MS-65
1464 (Brown)	$325	$410	$455	$625	$775	$1,100	$1,200	$1,600	$2,500
1465 (Red-Brown)	—	—	—	—	—	—	—	1,750	3,000
1466 (Red)	—	—	—	—	—	—	—	1,950	5,500

Varieties

No varieties are known for the 1909-S cent.

APPENDIX A
Levels of Collecting

When deciding to collect Flying Eagle and Indian Head cents, you can choose how much you want to expand or limit your collection. This chapter will give the collector ideas as to how far you want to take your collection and what should be included in each level of completion.

Level I: Major Design Types

To begin, we will start with the major design changes—the Flying Eagle design and the Indian Head cent types. This basic type set should include the following coins:

Flying Eagle cent (1856–1858).

Indian Head cent with the Laurel Wreath reverse (1859).

Indian Head cent with the Shield reverse, struck in copper-nickel alloy (1859–1864).

Indian Head cent with the Shield reverse, struck in bronze alloy (1864–1909).

These are the basic designs. This set includes the change in alloy in 1864. It doesn't take much to complete this set, unless you look for rare dates and/or high grades. This collection will usually be part of a full type set of United States coins. It can be assembled in both Mint State and Proof formats.

Level II: Major Design Types and Date Set

This set includes one of every date within the series. There are a few years where two examples from the same date are necessary. The 1864 date has the copper nickel and bronze example required. This set is collected in mint state as well as Proof format. The two regular production coins from San Francisco are also included.

The 1859 Shield Reverse cent is a new addition to this set, as it had been previously listed as a Pattern. It was struck in limited numbers and might be considered optional to the collection, especially if you are completing the set in circulated grades. See the catalog entry on the 1859 Shield Reverse cent for more information.

1859 Shield Reverse Cent

Level III: Minor Design Types and Date Set

This set includes all the dates produced as well as the popularly collected design and date differences within a given year's production. Some of these were minor to their maker's eyes, but to collectors they are very important differences. Some of these design changes were made to increase the life of the die by lowering the relief of the design. Other times the design was changed because the die's life no longer required shallow details. Some changes were just the Chief Engraver updating the design slightly. Changes in digit styles are also part of these minor design differences. Years with multiple design changes are as follows:

1856: 1856, High Leaves–1856, Low Leaves.

1857: 1857, Obverse of 1856–1857, Type of 1857.

1858: 1858, Large Letters–1858, Small Letters; and 1858, High Leaves–1858, Low Leaves.

1864: 1864, No L, Bronze–1864, With L on Ribbon.

1870: 1870, Shallow N–1870, Bold N.

1871: 1871, Shallow N–1871, Bold N.

1872: 1872, Shallow N–1872, Bold N.

1886: 1886, Variety 1–1886, Variety 2.

The history of what has been included in this set has evolved as the study of this series has evolved. In the 1870's, the 1864 design differences began to be noticed, with the "With L" design being called the "Thin Die" and the "No L" called the "Thick die," as in the January 1870 sale of the Longacre Estate by M. Thomas & Sons. The Large Letter and Small Letter design on the 1858 Flying Eagle cent began to be noticed in the 1910's. The design changes found in 1886 began to gain recognition after they were first described by Jim Reynolds in *Numismatic Scrapbook* in 1959. The 1860, Pointed Bust, cent was largely unknown until it was noted in *Walter Breen's Complete Encyclopedia of U.S. and Colonial Coins* in 1987. The earliest mention of the 1857, Obverse Style of 1856, is in a Joja Jemz pamphlet from 1988. Joja Jemz was the work of Bill "Zemo" Fivaz and J.T. "Bubba" Stanton.

The reverse design changes of the 1858 Flying Eagle cent were also not well known until 1977, when they were described in the 1856 Flying Eagle cent study in *Walter Breen's Encyclopedia of United States and Colonial Proof Coins, 1722–1977*, where he listed them as High Leaves and Low Leaves. The 1870 design change of the reverse of the Indian Head cent was first published in *Flying Eagle and Indian Cents*, 1992 by myself. At first, I called the 1870 redesign the Strong N, later changing it to Bold N. The pre-1870 design was called the Shallow N, as I was strongly opposed to it being called the "Weak N." So Bold and Shallow became the terms of choice instead of Strong and Weak.

These design differences are important for collectors to understand, so we will describe them here outside the context of the date by date analysis.

The terms High Leaves and Low Leaves refer to the leaves inside the wreath by the C and T of CENT. This design change was made in 1858 to lower the relief of the design. This would have the effect of increasing the life of the die by reducing the striking pressure needed to coin the cents. 1856 Flying Eagle cents were being restruck for sale to collectors beginning in 1858 and a few were struck with the die used to strike 1858, Small Letters, Proof cents and other 1858 patterns. The 1856, Low Leaves, cents are very rare, even compared to the rarity of the 1856 date. Only about 20 examples were struck. Because of their extreme rarity, most collectors will choose not to worry about completion here.

1856 High Leaves and 1856 Low Leaves

1857 Obverse of 1856 and 1857 Type of 1857

The diagnostic for the 1857, Style of 1856, is the squared O in OF. These dies were made at the same time as the other 1856 dies, but at least six were left undated and unused until 1857. These dies were then punched with the new date and put to use. The 1857, Obverse Style of 1856, is designated as a type in *The Flying Eagle and Indian Cent Attribution Guide*, 2014 by myself. Varieties within that type are listed with their own variety numbers. 1857 Snow-1, with a repunched date and 1857 Snow-2, without the repunched date. The Type of 1857 has an oval-shaped O in OF, among other subtle differences. All Proofs are the Type of 1857. *The Cherrypickers' Guide* lists these as FS-01-1857-401a for the repunched date and FS-01-1857-401b for those without the repunching. All grading services list the Style of 1857 as a variety and will attribute it if asked to do so.

1858, Large Letters, High Leaves & 1858, Large Letters and 1858, Large Letters, Low Leaves

The Large Letters design is the design in 1857 and the early half of 1858. You could say it is the Type of 1857, but that notation is never used. The eagle is quite bold and the letters are connected in places, notably the AM in AMERICA. Most collectors are used to collecting the obverse design differences. The popular albums have included spaces for them for years. Much more new is the inclusion of the reverse design changes. In *The Flying Eagle and Indian Cent Attribution Guide*, 2014 by myself, the obverse designs are grouped as their own type, with the reverse types attributed to the individual die varieties.

The High Leaves design is the same design used in 1857. The Low Leaves design was made in 1858 to try and make a lower-relief design so the striking pressure could be lessened and, as a result, the die life increased. The Large Letters dies are usually paired with the High Leaves reverse design, but a minority are also found paired with the Low Leaves reverse design. 1858, Large Letters, Proofs have the High Leaves reverse. The scarcer 1858, Large Letters, Low Leaves, combination is listed in *The Cherrypickers' Guide* (FS-01-1858-901). PCGS also labels these coins in Mint State when asked for the attribution (PCGS: 569232). All grading services list the obverse type.

1858, Small Letters, High Leaves and 1858 Small Letters and 1858, Small Letters, Low Leaves

The Small Letters obverse design was begun mid year. It is not just smaller letters, but a lower-relief eagle. This new low-relief design was intended to increase die life. It was designed along with the Low Leaves reverse. A few leftover High Leaves dies were also struck paired with this obverse. The majority of 1858, Small Letters, obverses are paired with the Low Leaves design. In *The Flying Eagle and Indian Cent Attribution Guide*, 2014 by myself, the obverse designs are grouped as their own type, following the convention used for the Large Letter examples. 1858, Small Letters, Proofs are mostly paired with the Low Leaves reverse and are very rare with the High Leaves reverse. The scarcer 1858, Small Letters, High Leaves, combinations is listed in *The Cherrypickers' Guide* (FS-01-1858-1901). PCGS also labels these coins in Mint State format only when asked for the attribution (PCGS: 569235). All grading services list the obverse type.

The dies used in 1859 had the pointed bust truncation (it points toward the U in UNITED). At least six of these dies were left undated at the end of 1859 and were later punched with the 1860 date and put into production. These are listed as a type in *The Flying Eagle and Indian Cent Attribution Guide*, 2014 by myself. Proofs are all the Rounded Bust type. Very few albums are updated to include this type. The scarcer Pointed Bust is listed in *The Cherrypickers' Guide* (FS-01-1860-401). It is listed as a type by all grading services.

1860, Pointed Bust and 1860, Rounded Bust

During the changeover to the bronze cent, Longacre redesigned the obverse, making it sharper. He also added his initial, "L", to the lower ribbon (below the last feather). At least 25 dies were made with the new design for regular production. Proofs exist for both types. The 1864, With L, Proof is very rare, with only 20 minted. The 1864, Bronze, No L, Proof is scarce, with an estimated 300 minted. These are both listed as separate types in *The Flying Eagle and Indian Cent Attribution Guide*, 2014 by myself. *The Cherrypickers' Guide* lists individual varieties in this type (see 1864, With L). The two types are popularly collected by most collectors. All popular albums include a space for both issues. They are listed as separate date entries by all grading services. (*PCGS:* Bronze BN: 2076, Bronze RB: 2077, Bronze RD: 2078; L on Ribbon BN: 2079, L on Ribbon RB: 2080, L on Ribbon RD: 2081).

1864, Bronze, No L and 1864, Bronze, With L

The Plain 5 has a banana-shaped top to the 5 while the Fancy 5 has a distinctively curved top. It is unknown why the change was made, but perhaps there were two engravers making digit punches. The same digit punches used for cents were used for the two-cent dies. All Proofs are Plain 5. Very few albums include both digit punch styles. In *The Flying Eagle and Indian Cent Attribution Guide*, 3rd edition, it is listed as a separate type. Grading services include these varieties in their regular date list. (*PCGS:* Plain 5 BN: 92082, Plain 5 RB: 92083, Plain 5 RD: 92084; Fancy 5 BN: 2082, Fancy 5 RB: 2083, Fancy 5 RD: 2084).

1865, Plain 5 and 1865, Fancy 5

The Shallow N reverse design was in use until 1869. It could be called the Type of 1869, but that designation is not commonly used. The Shallow N design was a modification done in 1861 where the N in ONE was lowered in relief to help strike up the obverse design. It was necessary when the metal alloy was nickel, but after the change to bronze, it was an unneeded feature. The Bold N was designed by William Barber in 1870. Remaining Shallow N dies were available for use in 1870, and they are fairly common for that date. At least 25 Shallow N dies were rehubbed with the Bold N design to create numerous doubled dies. These doubled dies could be considered a special case, and added to the date set, a situation similar to the 1878, 7 Over 8, Tail Feathers, Morgan Dollars. Proofs are of the Shallow N type. In *The Flying Eagle and Indian Cent Attribution Guide*, 3rd edition, it is listed as a separate type. Presently, no albums include a space for this reverse type. It is listed in *The Cherrypickers' Guide* (FS-01-1870-901). Grading services will attribute it as a variety. (*PCGS:* BN: 408017, RB: 408018, RD: 408019).

1870, Shallow N and 1870, Bold N

Most coins from 1871 are Bold N. Only two dies with the Shallow N were used this year for regular production and are found on Snow-4 and Snow-5. These are either dies left over from 1869 or new dies made erroneously with a Shallow N hub. Most proofs are Shallow N type. In *The Flying Eagle and Indian Cent Attribution Guide*, 3rd edition, it is listed as a separate type. Presently, no albums include a space for this reverse type. It is listed in *The Cherrypickers' Guide* (FS-01-1871-901). Grading services will attribute it as a variety. (*PCGS:* BN: 404549, RB: 404550, RD: 404551).

1871, Shallow N and 1871, Bold N

Most coins from 1872 are Bold N reverse. Only four Shallow N dies were used this year. As in 1871, these are either dies left over from 1869 or new dies made erroneously with a Shallow N hub. All Proofs are the Bold N type. In *The Flying Eagle and Indian Cent Attribution Guide*, 3rd edition, the Shallow N is listed as a separate type. Presently, no albums include a space for this reverse type. It is listed in *The Cherrypickers' Guide* (FS-01-1872-901). Grading services will attribute it as a variety. (*PCGS:* BN: 404546, RB: 404547, RD: 404548).

1872, Shallow N and 1872, Bold N

The Closed 3 digit punch looked too much like 1878, so it was opened up a bit. The 3 is still slightly open on the Closed 3, so recently it has been called the Close 3 instead of Closed 3. The Closed 3 is scarcer than the Open 3. All Proofs are Closed 3. In *The Flying Eagle and Indian Cent Attribution Guide*, 3rd edition, it is listed as a separate type. Many newer albums include a space for both digit styles. It is not listed in *The Cherrypickers' Guide*. Grading services will list it in their date listing. Grading services and all albums label the coin as "Closed 3". (*PCGS:* Open 3 BN: 2106, Open 3 RB: 2107, Open 3 RD: 2108; Closed 3 BN: 2109, Closed 3 RB: 2110, Closed 3 RD: 2111).

1873, Open 3 and 1873, Closed 3

The 1886, Variety 2, was Charles Barber's redesign of the Indian Head cent. The Indian Head was made slightly narrower on the Variety 2. To tell them apart, the last feather points to the IC of AMERICA on the Variety 1 and the CA of AMERICA on the Variety 2. Variety 2 examples are scarcer than Variety 1. Proofs exist for both types, with the Variety 2 being scarcer. PCGS calls these Variety I and Variety II. Grading services include in their regular date list. In *The Flying Eagle and Indian Cent Attribution Guide*, 3rd edition, Variety II is listed as a separate type. (*PCGS:* Variety I BN: 2154, Variety I RB: 2155, Variety I RD: 2156; Variety II BN: 92154, Variety II RB: 92155, Variety II RD: 92156).

1886, Variety 1 and 1886, Variety 2

Level IV: Major Die Variety Set—The Top 10 Varieties

The inclusion of die varieties in a regular set open up a whole other level to this fascinating series. Some die varieties have been long known and have been included in the regular date set—The 1858, 8 Over 7, Snow-1, and 1869, 69 Over 69, Snow-3, being the most often included varieties. These are special cases. In the 1960's the 1869, 69 Over 69 was touted as an overdate—1869, 9 Over 8—and many older albums included it under that designation. Overdates carry a special distinction and are widely collected as part of the date set. After the 1869, 9 Over 8, was changed to 1869, 69 Over 69, it still remained in albums, creating higher demand. Another overdate—the 1888, 8 Over 7, Snow-1—was long considered too rare to include in albums. There is, however, more to variety collecting than just overdates. This list includes the top die varieties for all Flying Eagle and Indian Head types. I will list them in a ranked order as compiled by the Fly-In Club in the April, 2014, issue of its journal, *Longacre's Ledger*. Almost all of these varieties are listed in *The Cherrypickers' Guide* (given a Fivaz-Stanton number). The CONECA number is the base numbering system used by all references.

1873, Closed 3, Doubled LIBERTY. Snow-1. This is the top variety in the series. There is bold doubling on the LIBERTY as well as the headband. A few albums will have a space for it. Most collectors desire to add it to a regular date set. Grading services have it listed in their date list. *CONECA:* DDO-001 (DDO = Doubled Die Obverse). Fivaz-Stanton– 01-1873-101. *PCGS:* BN: 2116; RB: 2117; RD: 2118.

1888, 8 Over 7. Snow-1. Although the overdate is only a small protrusion at the base of the last 8, this rare variety is one most collectors list. Grading services list it in their date list. Albums usually do not include it due to its rarity. *CONECA:* RPD-001 (RPD = Repunched Date). FS-01-1888-301. *PCGS:* BN: 2170; RB: 2171; RD: 2172.

1858, Large Letters, 8 Over 7. Snow-1. This overdate shows a bold 7 above and to the right of the last 8. Only early die states qualify for the variety designation. It is found in a few albums. Grading services list it in their date series. PCGS lists early die states as "Strong" and late die states as "Weak". *CONECA:* RPD-001. FS-01-1858-301. *PCGS:* Strong: 2022; Weak: 532214.

1894, Repunched Date. Snow-1. The boldest repunched date of the series. Many collectors add this to their regular-date set. It is not found in albums. Grading services list this variety and all that follow as varieties. *CONECA:* RPD-001. FS-01-1894-301. *PCGS:* BN: 92118; RB: 92119; RD: 92120.

1857, Obverse $20 Clash. Snow-7. A very highly prized and rare variety. The obverse shows clash marks from the obverse of a $20 Liberty Head double eagle. Only recently discovered, this variety grows more desirable as more collectors discover how rare it is. *CONECA:* WDC-001 (WDC = Wrong Die Clash). FS-01-1857-301. *PCGS:* 37376.

1880, Misaligned Die Clash. Snow-1. One of the most dramatic off-center die clashed dies known. Collectors pursue off-center clashed dies as their own collecting sub-category. *CONECA:* MAD-001 (MAD = Misaligned Die Clash), DDO-001. FS-01-1880-101. *PCGS:* BN: 37514; RB: 37515; RD: 37516.

1859, Repunched Date. Snow-1. Very dramatic repunching. A very popular variety. *CONECA:* RPD-001. FS-01-1859-301. *PCGS:* 37391.

1869, 69 Over 69. Snow-3. Initially attributed as an overdate: 1869, 9 Over 8. It is still included in most albums. Newer albums give the proper designation. It is widely collected for inclusion in albums. It is less-frequently collected as higher-grade examples that don't get put into an album. *CONECA:* RPD-004. FS-01-1869-301. *PCGS:* BN: 37475; RB: 37476; RD: 37477.

1873, Closed 3, Doubled IBERTY. Snow-2. Doubling is only on IBERTY. This variety is popular but overshadowed by the 1873, Closed 3, Doubled LIBERTY, Snow-1. *CONECA:* DDO-001. FS-01-1873-102. *PCGS:* BN: 37502; RB: 37503; RD: 37504.

1870, 0 in Denticles. Snow-5. Very scarce variety, considered a dramatic misplaced digit. The top misplaced digit variety in the series. *CONECA:* MPD-001 (Misplaced Digit), DDO-003. FS-01-1870-105. *PCGS:* BN: 73493; RB: 37493; RD: 37493.

APPENDIX B

The PDS Grading System: A New Path

By Rick Snow

Why The PDS Grading System?

The value of a coin is primarily determined based on its grade. This grade comes from applying the *Official ANA Grading Standards for United States Coins*, which were developed and first published in 1977. The adjectival grade (such as *Fine* or *About Uncirculated*) was combined with a 70-point scale developed in the 1950's by William Sheldon as a premium factor for 1794 large cents. The grading standards for this scale are fixed and authoritative, and the way they're interpreted should not change over time. If a dealer or collector grades a coin higher than the ANA Grading Standards would indicate, it is called an "overgraded" coin.

Before the mid-1980's, when professional third-party grading services began encapsulating coins in sealed holders indicating their assigned grades, a coin's grade would be reevaluated by each seller every time it was offered for sale. One mistake could be fixed by the next seller. Overgraded coins would not accumulate in the marketplace. Now coins are encapsulated, and the grade stays with the coin each time it sells. This would be great if every coin were accurately graded. But a coin owner who is dissatisfied with the grade assigned by a professional grading firm can always "crack" the coin out of its slab and resubmit it, hoping for a higher grade next time. As coins get regraded and upgraded over and over again, or as grading services relax their strict interpretation of grading standards, the certified coins seen in the marketplace will increasingly be overgraded. An overgraded coin might be, for example, a VF coin (by traditional ANA grading standards) in an EF holder or an AU coin in an MS holder. One could also be an MS-63 coin that has been overgraded to MS-65.

When a coin sells at auction, it leaves a *price realized* that will be studied by other buyers and sellers to determine the market value of comparable pieces. An undergraded coin might sell for more than the going market value for its assigned grade. If it is correctly graded, it should sell for the current market value. If it is overgraded, it will likely sell for less than the market value. Undergraded coins are very rare, and they do not affect market values very much. In my experience, accurately graded coins account for less than 50% of the certified coins in the market at any time, and overgraded coins may number more than 50%. Judging by recent trends, the percentage of overgraded coins can only increase in the future.

Sticker services, such as Certified Acceptance Corporation and Eagle Eye Photo Seal, were born out of the desire to identify coins that are accurately graded, and label them as such. A special sticker placed on a slab indicates this acceptance. QA, WINGS, and Modern Approved Coin (MAC) have followed this idea and label certified coins that meet their grading expectations.

However, coins that are overgraded remain out in the market. When these overgraded coins sell at auction, their prices realized typically are lower than those of stickered coins whose certified grades have been independently confirmed. These lower prices get reported as a reflection of the actual market, affecting the value of accurately graded coins. Each time an overgraded coin sells below what would otherwise be its market value, it adds to the whole market declining to that new lower level.

There are possible solutions to this problem. One would require selective reporting of auction prices realized. If only the coins that met the ANA Grading Standards were reported, then the prices garnered from these data points would accurately reflect the market. This kind of reporting would be very difficult to achieve in practice, because it would require market analysts to review every coin auctioned and apply their own judgment as to their grades.

I believe what we need is an alternative grading system that can work alongside the 70-point scale. This should be a system based on the ANA Grading Standards that can operate independently from the influence of changing interpretations and relaxed certified grading standards. This is where the PDS grading system comes in.

What is PDS grading? Instead of using the Sheldon 70-point scale to assign a number grade, we take the ANA Grading Standard and assign a quality qualifier.

The basic ANA Grading Standard grades are:

Poor
Fair
About Good
Good
Very Good
Fine
Very Fine
Choice Very Fine
Extremely Fine
Choice Extremely Fine
About Uncirculated
Choice About Uncirculated
Gem About Uncirculated
Uncirculated/Proof
Typical Uncirculated / Proof
Average Uncirculated / Proof
Choice Uncirculated / Proof
Gem Uncirculated / Proof
Superb Gem Uncirculated / Proof
Perfect Uncirculated / Proof

The definitions of these grade levels are found in the Official ANA Grading Standards. The latest version is the 7th edition published in 2013 by Whitman Publishing.

The PDS system uses these grades and qualifies them on a scale for each grade. The scale is a 0–15 number derived from three different graded factors: *Planchet*, *Die*, and *Strike*. Each of these factors is given a 0–5 ranking and then the qualifier is a sum of those numbers.

Parts of a PDS Grade

The factors considered in a PDS grade are given values, as assigned below.

Planchet

5 = Close to perfect. Very few marks—close to none.
4 = Fewer marks than average, with an original surface.
3 = Average number of marks; silver and gold might be dipped.
2 = More marks than average, and/or light hairlines from a past cleaning.
1 = Evidence of past cleaning.
0 = Cleaned, but not tooled or whizzed. (Tooling or whizzing disqualifies the coin.)

Die

5 = Very early die state—deep mirror or matte surfaces for Proofs.
4 = Early die state. Details are sharp. Some cartwheel effect. Mirrored fields or matte surfaces for Proofs.

3 = Average die state. Very little distortion of letters and devices. Moderate cartwheel effect. Dull mirrors for Proofs.
2 = Slightly late die state. Some distortion of the devices and/or letters.
1 = Late die state. Significant die wear. Heavy distortion on letters and/or design.
0 = Very late die state. Loss of major detail due to die wear.

Strike

5 = Full strike. Full details on letters and all devices.
4 = Good strike. Most of the design and letters fully stuck.
3 = Average strike. Some parts of the design lack definition due to strike.
2 = Below-average strike. Some detail is close to missing.
1 = Weak strike. Some details are missing due to strike.
0 = Very weak strike. Major design loss due to strike.

Color (copper or bronze coins only)

RD = Full red color.
RB (given as a percentage) = Red-brown, with a number indicating the percentage of red.
BN = Brown (this designation is optional, as coins of these metals are assumed to be brown unless otherwise stated).

Applying the PDS Grading System

The PDS grade is displayed in parentheses following the coin's adjectival grade. Inside the parentheses, first comes the composite PDS grade—or the *qualifier*, which tells you the coin's overall quality—then the individual grades broken down, as earlier, into the *factor for Planchet*, *factor for Die*, *factor for Strike*, and if the coin is copper or bronze the *color designation*.

As an example:

Gem AU (13: 4, 4, 5, RB 10%)

The adjectival grade is taken from the standards known to all and published in the ANA Grading Standards. The qualifier in the example above (13) is taken from a ranking of 4 for Planchet, 4 for Die, and 5 for Strike, and RB 10% for the color designation. The coin described is a very nice coin. It has just the slightest of wear. The planchet has fewer and less distracting marks than the average planchet and retains its original surface. The die was in an early die state, showing sharp detail. Almost all of the details are fully struck. It has a trace of original red color.

You can tell much more from this system than if I called the same coin an AU-58RB.

Suppose its owner resubmits this coin for third-party grading and it receives a grade of MS-62RB. Under strictly interpreted ANA Grading Standards a coin with slight wear would not be eligible for a Mint State grade, but "market grading" often is more relaxed, as discussed above. Now you can describe it as follows:

Typical Unc (9: 2, 4, 3, 10%)

This is the same coin, but now that we are assigning a different adjectival grade to it, some of the factors will change. The Planchet factor is lowered to a 2 to account for the light wear visible. The Die factor stays the same, and the Strike factor is lowered since some might argue that the wear is actually a strike deficiency. Thus the above-average Gem AU (13) is now just an average Typical Unc (9). If the same coin somehow received an MS-65RB grade, then maybe the factor would drop to Gem Unc (6).

Planchet grade 5 (Unc).

Planchet grade 4 (Unc).

Planchet grade 3 (Unc).

Planchet grade 2 (Unc).

Planchet grade 1 (Unc).

Die grade 5 (Unc).

Die grade 5 (Proof).

Die grade 3 (Proof).

Die grade 1 (Unc).

Die grade 1 (Proof).

Die grade 0 (Proof).

Strike grade 5 (Unc).

Strike grade 4 (Unc).

Strike grade 3 (Unc).

Strike grade 2 (Unc).

The same coin can have different qualifiers as its adjectival grade changes. The above example of a grade and qualifier changing might be an example of an undergraded coin reaching its proper level—despite the fact that it is not particularly well-struck, from excellent dies, or on a pristine planchet—or of a properly graded coin getting a grade it really doesn't deserve.

The key to preserving a market in properly graded coins is to identify above-average qualifiers for the grade against average or below-average qualifiers for the grade.

You can call a coin a 10 or a 13 PDS and we will know that it is an above-average coin for its grade. We can call a coin a 9 PDS and know it is average for the grade. The ones that have a PDS qualifier that falls below 9 are low-end, and likely overgraded or just not worthy of the price expected for the grade. It is these coins that would negatively affect the prices realized at auction and make the market suffer when those prices get reported as the actual market. It is also these coins you should avoid purchasing at retail market levels unless you are willing to pay more than what they are worth.

Coins with a PDS grade of 0 to 8, if eliminated from auction-price reporting, will not negatively affect the market. If an EF coin in an AU holder sells for half the going price, but everyone knows that it has a weak PDS rating, then your properly graded AU coin will maintain its true market value.

Using the PDS grading system, price editors (who study and compile average market prices for publications such as the *Coin Dealer Newsletter*, the *Red Book*, *Coin World*, *Numismatic News*, *Coins Magazine*, and online resources) would recognize the overgraded coins in the data points, eliminate them from their analysis, and be able to present a much more accurate snapshot of the real-world coin market. If everyone, especially auction catalogers used this grading system, perhaps the market will once again reflect the market for properly graded coins.

APPENDIX C
The Life of James B. Longacre

The Longacre family of Delaware County, Pennsylvania, had immigrated to the area from Sweden well before the establishment of the colony. James Barton Longacre was born on August 11, 1794, into a rural agrarian life. His mother died early in his life, and after his father remarried, young Longacre found the situation intolerable. At the age of 12, he ran away from his home for the city life of Philadelphia.

Longacre's Early Life

Longacre's first apprenticeship was in a bookstore owned by John F. Watson. He worked diligently for Watson for many years, learning the skills that he lacked from his early departure from home life. It was apparent to Watson that Longacre's talent was as a portrait artist. Watson gave James his leave in 1813 so that he could learn engraving from George Murray of Philadelphia. Teacher and apprentice remained close friends for many years, and Watson was later helpful in promoting Longacre's private works.

Longacre indentured himself with Murray as an apprentice. The contract held Longacre for a period of no fewer than three years and ten months. At the time, George Murray was a partner in Murray, Draper, Fairman & Co., a banknote-engraving firm acquired in 1810 from the demise of the engraving business started by Mint Engraver Robert Scot in 1795.

At the time, before the age of photography, the only way to mass produce any artistic work on the printed page was to have an engraving made in either wood or, preferably, copper or steel. Longacre proved a very capable artist in this process. Among his published works from this period were the portraits of Washington, Jefferson, and Hancock on a facsimile of the Declaration of Independence, published by John Binns in 1818. This plate was the largest engraving ever made up to that time in the United States. It measured 35" by 25" and cost the publishers $9,000. From this work and subsequent engravings, Longacre gained a very fine reputation for transferring other artist's portraiture to steel engravings. In 1819 he left Murray and set up his own business at 230 Pine Street in Philadelphia.

James B. Longacre at 41

The young engraver's first contract came from brothers John and Joseph Sanderson, who were assembling a collection of biographies entitled *Biography of the Signers to the Declaration of*

Independence. This work was published in nine volumes from 1820 through 1827. Almost immediately problems began with the project, primarily focusing on the writing (by John Sanderson), which suffered from a lack of proper editorial finishing. Also, accusations of plagiarism were thrown at them in the press, and ultimately, the Sanderson brothers quit the venture in 1822, after publishing only two of the nine volumes. The project, being underfinanced from the start, had not been producing satisfactory revenue. However, the first two volumes sold well enough that a continuation of the project was feasible. Also a new writer, Robert Waln Jr., and a new publisher, Ralph Pomeroy, were hired on. The time-consuming task of engraving the portraits continued to be done by Longacre, who produced nearly all of the 30-plus engravings.

It must have been evident to Longacre that the quality of his engravings was the main reason for the continued sales of this work. Unfortunately, he was still under contract, so he reaped no additional reward for the success of the books. During this time he also produced a set of engravings featuring actors in their character roles for *The American Theatre* (1826).

After the Sanderson-Pomeroy series ended, Longacre began the planning stages of his own biographical series of engravings. His idea was to make engravings from life of prominent persons, accompanied by brief biographical sketches. He weighed the good and bad from the *Biography of the Signers to the Declaration of Independence* and decided to place the emphasis on the portrait itself and not the biography. By 1831 publishing contracts were signed, subscriptions were issued, and sales agents were contacted. Longacre invested $1,000 of his own money to procure all the necessary equipment for the project, which was to be called *The American Portrait Gallery.*

Longacre's dream of producing a great portrait series was about to become a reality in 1831 when, to his great surprise, he discovered the existence of a rival project! He learned of it that February from an advertisement in a Washington newspaper, proclaiming the future publication of *An American Portrait Gallery*, which was to be issued by the summer of 1832 by James Herring of New York. Longacre must have been stunned by the appearance of a competing project. He quickly contacted Herring in October to strike a deal to collaborate on these identical projects.

John Herring was, at the time, secretary of the American Academy of Fine Arts. Although an artist, his business acumen was much more developed than Longacre's. One need only look as far as their engravings: Herring's invariably come with a copyright, while Longacre omitted this feature, as he would later regret. Herring's ideas for the series differed from Longacre's in that he was including all great Americans, not just living ones, and was giving each a lengthy biography.

Having learned many of the hardships associated with a project of this nature from his experiences with the Sanderson-Pomeroy series, Longacre showed Herring and the Academy that collaboration was essential to its success. The Academy accepted Longacre's contributions, and since they had already drawn up a plan, Longacre had to modify his own plans to fit theirs. He was really in no position to continue on his own, having sold only 20 or so subscriptions. The collaboration looked as if it would benefit all parties involved.

The project became *The National Portrait Gallery of Distinguished Americans.* This monumental work was published in four volumes between 1834 and 1839. It was in these works that Longacre began to show his own talent as an original portrait artist. The series contained 144 plates by 26 engravers. Longacre traveled extensively to fulfill his desire to make his engravings from life portraits. He would make a watercolor drawing from life, from which he would make his engraving plate. Among his original drawings are fine portraits of President Madison at age 82, and President Jackson, both completed from life in July of 1833.

Longacre made quite a name for himself with the political leaders of the day, many of whom were extremely flattered by his fine portraits. One of these individuals, former vice president John C. Calhoun, would later help Longacre secure the position of engraver at the Mint.

Eliza Stiles Longacre, 1835

James Longacre also built a fine family during these years, marrying Eliza Stiles in 1827. They had five children: Sarah in 1828, Andrew in 1831, James Madison in 1833, Eliza Huldah in 1837, and Orleans in 1840. The memories of his own disadvantaged and fractured childhood motivated James Longacre to create a sound environment for his children.

Lagging sales of *The Gallery* (due in part to the depression of 1837) forced Longacre to declare bankruptcy. To pay back his debts, he traveled to the South and Western Reserve states peddling his works from town to town. His wife, Eliza, and young daughter, Sarah, managed the business of shipping and accounting back in Philadelphia. Later that year, Longacre formed a banknote-engraving company, Toppan, Draper, Longacre & Co., with Charles Toppan and William Draper. Longacre, who by this time had gained a reputation as the best engraver in the country, had known William Draper since his time as an apprentice.

The Mint Hires Longacre

Director of the Mint Robert M. Patterson appointed Longacre to be chief engraver on September 16, 1844, after more than a month-long search following the death of the previous chief engraver, Christian Gobrecht.

The talents associated with engraving steel printing plates are quite different from those needed for the arts of coin design, hub and punch making, and die sinking. Longacre was not entirely trained in any of these talents. He was not under pressure to produce for the first five years of his work at the Mint, as all that was required during this time was die manufacture.

Many die errors occurred during Longacre's early years at the Mint. Examples of these early blunders are evident on the 1844/81 and 1851/81 cents, where the "18" date-punch was inadvertently used upside down. All 1851 half cents show an extra 1 to the right of the date. Some 1846 half dollars show the last 6 punched into the die lying horizontally, and then corrected. Double eagles of 1850 to 1858 indicate that LIBERTY (on the headband) was originally started as LLI, and then corrected.

It is unlikely that many of these errors should be attributed to Longacre himself. Engravers by the very nature of their work tend to develop the traits of a perfectionist. Moreover, the die shop was under the control of the chief coiner—at this time, Franklin Peale.

Franklin Peale (one of 17 children of famed artist/inventor Charles Willson Peale) was a gifted mechanical engineer, and was instrumental in upgrading the Mint's antiquated equipment. He brought the portrait lathe and steam coining press to the Mint from his travels to Europe. Peale had over the years become very comfortable in his position at the Mint, to the point that he considered himself to be irreplaceable. He had built a side business making hubs and dies for medals for special clients. Additionally, Peale and Mint Director Robert M. Patterson had been systematically skimming profits off of bullion deposits.

There were growing internal tensions between Longacre and Mint Director Patterson and his loyal chief coiner. Having an ethical chief engraver threatened their sideline. Peale used every opportunity to meddle in Longacre's work. The ultimate goal was the latter's replacement.

The attacks came to a head when the new denominations of the gold dollar and double eagle were called for in 1849. It began as a clash over the use of the Contamin portrait lathe, the single piece of machinery the two men used for die production. While Peale was dominating the machine, Longacre complained. Peale sabotaged many of Longacre's projects.

The development of the first double eagle was done in the midst of the battle between the two men. Peter F. Cross, a part-time assistant to Longacre from New York, made the first obverse die for the coin between November 6 and December 20,

Longacre Shortly After Joining the Mint

1849. Longacre produced the reverse die at the same time. When the first 1849 double eagle was made on December 22, Longacre noted in his diary, "The work did not come up as well as expected." Longacre reworked the obverse design and finished it on January 11, 1850. The die trial was left undated.

On January 26, 1850, several gold specimens were struck to test the dies. Peale complained about the new dies, declaring that the design was too deep to strike up correctly. Longacre needed one of the gold specimens to correct the problem, but Peale blocked their use, citing accounting problems, and had them melted. Longacre believed that this was an attack on his authority. Peale relented and allowed a piece in silver to be struck.

Longacre at 61

The conspiracy against Longacre also included Mint Director Patterson. Patterson had, on Christmas Day, 1849, gone so far as to secretly give a promise of appointment to Charles Cushing Wright, effective on the day Longacre was ousted. This promise was carried out in early February 1850. Longacre later related the matter in a deposition against Peale:

> [The Director} called on me privately in my room, when he stated that he had the painful intelligence to communicate to me that my removal from office had been determined on by the government, and advised me rather urgently to send in my resignation without delay. I was surprised and troubled at this communication, because it was, under the circumstances, a mortifying termination to a severe and painful effort to sustain, single handed, the arduous requirements of my office. I knew that I had labored faithfully, and I had never known my character as an artist to be seriously assailed. In the absence of positive information, these incidents were of a character to excite the suspicion of secret and unfriendly interference. I resolved not to use haste that was recommended in throwing up my commission, but first to seek an interview with the Secretary of the Treasury, who was Mr. Meridith of this city, and with whom, from my previous acquaintance, I had not the slightest cause to apprehend an unfriendly purpose.

Longacre went to Washington on February 12, 1850, to save his job. While there, he learned that all of the incriminating information that was given to Treasury Secretary Meridith was totally fabricated by Patterson and Peale. Longacre sought little retribution, satisfied only to continue his work at the Mint unimpaired. Patterson was replaced when the administration changed in 1853, and Peale was fired in 1854.

Longacre's wife, Eliza, died during 1850. This event and the problems at the Mint might have given him reason enough to leave Philadelphia and head for new opportunities in San Francisco, but he chose to stay with the Mint. His most productive years were just ahead.

Pioneer Gold and Federal Coins

There is a hypothesis given by some numismatists that Longacre worked on certain private pioneer gold dies. Some interesting entries in his diary during the next few months bring to light new information.

On April 16, 1850, Longacre traveled to New Brunswick, New Jersey, to meet with Peter Y. Cross. On April 17, he wrote: "Gave Mr. Cross the dies (1 pair) with the necessary directions to be made for Dobosq and Co." It is interesting that Longacre was now free to work on a private contract and apparently felt no apprehension to openly do so. Longacre's diary also notes that he used outside sources for various punches. An example of this outside work was detailed as he wrote that William Dougherty made a LIBERTY punch for use on the head of the gold dollar.

Longacre accomplished what his predecessors could not—he was able to add his initials to his new gold dollar and double eagle. His initials, JBL, are located on the truncation of the base of the bust of Liberty on the double eagle. His initial on the gold dollar is a single incuse L. No public objection has ever been noted to the addition of his initials.

During the next 15 years, James Longacre designed more new denominations than at any other time since the early years of the Mint. Among the new coin denominations designed by Longacre are the gold dollar and double eagle (1849), trime or silver three-cent piece (1850), $3 gold piece (1854), small cent (1856), two-cent piece (1864), nickel three-cent piece (1865), and nickel five-cent piece (1866).

Longacre's first designs for the gold dollar and double eagle used features for the head of Liberty that were inspired by a Greco-Roman statue, *Venus Accroupie* or Crouching Venus, which at the time was on display in Philadelphia (and is now located in the Vatican museum).

During the early 1850's, Longacre worked on new ideas for the small cent. Many of the designs for these patterns were utilitarian in their nature, the main emphasis being on the experimental materials used. The first patterns were small coins with center holes to increase the outside diameter. These annular cents contained a small amount of silver to maintain the metal value of the coin. Other small-cent patterns were made using already existing dies. An 1853 cent pattern was made using a current quarter eagle die for the obverse. Another cent pattern die was reduced directly from a silver dollar!

The next new denomination called for was the silver three-cent coin, in 1851. Peale and Longacre again were at odds. Peale created a pattern for the new denomination using a motif originally designed by Christian Gobrecht in 1836. It featured a liberty cap with rays. Longacre used very simple designs of a shield within a star for the obverse and a Roman numeral III encircled by the letter C for the reverse. Longacre's design was accepted. This simple design had to be reformatted more than once because of difficulties in striking it up.

During this time, gold from California was reaching the Mint in record quantities. This oversupply created an imbalance between gold and silver prices. Silver increased in value compared to the weakness in gold. This imbalance drove out of circulation all silver coinage except for the silver three-cent piece, which had less than its face value worth of silver. This problem was temporarily corrected by the Mint Act of February 21, 1853, which slightly reduced the amount of precious metal in the silver coinage from half dollars to half dimes. Longacre was required to show this change by altering the designs. For the quarter and half dollar dies, he made a punch that added rays to the reverse. For the obverse of these and the smaller denominations, he put arrows on either side of the date. The reverse dies with rays tended to crack early in their life, so they were dropped the following year.

The year 1854 brought the introduction of the new $3 coin Long-. acre's Liberty Head was crowned with a headdress of feathers inspired by the Indian tribes of northern Mexico, symbolizing the source of the majority of the gold used in the coins. This Indian Princess is of the same head design used later for the Indian Head cent, but with the headdress redesigned. The new reverse design was an innovative wreath balancing the agricultural products of the North and South. Corn and wheat from the North was combined with cotton and tobacco from the South. This wreath has been referred to as the "Agricultural Wreath." This design was also used later for the Flying Eagle cent, in 1856.

Longacre's Agricultural Wreath Design

The gold dollar was also redesigned to this Indian Princess theme, using the same head but altered by making the headband very wide and shortening the feathers. This design did not strike up well at all, and was redesigned to the same style as the $3 gold piece a few years later. The reverse also carried the new cornucopia wreath.

During 1854 and 1855 the Mint rejected the idea of changing the alloy of the cent and began experiments on a slightly-reduced-size copper large cent. Longacre started using an original design of a Flying Eagle motif on these cent patterns. They proved difficult to strike up fully.

It has long been numismatic lore that the model for the Indian Head cent was Longacre's first daughter, Sarah (born 1828, later Sarah Longacre Keen). The story was that as a young girl of 12, Sarah visited her father at the Mint when he was at work designing the new cent. A group of Indians were also visiting the Mint at the time, and the chief let the little girl try on his headgear. The effect was so striking that her father made a quick sketch and submitted it as the new cent design.

Unfortunately, over the years, the story has gotten so distorted that all credibility has been argued aside. The fact that Sarah was already 30 years old in 1858 is the first obvious error. The Indian headdress, Longacre wrote, was inspired by drawings of Indians of the Chippewa nation in the Lake Superior area, and not from any chance encounter at the Mint.

The cute story aside, the Indian Head cent may well carry the profile of Sarah Longacre. A sepia drawing done by Longacre around 1840 of Sarah shows all too well the similarities between her and the Indian princess. A later sketch, made from this earlier drawing, shows up in Longacre's sketchbook that also contains his other small-cent sketches, including the Indian Head cent prototype sketch. The most noticeable feature is the "Longacre nose," whose profile lines run straight from the tip to the forehead. The eyebrows, lips, and chin shape are very similar on all these sketches.

In late 1856 Mint Director Snowden was interested in getting Congress to pass a new cent coin, in a new metal and a new size. Longacre was instructed to create new working designs. The difficulties in striking coins in a harder nickel alloy would require a different design from his earlier Flying Eagle. Rather than devise a new design, he looked back 20 years to the Flying Eagle dollars of Christian Gobrecht. Gobrecht's design had in turn been based on drawings by the artist Titian Peale, brother of Franklin Peale.

On Longacre's original design the eagle is shown flying upwards holding a shield and arrows. This was probably considered a bit too busy for the small coin, and was dropped. On the finished coin the eagle is flying level.

In 1858, alterations were made to both the obverse and reverse designs of the cent to help the longevity of the dies. On the obverse, the eagle's relief was made shallower and the lettering smaller. It is believed that Assistant Engraver Anthony Paquet is responsible for this Small Letters design revision. The font used is very similar to punches used on medals by Paquet. The relief of the reverse was lowered and the design was also changed slightly. These changes did not, however, correct the problem of short die life. The inherent design flaw (having the head and tail of the eagle directly opposite the wreath) could only be solved with a totally different design.

Paquet tried to correct this problem with a modification of the Flying Eagle design. He proposed a new eagle that was bent in such a way that its head and tail would not oppose the wreath on the reverse. Unfortunately, this Small Eagle design looks more like a quail that has just been shot than a symbol of our national spirit.

Longacre's new Indian Head design was also created in 1858. A more accurate name for this design would be "Liberty With Indian Headdress," as the profile used on the Indian Head cent is obviously not a Native American. The source of the profile was borrowed from Longacre's earlier gold coinage designs.

Three new reverse designs were tested also at this time. The choices included a Plain Oak Wreath, an Oak Wreath with an ornamented shield, and a Laurel Wreath. Pattern coinage dated 1858 of all the design combinations were sold to collectors of the day. The Laurel Wreath and the Indian Head were adopted for use the next year with minor modifications.

Longacre's Laurel Wreath Design

The Laurel Wreath design is actually an olive wreath, but was dubbed *Laurel* by Mint Director Snowden, and has been know as such ever since. It survived only one year in production. A design with a more national character was desired starting in 1859 with patterns, and in 1860 for general circulation; an Oak Wreath and Shield design was used for the reverse. This design was used on the cent reverse until the change to the Lincoln design in 1909.

Longacre's longest-lasting design, however, was not the Indian Head cent, but his new Cereals Wreath design for the reverse of the dime, which was used from 1860 until 1916. The design was also used on the half dime until its demise in 1873.

Longacre's Cereal Wreath Design

Work had begun in the last part of 1863 for Longacre's next new project, the two-cent piece. Two original designs were made. The first was a revolutionary design of George Washington, facing right, with a motto GOD AND OUR COUNTRY above. Adoption of this design would have set a precedent of featuring famous Americans on the coinage of the United States.

The other design Longacre put forward was a shield with arrows and a laurel wreath, echoing the wartime posture of the country. Another motto, GOD OUR TRUST, was added to a ribbon above. This was later changed to IN GOD WE TRUST and eventually became a standard motto on all American coinage.

Minor modifications were made in the spring of 1864 to both the two-cent and one-cent pieces. The two-cent coin's motto lettering was made slightly larger and the cent design was changed by sharpening the details. Apparently, Longacre was satisfied with this latest change, vvvas he added his initial L to the ribbon below the headdress. This would be his last revision on the cent.

In March 1865, the issuance of a nickel three-cent coin was passed through Congress to help redeem the much derided paper Fractional Currency that had clogged up the commerce of the Civil War era. Longacre had not forgotten the difficulty of designing coins for this hard metal. His design incorporated the same head used on all his Liberty and Indian portraits, with the modification of a small coronet in the hair. The reverse was his laurel wreath from the 1859 cent design, with the addition of the Roman numeral III. Nowhere on the coin was the word "Cents."

Longacre's nightmare of preparing dies for striking coins in nickel alloy was only beginning. The next coin to fall to non-precious-metal "token" status was the five-cent piece. Longacre again tried his hand at portraying a famous American for the new nickel coin. This time he featured the recently assassinated and martyred President Lincoln. This was rejected as possibly being destructive to the Reconstruction process. He also resurrected the Washington design from the two-cent pattern of 1864. Various reverses using different wreath styles and lettering were tried. The design eventually settled on used the shield from the two-cent coin, minus the wartime arrows. The reverse was a simple "5" surrounded by 13 "stars and bars."

Longacre's other project for 1866 was the revision of the gold and silver coinage. The Act of March 3, 1865, called for the motto IN GOD WE TRUST to appear on all coinage large enough to permit the addition. Longacre added a scroll above the reverses of all silver coins larger than a dime and all gold coins larger than the $3 piece.

In 1867, with the silver and gold design revisions complete, Longacre began to correct the design of the five-cent coin. His Coronet-style head from the three-cent piece was tested with various wreath styles from the previous year. Another, more intricate, design was made featuring the typical Longacre Liberty Head. The design showed Liberty wearing a headdress of three large feathers and a four-star headband, with a ribbon featuring a new motto, UNION AND LIBERTY. No doubt very proud of this design, he added LONGACRE F. below the truncation of the bust. Although a beautiful design, the only change that was made to the five-cent coin was the removal of the rays.

1867 Five-Cent Pattern (Judd-561)

This same year Longacre redesigned the coinage of the Republic of Chile. His "Fine Style" designs were a great improvement over the crude coinage that preceded them. Longacre made these dies apparently on his own account, receiving $2,000 for this service.

Early in 1868, a bill was written that would· make the cent, three-cent, five-cent, and ten-cent coinage all from nickel alloy. The inclusion of the dime to this group seemed to doom yet another denomination to mere token status. Longacre made stereotypical designs, again using the Coronet style and various reverses from earlier designs. A large trial in nickel alloy for the ten-cent size was made using the old large-cent, Coronet-style Liberty. The idea was abandoned when it was decided that the ten-cent coin would be too large for the hard nickel alloy.

Longacre had begun work later in the year on other denominations utilizing the same Coronet design. The $10 piece was one that he had finished by year's end.

The End of "A Long and Useful Life"

James B. Longacre died very suddenly on January 1, 1869, at the age of 75. A memorial meeting was held at the Mint on January 5. Eulogies were given by Dr. H.R. Linderman, Charles Barber, and William DuBois. Also in attendance were James Booth, and A. Loudon Snowden, as well as the rest of the Mint staff.

Linderman said of Longacre:

> Mr. Longacre, my friends, was no ordinary man. His talents were of high order, and would, with his industrious and frugal habits, have enabled him to achieve success and distinction in any professional or business career. His refined nature, however, appeared to avoid the sharp conflicts of life, and he sought, in quiet devotion to art, a congenial field exercise of his powers, and in it he achieved a success sufficient to satisfy a reasonable ambition. He reached by merit the honorable position of engraver of the National Mint, and so discharged its duties for a period of a quarter of a century as to command the continued confidence of the government and the public.
>
> Mr. Longacre was a man of strong religious faith, and adorned that faith by his daily walk and conversation. Like all truly great and good men, he was modest in deportment. His official duties were performed with a faithfulness worthy of all commendation; whilst his intercourse with his brother officers and subordinates was characterized by dignity, frankness, and urbanity, and the utmost kindness. After a long and useful life, and with faculties unimpaired, our friend passed peacefully and contented to his rest. Let us ever cherish his memory, and strive to emulate his virtues.

APPENDIX D

Counterfeit and Altered Coins

Counterfeits were once a great detriment to the enjoyable pursuit of coin collecting. Throughout the 1950's until the mid-1970's, collectors had a good chance of buying a counterfeit if they strayed from traditional sources for their coins. The average collector was mostly ignorant about counterfeit detection, and there was nowhere to turn for protection. Venues not typically known for numismatic expertise (such as flea markets, estate auctions, and garage sales) were places where counterfeits could easily be found. At the typical coin show, counterfeits were offered knowingly by what one might call "fly-by-night" dealers, who gave no invoice and had no permanent place of business. Other established coin dealers may have unknowingly offered counterfeits as well. While the established dealers may have had more regard for their reputation and would probably refund the cost of a counterfeit if asked, it was still up to the collector to discover the counterfeit. It was buyer beware!

In the early 1970's Vigil Hancock, president of the American Numismatic Association from 1975 to 1977, along with noted collector John Jay Pittman and dealer Abe Kosoff, took on the problem of counterfeits in the marketplace. Together they created the ANA Certification Service, with Charles R. Hoskins as director. The sharing of knowledge of counterfeits made collectors aware of the extent of the problems. Coins that were commonly counterfeited were now issued authentication papers from ANACS. This slowed the traffic of counterfeits within the hobby, but they still were easily sold to inexperienced collectors looking for bargains.

The authentication of coins evolved into the certification of grades as well. This change to certified grading, with its automatic guarantee of authenticity, has been the main reason that the coin collecting hobby has grown dramatically over the last decade. Encapsulated grading (commonly called "slabbing" today) in 1986 was the idea that changed the coin hobby forever. Now, in addition to a guarantee of authenticity, there was a tamper-proof holder to ensure the coin's legitimacy. Today's collector who buys certified coins from established dealers or auction companies is assured of protection from buying counterfeits.

However, with the advent of Internet auctions, counterfeits are again being sold to the unwary. It is wise to be very cautious when buying uncertified coins from people you may not be able to locate later. If the bargain coin you bought turns out to be fake, there may be little recourse if the seller is in, for example, China.

The following examples are just a sampling of the pieces that have fooled collectors over the years. The Flying Eagle and Indian Cent Collectors Society (the Fly-In Club) maintains a "Counterfeit Library" of many of these coins, available for members to borrow as they would a book from a library.

Altered Dates (Typically 1856, 1877)

Most counterfeits were made to deceive collectors, so the scarcer dates are usually the target of counterfeiters. Many real coins are altered to look like a more valuable date. A common alteration is made by taking an 1858 Flying Eagle cent and changing the date to look like 1856. This is usually easily detected if you know the diagnostics and features of a real 1856 cent. Most alterations are made from lower-grade 1858 cents and may be artificially worn or corroded to hide the alteration work. The majority of 1856 cents grade VF or better, so the offering of a low-grade example is reason enough to be suspicious. Additionally, a quick check to see if the letters in the legend are not of the Small Letters style (used only in 1858) may eliminate an alteration. The digits of the genuine 1856 are much different from the digits on the 1858, especially in the shape of the 5. Genuine 1856 cents show the upright of the 5 pointing directly at the center of the ball at the end of the bottom loop. 1858 cents all have it pointing to the left of the ball.

The 1877 cent is also a target for an alteration from a more common coin, such as an 1879. On the example above, a few things should alert a collector right away. First, the reverse is from the wrong die used for 1877. All Mint State 1877 cents had a Shallow N in ONE. An 1879 cent (from which this piece was altered) always has a Bold N in ONE. Also the base of the digit 1 shows a slight bulge. This is found on all genuine 1879 Indian Head cents, and never on an 1877.

Of course a Bold N on an 1877 does not automatically condemn it as a counterfeit. Pictured is a circulated Proof example. All 1877 Proofs have a Bold N. Only a few dies are known for both the Proof and circulation-strike 1877 Indian Head cent, so basic knowledge of the die diagnostics will help authenticate any 1877.

Genuine 1856

Altered 1856

Altered 1856, Detail

Genuine 1877 Circulated Proof

Genuine 1877 Circulated Proof

Altered 1877, Detail

Spark Erosion Counterfeits (Patterns, Any Flying Eagle Cent, Most Better-Date Indian Head Cents)

A spark erosion counterfeit is made by transferring an image of a real coin to a die, by way of an electric current. The die is immersed in an electrolytic bath with the host coin held a slight distance off its face. As a current is passed between the coin and the die, tiny pits are etched into the die. The die is then polished to remove as much of the pitting as possible. By their nature, these coins are not difficult for moderately experienced collectors to spot. They usually have polished fields, and heavy pitting around and on the devices. The edges are normally very sharp, like those of a Proof issue.

The 1873 counterfeit on below is a very crudely made piece. Aside from the numerous raised pimples covering the coin, it may be noticed that it has a Shallow N reverse, a feature not known on genuine coins made this year.

The 1875 likewise has a Shallow N. This design is also not known on this date. There are fewer raised pimples on this one; perhaps the counterfeiter took extra care in preparing the die. However, it still has a very sharp edge and the details are very rough.

The 1878 counterfeit also bears telltale signs of the spark erosion process.

The 1908-S and 1909-S counterfeits shown share the same reverse. The dies are very well made. Maybe they would fool many collectors—and even some dealers—especially if they were included in a collection bought casually. The weakness in the denticles and the raised rim are two unusual aspects of these coins.

Spark Erosion 1873

Spark Erosion 1875

Spark Erosion 1878

Spark Erosion 1908-S

Spark Erosion 1909-S

Spark Erosion S Mintmark

Genuine S Mintmark

Transfer Dies (Any Flying Eagle or Better-Date Indian Head Cent)

The transfer die counterfeit is made by creating dies by directly transferring the design from a host coin. This is done by impacting the coin, and destroying it in the process, with a soft metal die. These counterfeits can be quite deceptive, if care is taken in making the dies. Knowledge of the characteristics of genuine coins will help identify possible counterfeits.

If all the details of the host coin get transferred to the die, so will any defects, such as contact marks. These will show up as depressions on all of the counterfeit coins made from this die. Unlike those on genuine coins, the depressions will have the same surface qualities as the surrounding areas of the coin. By noting the position of the depressions on multiple coins, you can identify counterfeits.

The 1869 cent above is obviously fake because it has a Bold N reverse, which was not used until the next year. If it were not for this oversight, this coin would probably remain undiscovered in many a collection.

Transfer Die 1869

Transfer Die 1873 S-6, Circulated

Transfer Die 1876

Transfer Die 1873 S-6, Uncirculated

Transfer Die 1877

Genuine 1873 S-6

Transfer Die 1909-S

Transfer Die S Mintmark

Genuine S Mintmark

The 1873 counterfeits pictured here are of a known variety: Snow-6, with a numeral 3 punched into the first pearl. Just by chance the counterfeiter used this variety as a host coin. The quality of these counterfeits is so good that they have escaped detection until very recently. Many examples of transfer dies counterfeits are artificially worn, perhaps in a rock tumbler, and recolored to hide much of the counterfeiter's work. The second 1873 cent is an unusual "Mint State" example of the counterfeit. Comparing the images, it may be difficult to say which is the counterfeit. Only careful inspection of the dies reveals the bottom one as the genuine example. Many of the raised pimples do not show up on the genuine example. A large transferred contact mark is visible on the O in ONE on both counterfeits (but not on the genuine).

The 1876 counterfeit pictured is also a very deceptive coin. No genuine 1876 Indian Head cent is known with a Shallow N reverse, so a specialist will immediately recognize it as fake. If this mistake had not been made, the counterfeit probably would have escaped detection for a long time.

The 1877 counterfeit (page 233) is very close to perfection. The obverse carries all the diagnostics of the genuine Mint State 1877 coin. The reverse features the Bold N, which, as mentioned earlier, is found only on the Proof of this year. Additionally, the reverse is rotated in medal alignment, top to top, rather than the usual coin alignment of top to bottom. While unusual alignments are not immediately reason to condemn a coin, on the 1877 cent it definitely cause for concern. Perhaps the counterfeiter lives in Canada, where medal alignment is natural on the coins in circulation.

The 1909-S cent would fool any casual observer. The surfaces look normal and even the mintmark looks right. However, there are numerous spike-like lines around the field just inside the denticles. This is unknown on any genuine 1909-S cent, so it is a dead giveaway that this is a fake.

Added Mintmarks (1908-S/1909-S)

A common counterfeit is made by adding an S mintmark to the more common 1908 and 1909 Philadelphia Mint coins. While both dates are found with added mintmarks, the 1909 is most commonly faked in this way. Again, by knowing the characteristics of the genuine coins, you can more easily detect counterfeits. For example, it is known by reading this book that all genuine 1909-S Indian Head cents have missing details on the left half of the first feather. This is not from a weak strike; it is part of the design. However, the 1909 cents from Philadelphia show full details on the first feather. If you want to buy a 1909-S with full feather details, be prepared to buy a counterfeit!

Added S Mintmark

Added S Mintmark, Detail

Genuine S Mintmark

Plating, Polishing, and Whizzing (Any Coin)

Although not actually counterfeits, coins that were "processed" to simulate a higher grade are as much a problem as the fakes and alterations described. It used to be very common to hear of people engaged in processing coins by the thousands! I hate to imagine how many beautiful VF, EF, and AU Indian Head cents have been ruined for the sake of a quick buck.

The simplest form of coin processing is polishing, illustrated by the 1896 coin below. The luster is gone and what remains is a very smooth surface. Comparison with an original Mint State coin will make a polished coin obvious for what it is. Some polish jobs are more difficult to detect.

The 1868 and 1871 pieces have been electroplated with copper to simulate mint red color. These are usually very bright and unnatural in appearance. If some of the plating wears off, the toned areas will have sharp outlines rather than a normal even shading between red and brown.

Whizzing is a problem that catches collectors all the time. The production and sale of these pieces is, in my opinion, as onerous a practice as selling counterfeits. Whizzed coins have their surfaces wire brushed in such a way as to simulate mint luster. These can be very deceptive, but familiarity with luster patterns of original Mint State coins will help you avoid whizzed pieces. Typically they will show a raised lip on the edge of the letters and devices (caused by the movement of the surface metal).

Polished 1896

Copper-Plated 1868

Copper-Plated 1871

Whizzed 1863

Whizzed 1863, Detail

Contemporary Counterfeits (Any Date)

Very rarely, we can find a fake made to circulate in commerce along with then-current Indian Head cents. These are usually crude pieces artificially worn to increase their acceptability in transactions. The 1891 piece pictured here was made from hand-engraved dies, and is very interesting. Here is one instance where the counterfeit is more interesting than the coin it hopes to mimic.

Contemporary Counterfeit 1891

Some Final Advice

Familiarity with the types of counterfeits will go a long way toward helping you avoid them. Buy from established dealers who will guarantee the authenticity of coins they sell. Learn what an original coin looks like; this will likewise help you avoid being taken by counterfeits and problem coins. If a coin look suspicious in any way, don't buy it. Even if it seems like a bargain and turns out to be genuine, there is no price too cheap for a problem coin!

APPENDIX

Market-Price History

Mint State Coins, By Date

This table shows historical prices for Flying Eagle and Indian Head cents in Mint State. Prices are taken from the *Guide Book of United States Coins* (the *Red Book*), from the *Unc.* listings in the 1947 and 1967 editions, the *MS-60* listings in the 1987 edition, and the *MS-63* listings in the 2007–2025 editions. (Due to "gradeflation," or the relaxation of grading standards over the years, the MS-60 of 1987 is often the MS-63 of today.)

Date	1947 ed.	1967 ed.	1987 ed.	2007 ed.	2017 ed.	2025 ed.	% Increase
1856	$150.00	$2,600.00	$3,500	$18,500	$24,000	$29,000	19,233%
1857	5.00	100.00	300	650	900	1,250	24,900%
1858, Large Letters	8.50	147.50	300	650	950	1,250	14,606%
1858, Small Letters	10.00	147.50	300	650	950	1,400	13,900%
1858, 8 Over 7	n/a	unpriced	1,000	1,000	10,000	8,250	725%
1859	4.50	90.00	300	500	625	875	19,344%
1860, Round Bust **(a)**	4.50	70.00	160	225	250	480	10,567%
1860, Pointed Bust **(a)**	4.50	70.00	160	500	575	725	16,011%
1861	8.00	100.00	235	275	325	480	5,900%
1862	1.10	35.00	130	160	200	415	37,627%
1863	1.00	30.00	130	160	200	415	41,400%
1864, Copper-Nickel	3.00	65.00	175	200	325	470	15,567%
1864, Bronze, No L	4.75	66.00	85	140	150	190	3,900%
1864, Bronze, With L	30.00	300.00	340	650	600	550	1,733%
1865	3.50	45.00	70	135	150	210	5,900%
1866	11.00	150.00	185	330	380	525	4,673%
1867	9.50	145.00	185	350	400	455	4,689%
1868	9.50	160.00	185	300	360	440	4,532%
1869	11.00	370.00	350	600	700	900	8,082%

a. The Pointed Bust and Round Bust varieties of 1860 were differentiated in the *Red Book* in 1994.

Date	1947 ed.	1967 ed.	1987 ed.	2007 ed.	2017 ed.	2025 ed.	% Increase
1870 (b)	$11.00	$175.00	$225	$565	$900	$750	6,718%
1871 (b)	16.00	220.00	275	600	950	850	5,213%
1872 (b)	22.50	300.00	350	925	1,250	1,000	4,344%
1873, Open 3 **(c)**	5.50	92.50	125	325	325	470	8,445%
1873, Closed 3 **(c)**	5.50	92.50	125	550	550	550	9,900%
1873, Doubled LIBERTY	n/a	n/a	1,200	13,000	13,500	7,750	546%
1874	5.50	92.50	115	250	250	275	4,900%
1875	6.50	92.50	100	250	260	305	4,592%
1876	6.50	115.00	135	380	390	365	5,515%
1877	37.50	950.00	1,500	4,000	4,500	6,250	16,567%
1878	6.50	100.00	135	380	380	390	5,900%
1879	2.75	42.50	55	120	140	170	6,082%
1880	2.50	32.50	45	130	130	100	3,900%
1881	2.75	32.50	45	90	90	105	3,718%
1882	2.00	32.50	45	90	90	115	5,650%
1883	2.00	30.00	45	90	90	120	5,900%
1884	2.50	40.00	55	120	120	130	5,100%
1885	6.50	62.50	75	200	200	180	2,669%
1886, Variety 1 **(d)**	2.50	45.00	60	225	250	280	11,100%
1886, Variety 2 **(d)**	2.50	45.00	60	475	500	525	20,900%
1887	1.65	25.00	40	80	80	115	6,870%
1888	1.65	30.00	40	125	130	175	10,506%
1888, 8 Over 7	n/a	n/a	unpriced	27,500	35,000	45,500	65%
1889	1.65	25.00	40	80	80	105	6,264%
1890	1.50	25.00	40	80	80	110	7,233%
1891	1.50	25.00	40	80	80	110	7,233%
1892	2.00	27.50	40	80	80	130	6,400%
1893	1.50	26.00	40	80	80	120	7,900%
1894	3.00	47.50	50	115	115	155	5,067%
1895	1.50	22.50	37	65	65	115	7,567%
1896	3.00	28.50	37	65	65	110	3,567%
1897	3.00	25.00	35	65	65	100	3,233%
1898	2.50	27.50	35	65	65	100	3,900%
1899	3.00	20.00	35	65	65	95	3,067%
1900	1.50	15.00	34	55	60	95	6,233%
1901	1.50	12.50	34	55	60	95	6,233%
1902	0.85	12.50	34	55	60	95	11,076%
1903	1.50	12.50	34	55	60	95	6,233%
1904	1.00	12.50	34	55	60	95	9,400%
1905	1.00	12.50	34	55	60	95	9,400%
1906	1.00	12.50	34	55	60	95	9,400%
1907	2.00	12.50	34	55	60	95	4,650%
1908	1.75	16.00	35	55	60	95	5,329%
1908-S	7.50	140.00	155	375	400	525	6,900%
1909	0.75	17.50	45	60	65	95	12,567%
1909-S	30.00	400.00	400	900	1,200	1,600	5,233%

b. Bold N. **c.** The Closed 3 and Open 3 varieties of 1873 were first differentiated by numismatists in the 1960's. **d.** Varieties 1 and 2 of 1886 were differentiated by numismatists in 1954.

APPENDIX

Flying Eagle and Indian Head Cent Patterns

The Mint has produced pattern coins ever since federal coinage for the United States began in 1792. Many different patterns from that first year leave a tangible trail of the problems the Mint faced early in its existence.

Most of the issues struck from the 1790's until the 1830's were utilitarian in nature. Patterns were made to test new designs, planchet sizes, and alloys. In the 1830's it became popular to strike presentation coins as gifts to dignitaries. The 1834 King of Siam Proof set, which included the previously non-existent 1804 dollar and Plain 4 eagle among the other (1834-dated) coins, is a prime example of a diplomatic gift of coins. (For more information, see *The Fantastic 1804 Dollar*, by Newman and Bressett.) When the Mint signed on the artistic dream team of Thomas Sully and Titian Peale in 1836 to work with Mint engraver Christian Gobrecht, increasingly artistic designs began to flow. Peale produced drawings of a flying eagle, which were brought to coin form by Gobrecht. After this flurry of activity in the development of the coinage redesign between 1836 and 1839, pattern-making largely went into a decade-long hibernation.

Early Small Cent Experiments

In 1850, inflation caused by increased availability of gold from the California gold rush caused the price of copper to rise. The Mint began to look into alternatives to the large 168-grain copper cent. In an era where the value of money was put into the metal content and given by the government stamp, a coin needed to be made with materials nearly equal to the value on its face. But given rising costs, the cent's metal value was rather quickly becoming greater than its face value (this also applied to the copper half cent).

In an attempt to remedy this problem, the Mint began experimenting with other alloys and sizes for the large cumbersome cent. A silver piece of .100 fineness was tried in 1850. This alloy, with its small amount of silver, is known as *billon*. The coins produced would have been quite small, so the Mint enlarged the diameter by adding a hole in the center. This would have also made the coins more easily recognized. It was a novel idea for U.S. coinage. Perhaps these odd coins could have been carried easily on a string, like a necklace, or mounted on a post. Although the coins were attractive and silvery-colored when first struck, they quickly turned a dull gray color. The patterns proved to the Mint that they could have been easily counterfeited with base metals.

In 1853, the melter and refiner of the Mint, Professor James C. Booth, resurrected an alloy that was first presented to the Mint by a Dr. Lewis Feuchtwanger in 1837. The alloy was then called *Feuchtwanger's alloy* or *Feuchtwanger's Composition.* It was a mixture of copper-nickel with the addition of zinc. When the alloy was first proposed, the Mint had requested an outside opinion. The report came back from the metallurgist at the Franklin Institute, condemning it on the grounds that it could not be reproduced reliably. That metallurgist was none other than Professor James C. Booth!

Although patterns are usually ascribed to the engraver (in this case James Longacre), it is clear from correspondence that Booth was the force behind these early experiments in copper-nickel at the Mint. The dies used to test this first copper-nickel alloy coin comprised of an 1853 Liberty Head quarter eagle die and a crudely engraved reverse die. As with the earliest American pattern coins, these were strictly utilitarian. No attempt was made to make them attractive. Tests showed that the silvery color of the alloy might be confused with that of the dime. In 1854 it was suggested that a larger size, between that of a quarter and a dime, would be more acceptable. More patterns were made to test this idea. This time the obverse die was quickly reduced from that of a regular 1854 silver dollar! The result was an extremely crude-looking piece. The date looked more like 1851 due to the lack of transferred detail. In addition to the copper-nickel alloys it was also struck in copper. In an odd move, the Mint even made electrotype copies, possibly to show how counterfeits could be made.

Booth's experiments in copper-nickel seemed to end in 1854 with the idea of a smaller copper cent being tested—about two-thirds the size of the large cent then in use. France had recently begun to issue large quantities of coins in an alloy of copper with a small amount of tin and zinc, called *French bronze.* This alloy was tested in various percentages at the Mint starting in 1854. The weights and alloys of these pieces vary wildly. The weight was to be 100 grains for the copper pieces and 96 grains for the bronze examples, according to official documentation. Later numismatists have given the term *originals* and *restrikes* to these, based on their weight differences. Testing has shown that the metallurgy of these pieces is all over the map and that such naming distinctions are problematic.

The initial design used for the reduced copper-cent patterns was closely related to the Coronet-style Liberty Head design then in circulation. Longacre then produced new dies showing a flying eagle. These were copied from the drawings done 18 years earlier by Titian Peale. The coins were made in slightly larger quantities than previous patterns. Longacre had engraved the eagle with too high a relief and many of the coins had to be struck again to bring up the details. This reflected a flaw in the design, not so much in the alloy.

1854 Small Cent Pattern

The experiments continued into 1855 with a lower-relief eagle. These patterns were also struck in copper, bronze, and various alloys of copper-nickel. Many of the bronze pieces have streaky planchets from improperly mixed alloy. The copper-nickel alloys were all just too hard for the large-diameter dies to strike up fully.

1855 Small Cent Pattern

The time was nearing when a decision on the new cent alloy had to be made. Congress was preparing to act based on these patterns, with legislation that would authorize the Mint to strike the new coins. In doing so it craftily moved the decision-making power over the alloy away from the Mint director and into the hands of Congress. James Ross Snowden, Mint director since early 1853, undoubtedly was not happy with that prospect.

Snowden had Professor Booth prepare more copper-nickel tests using smaller dies. Regular half-cent dies were used to strike examples in 88% copper and 12% nickel. The coins were sent to Treasury Secretary James Guthrie in July of 1856. Although still weakly struck around the edges, they showed that the alloy held promise as a coinage metal. These patterns forestalled action on the copper/bronze cent bill. By the end of the year Longacre had produced even smaller dies, which featured a redesign of the flying eagle from Gobrecht's dollar coinage from the 1830's. The reverse used was taken from the current three-dollar gold piece, also designed by Longacre. This proved to be an adequate size for the alloy. The first 1856 Flying Eagle cents were struck late that year and when Congress resumed the next year they were distributed to every senator and representative.

We know the coins were a hit because more were requested and a new bill authorizing the copper-nickel cent (and giving the Mint director authorization over any changes) was written and passed in February of 1857. This six-year process was now complete, culminating in the biggest change yet to hit United States coinage. The patterns survive as statements on that process. The 1850–1856 patterns were not struck for sale to collectors, and the ones that survived did so because they were held by the persons in the decision-making process. The era of utilitarian patterns ended with the 1856 Flying Eagle cent.

A Coin Collecting Boom

When the new nickel cents dated 1857 entered circulation, there was a general recall of all earlier copper cents and half cents. Legislation also called for the expiration of the legal-tender status of foreign silver coins, and their removal from circulation. This withdrawal spurred many people to begin collecting the old copper coinage. Collector societies were formed and antiquarian dealers began to stock American coins. In these circles, it began to be known that there were "rare" coins of the new design, dated 1856. The premiums on this coin rose so dramatically that demand soon outpaced the supply. It should be remembered that the 1856 Flying Eagle cents were not initially struck for collectors. They were made to encourage passage of the coinage bill in Congress. When these coins trickled out of official hands into dealers' inventories they created a frenzy of activity—in 1858, auction records show a 200% premium for these coins! The birth of coin collecting in America was kicked into high gear due to the 1856 Flying Eagle pattern cent.

The Mint started to get numerous requests from collectors for these and other pattern coins, and was happy to oblige. They began striking additional 1856 Flying Eagle cents for sale to those who applied. Sales of Proof coins began on a routine basis and the Mint's collector sales business began to get very big. There was, it seems, little or no moral obstruction to restriking coins made in earlier years. Silver dollars dated 1836 to 1839, Proof half cents dated 1836 to 1852, and other rarities were restruck and sold or traded to collectors. There were complaints, especially when the 1804 dollars were restruck over foreign silver coins and marketed to Philadelphia dealers at exceedingly high prices. These were seemingly not struck on an official level, but with so much money to be made in the restriking business, everyone who had access to the Mint had an opportunity to make some extra money. Those 1804 dollars (now known as Class II) had to be rounded up by the Mint and destroyed. It was a wild and crazy time for the Mint and the coin-collecting hobby.

New Patterns and Possibilities

Right from the start, the Mint was having trouble with Longacre's Flying Eagle design. The presses had to strike the hard nickel alloy with higher than normal pressure to bring up the design properly. This destroyed the dies quickly and added to the production costs. From a design perspective, the head and tail of the eagle are opposite the wreath on the reverse. During striking, the metal didn't flow easily into these opposing designs. More pattern cent designs had to be made to solve this problem. Longacre and his assistant engraver, Anthony Paquet, worked on various changes to both sides of the coin.

Three basic obverse designs were presented. A design very similar to Longacre's Flying Eagle, but with a lower relief, is attributed to Paquet. It has smaller letters, similar to those on medals he is known to have made. This obverse was deemed to be an acceptable short-term solution and was put into production that same year, 1858. Collectors know it as the 1858 Small Letters type. Another obverse, also ascribed to Paquet, showed a very low-relief small eagle scrunched into a distorted pose. While it did much to eliminate the opposing detail of the dies, the visual effect left much to be desired. A third obverse design was the Indian Head by Longacre, which ultimately answered the problem of the opposing detail when it was paired with a wreath on the reverse.

The reverse designs proposed included the current agricultural wreath but in a lower relief. This design change is known as the *low leaf* due to the shorter length of the inner leaves by the C and T of CENT. This was used right away for production in 1858, so it is considered a regular-issue design. Other reverse dies include a plain oak wreath with a few olive leaves gathered with a ribbon at the base. Another similar wreath adds an ornamental shield to the design at the top. A fourth design featured a wreath of olive, which was called a *wreath of laurel* in official correspondence by Mint Director Snowden. That name has been attached to this wreath ever since.

With these three obverse dies and the four reverse dies, paired in every possible combination, the Mint made 12-piece sets. The 1858 Small Letters obverse paired with the agricultural wreath is considered a regular issue while all the rest are patterns. At least 75 sets were struck with some of certain popular combinations made in larger quantities. The design ultimately adopted, the 1858 Indian Head / laurel wreath, was made in the greatest quantities. With the change to the Indian Head cent, the 1858 12-piece set became another hot item for the Mint. When word got out about the sets, collectors requested more examples. However, things soon got out of hand. On January 22, 1859, a collector wrote to Snowden:

> If you have specimens in copper of the new $20, also model half & quarter dollars & specimen cents struck last year before settling on the new device now used – & can spare them without detriment to the public interest, I would like to have them – My object is to give them to a friend who seems to have a passion for specimens of coins.

Snowden replied on January 24, 1859, in a letter marked "Unofficial":

> I have rec'd your note of the 22nd inst. and learn from it that you are acquiring a personal knowledge of the 'passion for specimen coins' which possesses so many people in our country.
>
> On Saturday I had nine applications of a similar character – today (now 12 o'clock) I have had three. It was in view of this increasing, as well as troublesome, taste that I made the request mentioned in my official letter of last Saturday (22nd inst.) which I hope will deserve the sanction of the department.
>
> In reference to the specimens you ask for I have to state that the trial piece in copper of the double eagle of 1859 which I left at the Department is the only one I had: I have a few of the specimen cents but not all the varieties. I could send you two or three of these, but perhaps it will be best to defer sending them, until the new arrangement is made, when your friend, and all other collectors of Coins, AND THEIR NAME IS LEGION, can be supplied to their heart's content.

Within a few months the Mint's pattern business was causing problems for collectors and dealers. Coin dealer Edward Cogan wrote to Snowden on June 14, 1859:

> I have been applied to by a great many collectors of American coins wishing to be informed whether the report now current—that there are many of the Pattern Cents being restruck at the Mint for the purpose of exchanging them for Washington pieces is true—the only answer I can give is that the many pieces shown to me lately would tend to confirm the report. A rumor of this kind uncontradicted will tend to depreciate the value of every fine piece in whatever collection it may be found and I should be glad if you would give it the most unqualified denial.

Three obverse options of 1858

Four reverse options of 1858

Apparently Snowden's activities in restriking patterns were continuing, to the dismay of many. His reply gave no comfort:

> It is quite true that I have caused a number of pattern or specimen cents to be struck for the purpose of exchanging them for Washington pieces whenever opportunities to do so occur. If you possess any Washington pieces I would be much obliged if you will send me a list of them, and if there are any among them which I desire for the Cabinet I would be pleased to procure them by giving you in exchange other interesting medals and coins.

The adopted design of the Indian Head cent in 1859 was slightly different from the patterns used in 1858. The adopted obverse (actually Lady Liberty wearing an Indian headdress) had sharper details, with a pointed truncation of the bust. The reverse that was adopted had the laurel wreath in bunches of six leaves rather than the wreath with bunches of five leaves used in the initial patterns. Both of these designs do show up on 1858-dated patterns. These were likely struck in 1859 and are very scarce.

The 1859 laurel wreath reverse was given a short lifespan by the Treasury secretary, who wanted a more national character presented on the coin. Along with the remaining oak and ornamental shield reverse dies was introduced an oak wreath with a federal shield above. More patterns were struck, but not in the quantities seen for the previous issues. The adopted type, bearing the new shield, was struck in large quantities in the same format as regular issues—unusual for patterns, which are typically struck in Proof format.

After 1859, the utilitarian nature of patterns returned to the Mint. During the Civil War there was no interest in creating rarities for public sale. In 1863, a request was made to put some reference to God on our coinage. The initial GOD OUR TRUST became IN GOD WE TRUST and first appeared on the first available new design—the two-cent piece. The Indian Head cent and the two-cent piece were born of the same problem that came to a pinnacle in 1863. The government's financing of the war and the bad turns that the conflict was taking for the Union created a situation where all metallic money disappeared from circulation. The nickel cents were replaced by privately produced cheap copper tokens. These circulated in many Northern cities primarily because there was no other hard money available. Mint Director James Pollock saw that a solution might be to imitate these tokens and for the Mint to strike its own cheap copper coins. In 1863 copper cent patterns were struck in sizable quantities. These proved to be acceptable and the next year a law was enacted that made the private tokens illegal and authorized the nation's own official bronze cents and two-cent pieces. That bronze alloy stayed in the cent mostly unchanged until 1982.

A Pattern of Manipulations

Beginning in 1867 and continuing for a few more years, another period of restriking began. Under Mint director Dr. Henry Linderman, strange patterns that did not earlier exist were made for his personal collection and also for surreptitious sale to certain dealer friends. Pieces bearing GOD OUR TRUST, but now on coins dated prior to the initial request for consideration of the motto, came into existence. Coins in aluminum (which was not available unalloyed until 1867) now showed up with dates like 1864 and 1863. Coins like the 1863 Indian Head cent with an L on the headdress ribbon were struck at this time. More 1804 dollars were made (today called Class III). An unusual coin bearing the Coronet Liberty Head from the earlier large cent now returned on a large planchet, dated 1868. The days of the Mint being a source for rare collector coins came back to life under Dr. Linderman.

In the late 1860's the interests of businessman Joseph Wharton, who owned a monopoly on nickel production in the United States, had the Mint experimenting with an all-nickel coinage of the cent, three-cent piece, and five-cent piece. Pattern sets were given as gifts and sold to collectors. Legislation authorizing the coins never materialized, but the idea of a uniform coinage in nickel was proposed in 1868 and 1869. The small nickel cent would have required yet another odd coin in our coinage system, which already had nickel cents, bronze cents, copper two-cent pieces, silver three-cent pieces, nickel three-cent pieces, silver half dimes, and nickel five-cent pieces, as well as paper currency in three- and five-cent denominations.

The cent was left alone for a while and no cent pattern designs were made between 1869 and 1881, with the exception of some aluminum pieces made for sets. In 1881, the Mint resurrected the idea of a uniform nickel cent, three-cent, and five-cent coinage, to be designed by Charles Barber. To show that the size was the only important factor in determining the value, the denomination was left off these patterns. When Barber's five-cent design was officially adopted in 1883, sure enough, the denomination was left off, to the embarrassment of the Mint.

The last cent patterns of the Indian Head cent era are a series of Shield cents struck in 1896. This was an attempt to change the cent to nickel or possibly even change both the cent and five-cent denominations to aluminum.

Collecting Small Cent Patterns Today

Collecting these fascinating pieces of U.S. Mint history is a very challenging endeavor. Collectors should arm themselves with the standard reference, *United States Pattern Coins*, by J. Hewitt Judd, edited in the most recent edition by Q. David Bowers. This book was first published in 1959 and was researched by Abe Kosoff and Walter Breen. It supplanted the 1913 reference by Edgar H. Adams and William H. Woodin, *United States Pattern, Trial and Experimental Pieces.* Andrew Pollock's 1994 *United States Patterns and Related Pieces* expanded the knowledge base of patterns. The Judd numbering system, which uses the J- prefix, is the primary attribution system used today. The Web site maintained by Saul Teichman and Andrew Lustig for the Society of U.S. Pattern Collectors (www.uspatterns.com) is also a very useful reference.

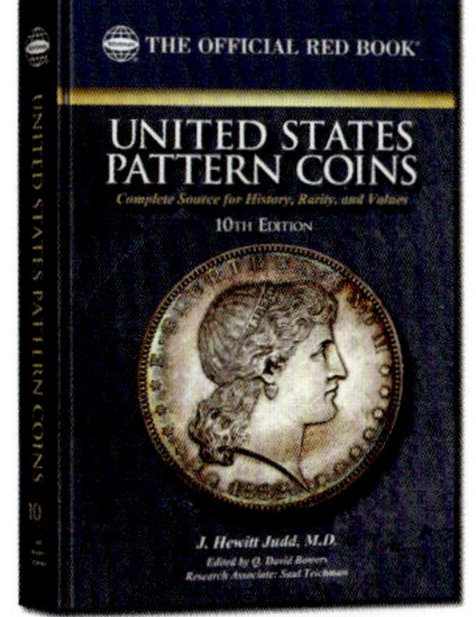

Many of the cent patterns are more readily available than other denominations. Because of this there are more collectors of this denomination than any other. Their prices typically begin at $1,000 and go up to $7,500 for the most common pieces. This makes building a collection a financial challenge as well. An exciting set that many collectors attempt when

Judd-406

first starting out is the *simulated series* set. It encompasses all the issues that were eventually adopted for circulating coinage: the 1856 Flying Eagle cent (J-180), 1858 Indian Head cent (J-208), 1859 type of 1860 (J-228), and 1863 copper cent (J-299). The rare 1863 With L in bronze (J-301) could also be added here, but these are very rare and only a select few could hope to own one. Many collectors expand this set by adding the *transitional* patterns, which are combinations of adopted designs but not issued together. The 1858 Small Letters obverse paired with the laurel wreath (J-191) is one of these. The 1858 Indian Head paired with the regular 1858 reverse (J-213) is another. The rare 1863 With L in copper-nickel (J-302) and 1864 With L in copper-nickel (J-358) also fit into this collection, but are very rare and only a few can hope to own them.

The early pieces from 1850 to 1854 make a haphazard collection of shapes and sizes and are not as given to building a uniform set, but that makes them more enjoyable to those who seek to collect off the beaten path. Many of these will cost in the $1,000 to $5,000 range, although sometimes a bargain gets offered.

The 1854 and 1855 copper cents are a very interesting field of study. A basic set of the 1854 Liberty Head and two Flying Eagle obverse dies is an attainable goal for many collectors. Prices are typically between $1,000 and $2,500 for the Liberty Head and $2,000 and $5,000 for the more popular Flying Eagles, unless they are cleaned or circulated. Many of these coins were abused, as the original owners were not coin collectors. Collecting the various alloys and minor reverse wreath differences can be daunting. Numismatic researcher Rick Kay is doing an exhaustive study of these patterns.

The 1858 12-piece set has long been the main focus for Indian Head cent pattern collectors. Only 75 sets are possible, so demand outstrips supply on these. In the scale usually used to measure pattern rarity, these are considered common. Their availability creates more collector activity and demand. There are also the scarcer die combinations, which include the Pointed Bust Indian Head design and the six-leaf laurel wreath. An extended set including these is very challenging. The main resource for these coins is *The Flying Eagle and Indian Cent Attribution Guide 1856–1858* (Snow).

Also ancillary to the various pattern sets are the off-metal pieces. These include copper examples of the copper-nickel series and nickel or aluminum examples of the bronze series. These are mostly very rare and can be picked up only occasionally. They usually cost more than $5,000, with prices well over $10,000 quite typical. Perhaps the only pieces generally available are the 1865 cents struck in nickel alloy (J-404 and J-406). These are found with a Fancy 5 or a Plain 5 date. They typically can be found for $2,000 to $5,000.

The 1859 set uses some of the reverse dies from the 1858 12-piece set, but is only a 3-piece set. This set is easy to start, as the common 1859 type of 1860 (J-228) is typically available. This should cost $1,000 to $2,500. The two other die pairings—the 1859 Indian Head with the oak wreath reverse (J-226) and the 1859 Indian Head with the ornamental shield reverse (J-227) are both pretty scarce. Expect to pay $3,000 to $6,000 for these.

An interesting set can be built around the three-piece nickel sets of 1868 (two types of

The denominational pattern set from 1881.

reverses), 1869 and 1881. These include the three-cent and five-cent nickel patterns. The diminutive nickel cents of 1868 (J-605 and J-608) and 1869 (J-666) using Longacre's Coronet design from the three-cent nickel of 1865 and the reverse designs from the 1858 and 1859 cents are interesting on their own. Perhaps only when you add the other denominations do the coins show their real purpose. The 1881 cent (J-1665) with Barber's Liberty Head is also better exhibited in a denominational set. The cents will cost between $1,000 and $2,500 and the other denominations slightly more.

Lastly, the 1896 Shield design patterns (J-1767, J-1768, and J-1769) can be collected in the various alloys together with the five-cent denominations (J-1770, J-1771, and J-1772). These exist in copper, nickel, and aluminum. Prices are generally in the $2,000 to $7,500 range.

Any single pattern can excite a collector. They are evocative of the problems and ideas the Mint wrestled with throughout its history. They speak of a time when our coinage system was changing. Collectors appreciate this and the addition of pattern coins to a Flying Eagle and Indian Head cent collection certainly enhances it, giving it that *wow* factor.

APPENDIX G

Toned Indian Head Cent Proofs

Collectors who delve into the Proof Indian Head cent series will at some point run into vividly toned Proofs with iridescent hues of magenta, lavender, emerald, and rose. These coins can be very beautiful and are targeted by some collectors for their beauty. They are also very misunderstood. Questions about their legitimacy have arisen from time to time because it has been shown that coins with little or no natural toning can be artificially made to show various colors. Because the iridescent toned Proofs garner higher premiums than non-toned Proofs, artificially toned pieces will certainly hurt the market.

The iridescent Proofs that we are discussing here are invariably toned a deep chocolate brown with colored highlights. This type of toning has been well documented on Proof Indian Head cents that started showing up in large quantities in the 1930's. Similar toning is also occasionally found on Matte Proof Lincoln cents, Proof large cents, Proof half cents, Proof two-cent pieces, and pattern issues struck in copper. The toning is believed to have formed by more than 50 years of the coins sitting in Mint tissue wrappers or envelopes that contained a toning agent, typically sulphur.

How the Toning Came About

The distribution of Proofs has changed over time. Early pieces, prior to 1858, were made for various reasons, sometimes sold to interested collectors, sometimes included in presentation sets. Beginning in 1858 Proof coins were sold to collectors at standardized prices and were available each year. These coins were struck in small lots and unsold examples were destroyed. Mintage figures were not reported in the Mint director's report and have had to be pieced together through years of research by numismatists such as Robert W. Julian, Walter Breen, Don Taxay, and Eric P. Newman.

Coin collecting subsided during the Civil War, but during the Reconstruction period (from the end of the war through 1877), the hobby steadily grew, as did sales of Proof coins. At this time many newly wealthy industrialists

1875 Toned Indian Head Cent

1880 Toned Indian Head Cent

were becoming interested in coins: T. Harrison Garrett, Virgil Brand, and John Beck, to name a few. The expansion of the market also brought many new coin dealers onto the scene.

In 1878 the Mint began publishing mintage figures for minor coins. Mintages of minor coins began to climb higher than those of silver coins as the option of buying just the cent, three-cent nickel, and five-cent nickel was offered. These minor sets were affordable to all collectors. For some years the demand for one denomination caused others to be overproduced. This happened in 1883, when three types of five-cent nickels were produced and included in the minor set at different times of the year. Collectors wound up with duplicates of the cent and three-cent nickel. Dealers typically bought up this overproduction for little or no premium over the face value.

A.M. Smith, a onetime wine merchant from Salt Lake City, set up shop in Philadelphia in 1879. From that time until 1889 he purchased large quantities of Proof sets from the Mint. While he made a business by selling these coins and others, by the time of his death in 1915 he had accumulated more than 1,500 Proof sets. These were sold through M.H. Bolender, then of Orangeville, Illinois, in 1935.

Another Philadelphia dealer, David U. Proskey, who started business in 1873, is known to have had a relationship at the Mint where in early January he would stop in and buy the unsold minor coins of the previous year for face value. By the time of his death in 1929, his holdings of Proof cents, three-cent pieces, and five-cent pieces were in the hundreds of each date.

As told by Q. David Bowers in *Abe Kosoff: Dean of Numismatics*, many of these coins were flooding the market in the late 1930's.

> One of [Kosoff's] first transactions after making the decision [to set up a coin business] was with I. Silverman, who operated a shop on 1 East 29th St. and who acquired a large quantity of minor United States Proof coins. Such pieces were abundant in New York City in the 1930's and for the most part came from the estate of David U. Proskey. Wayte Raymond had large batches of them, Proskey's son had many in his possession, and other groups existed here and there. It could have been his first day of business, but it was certainly in the first week, when he bought $1,000 worth of Proofs from Silverman, ran an ad in *Numismatic Scrapbook Magazine*, and was overwhelmed with orders.

Many or most of these hoards of Proof minor coins were apparently stored in their original tissues for 30 to 50 years. The nickel coins, being less reactive, stayed mostly bright. The bronze cent toned to a deep chocolate brown with multicolored toning. These were advertised throughout the 1940's and 1950's as iridescent Proofs.

Some comments by Walter Breen throughout his *Encyclopedia of U.S. Proof Coins* are as follows:

> 1882, 1883—Iridescent ones come from Wayte Raymond (1880–90's mostly).
>
> 1884—Many iridescent ones—featuring greens, lilacs and mauves.
>
> 1887—Often toned to an odd assortment of pinks and greens, different from the 1884–85 group; Did the Mint use a different supplier for its paper wrappers?

There was not much more of a study made by Breen, but he does mention weirdly iridescent toning clear through to the Matte Proof Lincoln cents. Other copper and bronze coins turn up with a similar patina. Certain other Mint issues tend to show up more often than others with this type of toning. Pattern 1863 bronze cents (J-299) and pattern two-cent pieces are typically toned brown with iridescent highlights.

For the Indian Head cent series, certain dates tend to be found with this type of toning in larger numbers than others. This suggests that the number of coins that were put aside from year to year varied. Dates such as 1883 and 1885 are often found with iridescent toning while other dates, like 1894, are not. The percentage of each date included in the various hoards can be approximated by comparing certified populations for Red (RD) and Red Brown (RB) versus those for Brown (BN), as illustrated in the chart below for the 1870 to 1916 Proof cents. The figures include PCGS and NGC populations from June 2008. The ratio of RD/RB to BN Proofs shows the likely percentage of coins held in the various hoards. We are assuming that the Brown pieces got their tone from these hoards, which is really impossible to know for sure.

Toned Proofs Today

In recent times, some 80 years after these coins last acquired their toning, they have been coming out of various old-time collections, especially that of Louis Eliasberg. When it was sold by Bowers and Merena in 1996, many of the 1868–1892 cents were brown with iridescent toning, which was absent on the Proofs of 1893–1906. This was because the latter, formerly part of the J.M. Clapp collection, had been purchased directly from the Mint; the former had not.

1885 Toned Indian Head Cent

Prior to the Eliasberg sale, grading services were uncomfortable grading these toned coins. Starting in 1996, they accepted them as having original toning. Eliasberg's coins were certainly not an isolated case. Many other older collections that were put together in the 1930's and 1940's had iridescent toned Proofs as well. Not all were cared for as well as the Eliasberg collection coins.

To preserve the quality of their copper Proofs, collectors prior to the late 1950's sometimes coated them with lacquer. This protected the coins, but covered up their toning. In today's climate of third-party certification, these coins must be conserved of the protecting lacquer prior to encapsulation. During the 1960's and 1970's collectors put their coins in soft plastic holders made out of polyvinyl chloride (PVC). A plasticizer in PVC makes it soft and flexible. Unfortunately, the plasticizer leeches out onto coins in the form of a sticky, oily substance. This was the fate of some coins stored long-term in these holders. PVC residue can damage a coin and also must be removed prior to certification. Other coins fared better, but the long-term storage of copper is always a problem. Copper acts like an oil magnet. When oils from the surrounding environment coat the coin, dirt and dust follow and build up. The effect this all had on the iridescent toned Proof copper coins was to mute the brilliance of their toning.

Now, more than 100 years after minting, these coins usually end up looking dingy brown with only a hint of colorful toning. A rinse in acetone and other soaps and solvents can remove the gunk and show the true colors underneath. The difference can sometimes be astounding! Unfortunately these soaps and solvents can also harm the surface of the underlying coin. When the protecting surface dirt or lacquer is removed, the coin is exposed to the atmosphere for the first time in decades. The chance of the coin reacting to the atmosphere anew is great.

Another phenomenon that changes the appearance of copper is the *acetone effect*, which is an additional blue-purple tone that sometimes comes from the removal of oils on the surface of a copper coin. This is seen on non-Proof coins (which don't typically tone iridescently) as well as on full Red and Red-Brown Proofs that didn't have colored toning prior to conservation. A light application of oil, such as Blue Ribbon Coin Preserver, will negate this unnatural toning. In a well-publicized effort to thwart artificial enhancement of all coins, certified grading services frown upon adding oils to coins. However, longtime copper collectors know that most copper coins benefit from a proper application of some oil-based protectant every ten to 20 years. This is one reason many early copper collectors keep their coins uncertified.

1896 Toned Indian Head Cent

1897 Toned Indian Head Cent

1902 Toned Indian Head Cent

Looking Back—And Forward

As the prices for toned coins have increased, so have the appearances of artificially toned coins. These are manufactured for the purpose of making an additional buck from the collecting public. They tend to have very unnatural colors, much different from the examples cited above.

Which are real? Which are curated? Which are enhanced? Which are fake? The pendulum has swung widely over the past 30 years. The grading services have experts who have learned over time to tell coins with original patina from those artificially toned. As with any judgment call, a few mistakes can be expected. After looking at many original toned coins, you get a sense when something about a coin is not quite right. It is important to understand the history of the coins you are collecting and not to condemn original toned coins because of the existence of a few that are questionable.

APPENDIX H
Mint Error Cents

Throughout the 19th century, increasing quantities of coins were minted. The discovery of gold in quantity in California in 1848 resulted in immense quantities of the precious metal being shipped to the eastern mints, particularly to Philadelphia, during the next decade. Production of silver coins increased as well. Most attention was paid to the careful striking of these coins in precious metals, while copper output was not considered as important. Accordingly, misstrikes of cents were frequent (although but a tiny fraction of the current mintages) and often went into circulation. Nearly all errors in the making of silver and gold were caught by mint employees. Today, as a class, 19th-century misstrikes are rare, but copper errors are much more common than gold errors from that era.

Into the 20th century, processes continued to be improved. Mintages increased. Careful oversight continued to be practiced for silver and gold coins, but Indian Head and early Lincoln cents were not given as close scrutiny.

The following error cents are from the *100 Greatest U.S. Error Coins:*

1906 Indian Head Cent Struck on a Liberty Head Quarter Eagle Planchet. This is perhaps the most remarkable Indian Head cent error. Speculation abounds as to the origin of the gold Indian Head cents. Due to the extra care that was taken at the Mint when accounting for precious metals, it is difficult to believe that a gold planchet intended for a Liberty Head $2.50 gold piece accidentally ended up in the tote bin or collar for Indian Head cents. Were these pieces struck deliberately, perhaps for Colonel Green, who owned all five specimens of the 1913 Liberty Head nickel?

Only a handful of genuine examples have been confirmed in the past 50-plus years. There is mention of three or four additional gold Indian Head cents, but it's been impossible to verify and authenticate these others. One or two of those reported may be gold plated, some other type of error, or just plain counterfeit.

1862 Indian Head Cent Obverse Die Cap. With an appearance unlike any other die-cap coin of any type known, this unique 1862 copper-nickel cent has eight distinct "arms," caused by repeated striking pressure. Instead of being ejected after striking, this coin stuck to the top obverse die and continued to strike planchets that were fed into the coining chamber. For unknown reasons, this piece did not wrap itself around the top obverse die; instead, it spread out along the top of the collar, remaining relatively flat and eventually cracking in eight separate areas of the planchet. It continued to act as an obverse die, with the reverse design causing full brockage strikes on the coins struck subsequently. Each strike spread the coin further, and by the time this coin was dislodged from the striking chamber, the reverse design was wiped out.

1859 Indian Head Cent Struck on an 1857 Liberty Seated Half Dime A wonderful, unique overstrike, this is a first-year Indian Head cent that was struck over an 1857 half dime. The reverse of the coin shows a fairly normal half dime reverse, but it is distorted due to the copper-nickel cent planchet that lay in the lower, Indian Head cent reverse die. This thereby prevented the cent reverse design from being struck on the coin. On the obverse, the 1857 date can be seen in the field in front of Liberty's forehead, just under the word STATES. Some stars, as well as the outline of the Liberty Seated design, are also visible. The weight of this specimen is 19.2 grains. It is a rare double denomination ("six-cent piece") and the only such type struck on a half dime for the entire Indian Head cent series.

1909 Indian Head Cent Struck on a 1906 Barber Dime. Two examples of this error are known. In this example, a Barber Liberty Head dime was struck in 1906 and probably ended up in the bottom of one of the large tote bins used to move planchets and struck coins around the floor of the Mint. Three years later, when the bin was filled with bronze cent planchets, the struck dime was found in or near the bin and tossed into it, and subsequently overstruck with cent dies.

This frosty gem example—now in an NGC MS-66 holder—must have been found immediately after release, as its luster, strike, and overall condition say that it did not make it into someone's pocket change, even for a short time. Large portions of the original 1906 dime design show clearly. The dime's date is easily visible at 4:00 on the obverse, rotated about 45 degrees from the second strike. Both denominations show on the reverse side, with other details from the dime strike visible on both sides of the coin.

1872 Indian Head Cent Struck on a Nickel Three-Cent Piece Planchet. There are fewer than six examples of this error known. The eye appeal of an Indian Head cent in nickel, as opposed to a normal copper-colored planchet, is what makes these Indian Head cent off-metal errors so desirable, in addition to their overall rarity.

1877 Indian Head Cent Struck on a Venezuelan 1-Centavo Planchet. Listed until 2003 as a pattern (Judd-1496, Pollock-1649), this Indian Head cent is today recognized as a mint error. Records from the Philadelphia Mint show that eight million 1-centavo coins were minted for Venezuela in 1876 and another two million in 1877. This errant 1-centavo planchet evidently got mixed in with the normal bronze planchets intended for cents. Interestingly enough, only 852,500 Indian Head cents were struck by the Mint in 1877, making it the key date in the series already.

Today, with the understanding of just how rare any type-coin error is—especially on a key date—a coin like this would bring upward of ten times its value as a normal coin. As 1876 was the first year in which the U.S. Mint struck foreign coins, this is the earliest officially recognized error of a U.S. coin on a foreign planchet. It's also the earliest Indian Head cent of such renown.

APPENDIX I

Flying Eagle and Indian Head Cent Exonumia: A Meditation

By Charmy Harker, The Penny Lady®
Photos by Todd Pollock of BluCC Photos

Over the centuries, people have made a great variety of interesting and unique items using coins, especially pennies. "Penny" is the slang term often used interchangeably with "cent," and the term most often used when discussing these kinds of pieces. These coin creations have been described as "folk art," "outsider art," and "prison art," but in the numismatic world they are known as "exonumia," which means "outside the realm of coins."

I have been hunting and gathering penny exonumia for more than 15 years. Some of the pieces in my collection were so difficult to locate that I believe them to be rare and perhaps even unique, such as my Indian Head cent watch fob and the cardboard-encased cent. As a result of the scarcity of these pieces, pricing and values can be difficult to determine, and these are often the first things people ask about when they see my collection. Here I have included estimated retail values based on my personal experience, research, and observations and the rarity of the piece.

Prison Art Cents: Teapots, Charms, and More

One fascinating and popular part of my penny exonumia collection is "Prison Art." Prisoners often had an abundance of free time, yet were restricted in the availability of tools and materials with which to create arts and crafts. Thus, inmates in the 1930's and 1940's began fashioning tools from whatever items they could gather such as spoons, which they used to carefully tap, bend, mold and shape art objects. They also used whatever materials they had on hand, in this case pennies, to create tiny teapots, pans, charms, and other delightful objects. They were usually made from Indian, Wheat, and Canadian cents, but rare dime and other foreign-coin teapot examples are also known. The reverse of the coin is usually obvious on the bottom of the teapot, which allows identification of the type of coin used.

Prison art cent charms.

Officially, the teapots were not made for sale by the prisoners. They were usually given out as a gift or souvenir to thank a contributor for their "support" of the prison. However, it is known that teapots were sold at some of the prison gift shops. There is also evidence that some prison guards would take the teapots and charms into the nearby communities and sell them for 10 to 25 cents each. According to an article appearing in the December 2005 issue of *The Numismatist*, ANA Executive Director Emeritus Ed Rochette said exchanges of these little teapots regularly took place at the Massachusetts' Bridgewater State Prison between the guards and patrons at his uncle's Bridge Diner on Pope's Island, Massachusetts. The Indian Head cent teapots sell for $75 to $100, depending on whether the handle and spout are intact. Pieces with a removable lid are scarce and sell for over $100.

In addition to teapots, prison inmates (although similar pieces were sometimes made by soldiers) also created miniature charms out of pennies (Lincoln cents were more commonly used for these than their earlier counterparts) such as mugs, pots, pans, irons, hearts, bells, salt and pepper shakers, and even working padlocks. Sometimes these tiny creations were attached to a chain and used as a charm bracelet. The charms sell for between $20 and $75, with the complete charm bracelet worth over $200.

"Hartford, Conn., January, 1924.

TO OUR CONTRIBUTORS:

We acknowledged your gift received for the purpose of assisting in the work of this Association with thanks. The enclosed souvenir shows what "genius" many unfortunates possess. We encourage their thrift and present to you with the compliments of the Association and with an earnest appeal for your continued support and interest.

Sincerely yours,

W. G. BAXTER, *Secretary.*"

P. S. This "Kettle" is made from "ONE CENT" (trade mark on under side.) Lid is movable.

Note from the packaging of a souvenir cent kettle.

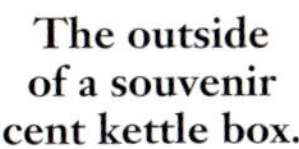

The outside of a souvenir cent kettle box.

Box with inscription storing a cent kettle.

Teapot Card, Box, and Letter

Prison teapots sometimes came in a small box with the inscription "This Kettle made from One Cent by 'Lifers'" printed on the top and included a card from the penitentiary where the teapot was made. The notecard thanked the purchaser for their "gift" to the prisoners and contained an appeal for their continued support. The original teapot card and box are very rare, and I was very fortunate to have recently acquired the only one I've ever seen to exist. I also received from a fellow collector a copy of a 1936 letter from the Warden at the Ohio Penitentiary to a numismatist trying to purchase teapot charms:

Prison art cent teapots.

We are mailing you under separate cover four (4) of the copper kettles made from pennies. The *Numismatic Scrap Book* was in error if they had an ad in their publication that these kettles were made here for sale. Such a statement was not authorized by us and we could not mail out any more [than what we are sending you now]. Just a few of our inmates make them for souvenirs.

Conservation Corps Teapots

There is also evidence that some penny teapots may have been made by workers in the Civilian Conservation Corps (CCC) during their spare time. The CCC program was a public work relief program that operated from 1933 to 1942 in the United States. It focused on the improvement and development of state park resources and included 68 camps of workers with nearly 100,000 men. According to an article from the Original Hobo Nickel Society website a penny teapot was discovered in a small box with a note on the inside of the box: "William A. Holbrook Co 11J3 CCC Warwick, MASS."

Fancy Rim Cents: Tools, Toys, and Gears

Many early cents were altered and used as tools such as pastry crimpers, pie cutters, clock gears, washers, buttons, and even children's toys such as a whirligig (also known as a button spinner). The rim of the coin was notched, a hole or two was punched or drilled into the center, and, in the case of pastry crimpers, a wooden or metal handle was attached through the hole so the jagged coin could roll across the pastry to crimp the edges of the dough together or to cut it, leaving a fancy serrated edge. Large cents were more commonly fashioned as pastry crimpers, but Flying Eagle and Indian Head cents were used for tools and gears as well. Over the years, I have come across many different carved designs on the rims of pennies. Some of these may have been carved just for fun, but their true purpose is left to the imagination! The value of these carved cents depends on the quality of the piece and how fancy the design is, and can range from $50 to $200.

Cents with designs carved into the edges to form gears, pie-cutters, decorations, and more.

Encased Cents

Coin encasements were a popular advertising medium, usually containing an Indian Head or Lincoln cent. The coin was inserted into a ring or other shape, often made from aluminum, but other materials were used such as cardboard, brass, copper, silver, gold, wood, celluloid, and even mirrors (creating "pocket mirrors"). One side of the ring usually had a good luck symbol, such as a horseshoe or four leaf clover, and the words "Keep Me and Never Go Broke" or "Keep Me and Have Good Luck" pressed onto the encasement. The other side had whatever inscription the customer wanted, such as a business advertisement, a souvenir message, or someone's personal information to be used as their calling card. Encased cents can be found advertising expositions, world fairs, restaurants, jewelers, and many other types of businesses. Uncirculated examples generally range from $100 to $300, depending on the quality and rarity of the encasement, as well as the quality of the Indian Head cent.

Although typical encased cents, such as aluminum pieces, were first created in 1901 at the Pan American Exposition in New York, the very rare 1895 cardboard encased cent (opposite) from the Philadelphia Times is an early example of an advertising encased cent, valued at over $400.

One of the most popular and less common encased cents is the 1908 Kolb's Bakeries Indian Head, cent with its teddy bear–shaped encasement (page 241). The obverse reads "Bear Us In Mind," and the reverse states "'Teddy Bear Bread Kolb's Bakeries, Philadelphia." Prior to 2008, gem Teddy Bear encasements were especially difficult to locate and often sold for over $500. However, since then, the Kolb family released a "hoard" of over 200 of these encasements, so the values have dropped. Despite this, these endearing "Teddy Bears" are still one of the most favored and sought-after aluminum-encased cents, and gem pieces are valued at $250.

1908 Kolb's Bakeries encased Indian Head cent.

1904 St. Louis World's Fair "chamber pot" encased cent.

Rare encased cents.

A goblet-shaped encasement from Ohio and a keystone-shaped encasement from Washington D.C. are very rare—encasements from Washington, D.C., are especially rare. The examples below are the finest known of these particular encasements and are valued at $700 and $400, respectively.

Cents encased in aluminum.

A cent encased in cardboard, a great rarity.

A 1904 St. Louis World's Fair encasement with the Indian Head cent appearing to be inserted into the "chamber pot" is very different from other encasements. I have only come across a few of these in the past 15 years, so they are a more scarce style compared to the typical aluminum-encased cents, where the entire coin is visible. The example shown is valued at $75.

A very rare 1905 wooden encasement (next page) was issued for the Lewis & Clark Exposition in Portland, Oregon, to celebrate the centennial of their famous expedition. This encasement is made from fir tree wood, probably because lumber was Oregon's chief export at the time. These wooden Lewis & Clark encasements are the only encased cents known to have been made out of wood, with perhaps six to seven remaining in existence. Unique to these wooden encasements, the penny was manually squeezed down into the encasement, unlike the aluminum encasements where the coin would be inserted before the encasement dies struck. This particular example contains a gem red Indian Head cent, the wood is in excellent condition as it is not cracked or dirty, and the printing on the encasement is still bold and colorful, thus, making it the *finest known*. Its value is over $800.

Frying Pan encasements were popular at the 1901 Pan American Exposition and were likely created in keeping with the "Pan" theme of the exposition. They are a fun variation of the usual aluminum ring encasement and are very difficult to find intact, with the stem unbent and still containing the stick pin. Uncirculated complete examples sell for $200 up.

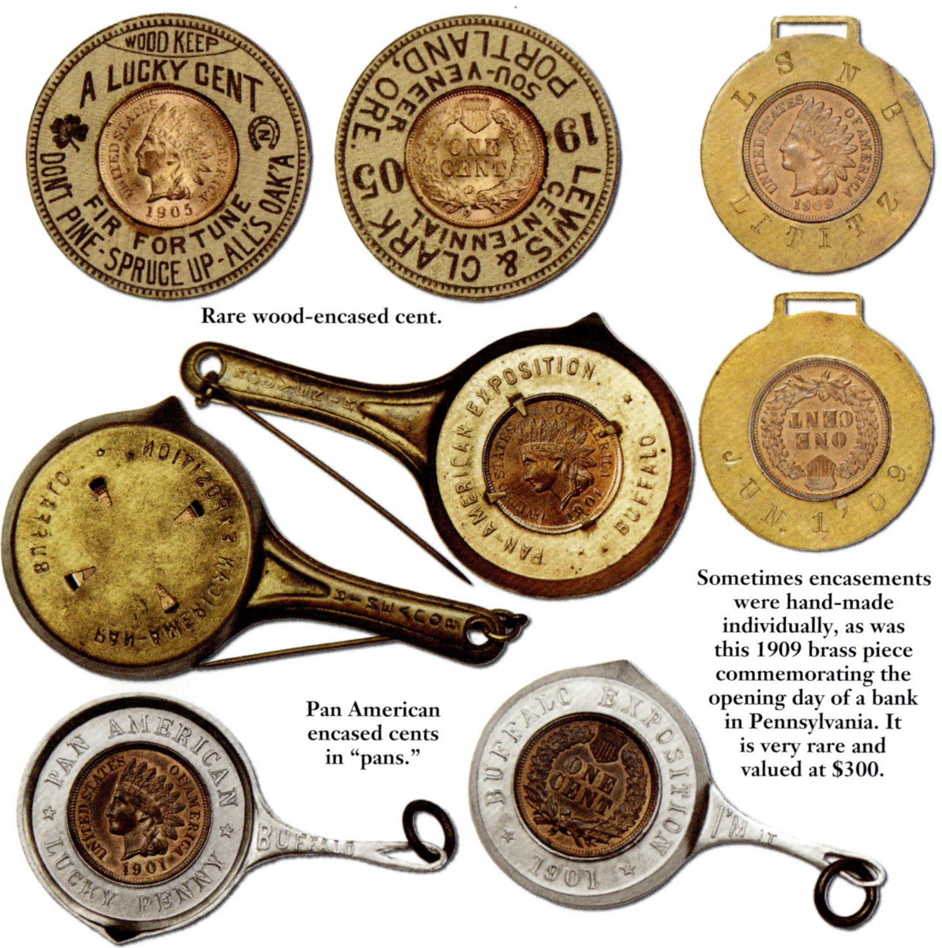

Rare wood-encased cent.

Pan American encased cents in "pans."

Sometimes encasements were hand-made individually, as was this 1909 brass piece commemorating the opening day of a bank in Pennsylvania. It is very rare and valued at $300.

Celluloid Encasements

Whitehead & Hoag (1892–1921) was one of the largest advertisement firms in the world at the turn of the century. They became famous for developing and patenting celluloid, a high-quality compound used for printing that created prints more durable and vibrant in color. They made many different types of advertising, political, and fraternal items such as buttons, pins, and pocket mirrors that are now very collectible.

A beautiful A.F. Fox Company encasement containing a gem red 1902 Indian Head cent (next page) is made out of blue celluloid and is very scarce. It is valued at $450. Also scarce is a cream-colored George Washington "Keep Me and Never Go Broke" celluloid, which contains an original 1902 Indian Head cent and is valued at $250. The other advertisement celluloid encasements shown on the next page are also scarce, especially in gem red, and are valued at $250 each.

Another scarce encasement is a 1901 Pan American Expo celluloid (next page) with a gem Indian Head cent on one side and an image of the Triumphal Arch usually on the other usually comes with a faded or torn image. This one is the finest one I've ever seen and is rare in such perfect condition. Its value is $200. The 1904 Indian Head cent charm shown on the next page, also encased in brass and celluloid, contains an embossed design on the reverse from the St. Louis World's Fair. It is quite scarce but obtainable in lesser condition. This piece is worth $300.

KEEP ME AND NEVER GO BROKE.
WASHINGTON'S LUCKY SOUVENIR.
YOU WILL NEVER GO BROKE IF YOUR
REAL ESTATE
IS MANAGED
BY A RELIABLE FIRM.
A.F. FOX COMPANY,
INCORPORATED:
REAL ESTATE
AGENTS,
BROKERS, APPRAISERS.
WASHINGTON, D.C.
SALES, RENTS, LOANS, INSURANCE.
KEEP ME AND NEVER GO BROKE
YOU'LL NEVER GO BROKE
WHEN USING
THE C.G.CONN INSTRUMENTS
ELKHART, INDIANA.
DID YOU EVER STOP TO THINK
10
of these Saved
Each Day will make
$36.50 per year
or $182.50 in Five Years?
You can also add
3%
Semi-Annual Interest to your Savings
by depositing them at
The Second National Bank,
COOPERSTOWN, NEW YORK

A 1900 Indian Head cent political campaign charm (opposite) is encased in brass and celluloid and is very scarce, especially in this condition. It contains a gem red Indian Head cent on one side and an albumen photo of William McKinley and Theodore Roosevelt on the other. Rather than the typical free souvenir token that was usually given away during campaigns, these were actually *sold* during the 1900 presidential campaign, probably for $1 each. This charm is one of only about a dozen known to exist in choice condition with the celluloid intact. Another similar piece in a lesser condition recently sold at auction for over $500, so this piece would retail at over $600.

This 1900 turn-of-the-century watch fob is extremely rare and perhaps unique. Each of the Indian Head cents is original and uncirculated. Except for one, the pennies are covered on both sides with a transparent piece of celluloid. I originally saw this watch fob for sale on eBay back in the late 1990's, and I was disappointed to be outbid. Then, just a few years ago, I was very surprised when a customer walked up to my table at a coin show and offered to sell me the *exact same* watch fob I had seen on eBay! Of course, I was thrilled and gladly paid the asking price. Its value is at least $200, though it is probably one of the last pieces I would ever part with.

Pocket-Mirror Encasements

Pocket-mirror encasements were another popular form of marketing and advertising using coins, especially pennies, placed on one side of a small mirror. Quality intact Indian Head cent pocket mirrors can be difficult to locate compared to the more common aluminum-encased cents since they are often found with the mirror damaged or missing, or the celluloid over the coin cracked or missing.

The value of round gem Indian Head cent mirrors ranges from $150 to $200, depending on the quality of the coin and the rarity and quality of the encasement.

Oval pocket mirrors with uncirculated Indian Head cents that are fully intact are particularly scarce pieces. The pocket mirror shown at right, from C.G. Conn Instruments (founded in the 1870's and eventually bought out by Steinway Musical Instruments), has an original red 1909 Indian Head cent and is valued at $250.

The Second National Bank of Cooperstown, New York, (operated from 1864 to 1935) pocket mirror, also shown on the following page, contains another gem full-red 1908 Indian Head cent and is valued at $300.

Elongated Cents

The first elongated cents (also known as pressed or rolled cents) in the United States were created in 1893 at the World's Columbian Exposition in Chicago, Illinois. These flattened pennies became very popular and were widely made at various expositions and fairs, including the 1901 Pan American Exposition in Buffalo, New York, and the 1904 World's Fair in St. Louis, Missouri. Machines to make elongated coins ("pressed penny" machines) can be found today in amusement parks; at museums, national landmarks, and parks; near tourist attractions; and even at special events. Elongates that still have the original coin image visible are more sought after and thus more valuable. The two attached 1893 Columbian Expo elongated pieces shown (next page) were made from 1881 and 1886 Canadian large cents and soldered together, possibly as the beginning pieces of a bracelet. Columbian Expo pieces on Canadian large cents are a lot less common than their Indian Head cent counterparts. Columbian Expo pieces in general are more valuable than other elongates, and this special double piece is worth $200. Quality uncirculated Indian Head cent elongates sell from $75 to $150, and $20 to $50 for gem Lincoln cent examples.

Elongated Cents

Hobo Cents

The hobo coins are created by creative carving on small-denomination coins, both U.S. and foreign. This art form became popular in the 1930's as a result of the scarcity of jobs. Because of the low cost and easy-to-carry size of nickels and other coins for carving, indigent people such as hobos often took up the art form, hence the name "hobo nickel." Carvings have been made on many different denominations of coins, including cents, which are less common compared to their nickel counterparts.

This 1900 "Skull Chief" hobo Indian Head cent carved by Andrew Tamburin is most likely a later-date carving, yet hobo cents remain very popular and sought after by hobo coin collectors. They range from $100 to $200.

Hobo Cent

Repoussé Cents (Pop Out or Push Up Cents)

The term "repoussé" refers to a technique in which a high- or low-relief design is created by striking malleable metal with a hammer on the opposite side of the metal from the design. These pieces are also known as "pop outs" or "push ups." These interesting pieces of exonumia were created with various types of coins, but cents were more common. Many varieties exist, including Liberty and Presidents, with Lincoln being the most common. Indians, animals, political, religious, fraternal clubs, and foreign themes were also popular. The value of these pieces depends on their craftsmanship, but, in general, individual pieces range from $30 to $75.

Repoussé coins and cents in particular were made into jewelry, such as fobs, pins, pendants, cufflinks, and even buttons. The mated cufflinks are valued at $100 to $150.

Repoussé Cents

Love Tokens

A love token is a coin that was smoothed or sanded down and then etched or engraved with the name or initials of the giver, special date, place, or event. The coins sometimes also had fancy etched borders or other designs. From the late 18th century throughout the 19th century, love tokens were widely given as an expression of love. Men who could not afford to buy their sweetheart a ring would purchase the largest coin denomination they could afford, personalize it, and give it to her as a token of their affection. The value of these carved coins varies widely depending on the rarity and condition of the host coin, the elaborateness of the engraving, and the token's special story or history. The price can range from $20 for simple designs on a common coin, up to $200 for more detailed designs on better-date, quality pieces.

Copper coins were especially popular among less-affluent men who would sometimes gold plate or gold fill the penny, making it look like a real gold coin.

Many times a pin back was added to be worn near the heart, or a hole or bezel was added to be worn around the neck.

Sometimes a coin would be carved into a love token along with the name of a business. Dual love token / store cards are very scarce. The example shown at the end of the gallery on the next page is valued at $250.

Love Tokens

Counterstamped Cents

Starting in the early 1800's, a simple and popular method of advertising a merchant's wares and services was to counterstamp coins. This practice began with large cents, and later small cents were used, as well as other denominations and foreign coins. The merchant would stamp the store's name or hallmark onto the coin and put the coin back into circulation. By the late 1800's, the use of counterstamped coins was eventually replaced by cardboard- and celluloid-encased coins, followed by elongated and ring-encased coins. The value of counterstamped cents varies widely, depending on the age, quality, and rarity of each piece, ranging from $20 to hundreds of dollars.

Cut-Out Cents

The fine art of piercing coins is more commonly referred to as cut-out coins and originated in the 17th century. At that time noblemen would give pierced coins as gifts to their sweethearts, who would wear them as jewelry. It is a highly skilled art requiring a great deal of patience and a steady hand to control the blade. They are made using any denomination and type of coin, both U.S. and foreign. The finished piece will look like the cut-out design is floating inside the edge of the coin. They usually range in value from $40 to $75.

Sticker Cents

Even though stickers on coins are a very simplistic advertising medium, not many have survived, and examples seem rather hard to find. This is probably due to the Secret Service banning them as violating federal law (*1951 - Act of July 16, 1951*), since the law prohibited attaching notices, advertisements, or labels on United States coins and currency, and required violators to remove any such stickers or face stiff fines. They are usually found on Lincoln cents, but Indian Head cent sticker cents can still be found. Such examples are valued at $75 and up.

Enameled Cents

Enameling is the art of fusing glass to metal, which arose from the Victorian love of unusual jewelry. The most popular year of production was 1887, during Queen Victoria's Golden Jubilee. Enameled buttons, cufflinks, and other jewelry pieces were popular, and the skill of enameling was also applied to coins like this Indian Head cent stick pin valued at $75.

Novelties

As you can see, penny exonumia can encompass many interesting forms of coin creations that were made for tools, toys, advertising, jewelry, souvenirs, decorations, or just for the fun of it, including this hand-made whistle decorated with Indian Head cents, or this glittery postcard with a penny glued to it.

Each time I find a new piece to add to my collection, especially one I hadn't previously encountered, it brings me great joy. I know my collection will never be complete, as there are many more creations made from pennies that are still waiting for me to discover, so the hunt goes on. But whatever their design or purpose, I hope you find these little copper creations as fascinating and entertaining as I do!

Charmy Harker eventually turned her passion into a full-time business, The Penny Lady®, buying and selling high-quality coins at most of the major shows, and on her website, thepennylady.com. She currently serves as President of Women in Numismatics (WIN) and chairs the ANA's Dealer Relations Committee, has received the ANA Presidential Award, and writes for various coin publications.

Post card Postkarte Carte postale
Cartolina Postale — Levelezö Lap — Dopisnice — Brefkort
Briefkaart — Brevkort — ОТКРЫТОЕ ПИСЬМО —
Tarjeta postal — Cartão postal
Union postale Universelle.

10-20-07.
Birthday greetings from George.

Miss Julia Larsson
1331 Montgomery Ave
Local

Notes

The reader may view reference citations, if desired, via the QR code at right.

Bibliography

Alexander, David T., Thomas K. DeLorey, and Brad Reed. *Coin World Comprehensive Catalog & Encyclopedia of United States Coins.* Sidney, OH: Coin World, 1995.

ANACS Population Report. Columbus, OH: ANACS. Various issues.

Bowers, Q. David. *A Buyer's and Enthusiast's Guide to Flying Eagle and Indian Cents.* Bowers and Merena Galleries, 1996.

Bowers, Q. David, with Douglas Winter. *The United States $3 Gold Piece.* Wolfeboro, NH: American Numismatic Rarities, 2005.

Breen, Walter H. *The United States Minor Coinage 1793–1916.* New York, NY: Wayte Raymond, Inc., 1954.

———. *The Secret History of the Gobrecht Coinages 1836–1840.* New York, NY: Wayte Raymond, Inc., 1954.

———. "Blundered Dies of U.S. and Colonial Coins." *Empire Topics*, October 1958. (First publication of the 1873 Doubled LIBERTY cent.)

———. *Complete Encyclopedia of U.S. and Colonial Proof Coins.* Albertson, NY: F.C.I. Press, 1977.

———. *Walter Breen's Complete Encyclopedia of U.S. and Colonial Coins.* New York, NY: Doubleday & Co., 1988.

Bressett, Kenneth (editor). *A Guide Book of United States Coins*, 2006 edition. Atlanta, GA: Whitman Publishing, LLC, 2005.

Bressett, Kenneth E., with narrative by Q. David Bowers. *The Official American Numismatic Association Grading Standards for United States Coins*, sixth edition. Atlanta, GA: Whitman Publishing, LLC, 2005.

Carothers, Neil. *Fractional Money.* New York, NY: John Wiley & Sons, Inc., 1930.

Cartwright, Timothy. "The Thrill of Discovering the 1871 S4, Shallow N Reverse." *Longacre's Ledger*, December 1999.

Coin World Almanac. Sidney, OH: Coin World, 1976 and later editions.

Coin World. Sidney, OH: Amos Press. Various issues.

COINage. Ventura, CA: Miller Publications. Various issues.

Coins Magazine. Iola, WI: Krause Publications. Various issues.

Conger, George R. "The Controversial Feathered Headdress." *Longacre's Ledger*, April 1992.

———. "An Argument Favoring Sarah as Longacre's Model." *Longacre's Ledger*, July 1992.

DeLorey, Thomas K. "Was Mischief Afoot in 1857 Die Clashes?" "Collectors' Clearinghouse," *Coin World*, July 1, 1977.

———. "Longacre, Unsung Engraver of the U.S. Mint." *Longacre's Ledger*, January 1992. Reprinted from *The Numismatist*, October 1985.

Eaton, W.C. "The Eagle Cents of 1858." *The Numismatist*, January 1916. Updated in *The Numismatist*, November 1920, and further in *The Numismatist*, March 1921.

———. "The Eagle Cents of 1857." *The Numismatist*, May 1921. Most research for this article was done by E.R. Alvord.

Fivaz, Bill. "Never In My Wildest Dreams." *Rare Coin Review* No. 62. Description of the discovery of the 1857 Flying Eagle cent with clash marks from a Liberty Seated quarter dollar.

———. "Definitely a Difference!" *Longacre's Ledger*, Summer 1994. Description of the differences in the neck feathers on the letter size varieties of the 1858 Flying Eagle cent.

Fivaz, Bill, and J.T. Stanton. *The Cherrypickers' Guide to Rare Die Varieties*, fourth edition, volume 1. Mike Ellis, editor. Savannah, GA: Stanton Books and Supplies, 2000.

Fuld, George, and Melvin Fuld. *U.S. Civil War Store Cards*. Token and Medal Society, 1972.

———. *Patriotic Civil War Tokens*, fourth edition. Token and Medal Society, 1982.

Goe, Rusty. *The Mint on Carson Street*. Reno, NV: Southgate Coins and Collectables, 2005.

Hettger, Henry T. "Collusive Bidding on Indian Head Cent Planchets in 1892." *Longacre's Ledger*, October 1991.

Jones, John F. "The1856 Flying Eagle Cent." *The Numismatist*, April 1944.

Judd, J. Hewitt. *United States Pattern Coins*, 9th edition, edited by Q. David Bowers. Atlanta, GA: Whitman Publishing, LLC, 2005.

Julian, R.W. *Medals of the United States Mint: The First Century 1792–1892*. El Cajon, CA: Token and Medal Society, Inc., 1977.

———. "The Flying Eagle Cent." *COINage*, October 1987.

———. "The Indian Head Cent." *COINage*, May 1988.

———. "The Cent Becomes Bronze: 1864." *FUN-Topics*, Summer 1987.

———. "The 1877 Indian Head Cent." *Coins Magazine*, October 1992.

Kross, Herman E. *Documentary History of Banking and Currency in the United States*. Volumes 1–4. New York, NY: Chelsea House Publishers, 1983.

Larson, Dr. Timothy. "The 1888/7 S2 – Is it an Overdate?" *Longacre's Ledger*, June 2000.

Longacre's Ledger. Journal of the Fly-In Club. Contains much information on die varieties, rarity ratings, etc.

Numismatic Guaranty Corporation of America Census Report. Parsippany, NJ: Numismatic Guaranty Corporation of America. Various issues.

Numismatic News. Iola, WI: Krause Publications. Various issues.

Numismatist, The. Colorado Springs, CO. Various issues.

Pilliod, Chris. "What Error Coins Can Teach Us About Die Settings." *The Numismatist*, April 1996.

———. "Can a Two-Headed Cent Really Exist? Yes, But Only in 1859." *Longacre's Ledger*, Dec. 2000.

PCGS Population Report. Newport Beach, CA: Professional Coin Grading Service. Various issues.

Pollock, Andrew W. III. *United States Patterns and Related Issues*. Wolfeboro, NH: Bowers and Merena Galleries, 1994.

Rare Coin Review. Wolfeboro, NH: Bowers and Merena Galleries, Inc. Various issues.

Sebby, Vernon. "A Discussion of High Grade, Mint State Indian Cents," four-part series. *Longacre's Ledger*, 2001–2002.

Sirna, Ronald R. "Collecting Proof Indian Cents for Fun." *Longacre's Ledger*, December 2002.

Smithsonian Institution, National Portrait Gallery. *American Portrait Prints*. Wendy Wick Reaves, ed. 1984.

Snow, Richard. "The Midnight Minter." *Longacre's Ledger*, January 1991.

———. "High Leaves, Low Leaves." *Longacre's Ledger*, April 1991.

———. "The Indian Head Cent of 1877." *The Numismatist*, March 1998.

———. "The Showdown." *Longacre's Ledger*, September 2002.

———. *Flying Eagle and Indian Cents*. Tucson, AZ: Eagle Eye Press, 1992.

———. *Flying Eagle and Indian Cent Attribution Guide*, Vol. 1, 1856–1858, second edition. Tucson, AZ: Eagle Eye Rare Coins Inc., 2001.

———. *Flying Eagle and Indian Cent Attribution Guide*, Vol. 1, 1859–1869, second edition. Tucson, AZ: Eagle Eye Rare Coins Inc., 2003.

———. "Proof Die Identification for Indian Cents." *Longacre's Ledger*, Fall 1994.

Snowden, James Ross. *A Description of Ancient and Modern Coins in the Cabinet Collection at the Mint of the United States.* Philadelphia: J.B. Lippincott & Co., 1860.

Steinberger, Otto C. "Indian Cent Date Varieties." *Numismatic Scrapbook Magazine.* Serial feature commencing with the December 1961 issue, later reprinted as a monograph.

Steve, Larry R. "THE F.IND.ERS REPORT." *Longacre's Ledger*, various issues.

———. "An Analysis of the 1867 Over 67." *Longacre's Ledger*, June 2001.

Steve, Larry R., and Kevin J. Flynn. *A Comprehensive Guide to Selected Rare Flying Eagle and Indian Cent Varieties.* Jarrettsville, MD: Nuvista Press, 1995.

Taxay, Don. *Counterfeit, Mis-Struck and Unofficial U.S. Coins.* New York, NY: Arco Publishing, 1963.

———. *Scott's Comprehensive Catalogue and Encyclopedia of U.S. Coins.* New York, NY: Scott Publishing, 1971.

———. *U.S. Mint and Coinage.* New York, NY: Arco Publishing, 1966.

Travers, Scott A. *Official Guide to Coin Grading and Counterfeit Detection*, edited by Q. David Bowers. Professional Coin Grading Service, 1997.

Van Ryzin, Robert R. *The Crime of 1873.* Iola, WI: Kruse Publications, 2001.

Vermeule, Cornelius. *Numismatic Art in America.* Cambridge, MA: Belknap Press, 1971.

Wharton, Joseph. "Project for Reorganizing the Small Coinage of the United States of America." April 15, 1864.

Yeoman, R.S. (editor). *A Guide Book of United States Coins.* Racine, WI; New York, NY; and Atlanta, GA: various editions beginning with 1947.

Credits and Acknowledgments

Creative Director and Cover Designer, Matt Jeffirs
Editorial Director, Diana Plattner
Graphic Designers, Matt Heller and Thinh Bui
Pricing Editors, John Feigenbaum and Patrick Ian Perez

This book is the culmination of many years of work by many dedicated numismatists. My own interest in Flying Eagle and Indian Head cents started with the publication of **Walter Breen**'s *Complete Encyclopedia of U.S. and Colonial Coins*. Early research into this series included help from **Elvira Clain-Stefanelli** at the Smithsonian Institution. **Robert G. Stewart**, senior curator of the National Portrait Gallery, helped with access to the James Longacre collection, including Longacre's sketchbooks and diary. **Dr. Harriett Longacre Phelps** helped with many previously unknown aspects of Longacre's life and information on the family's history. **Andrew Longacre Jr.** furnished the life portraits of James and Eliza Longacre in Appendix A.

Much of this work is built on my 1992 book, *Flying Eagle and Indian Cents*, which was assisted greatly by the photo file of **Christopher Pilliod**, who also wrote a foreword for this edition. **Larry R. Steve** helped with gathering information through the Fly-In Club. Larry's 1995 book with **Kevin J. Flynn**, *Flying Eagle and Indian Cent Die Varieties*, added much-needed depth to the Flying Eagle and Indian Head cent variety field. Bill Fivaz also wrote a foreword for this edition.

Charmy Harker, The Penny Lady®, wrote a beautiful appendix on Flying Eagle and Indian Head cent exonumia, illustrated with photos taken by Todd Pollock of BluCC Photos. More of her collections can be seen at thepennylady.com.

Q. David Bowers helped greatly over the years with this project. When Dave wrote the *Buyer's and Enthusiast's Guide to Flying Eagle and Indian Cents* in 1996, I was relieved of the pressure of writing another book and contributed all my notes to that project. Now, Dave has graciously returned the favor with his continuous help and suggestions.

The active participation of the membership of the Fly-In Club was a great help, notably: **William Affanato, Ralph Bergholtz, Larry Briggs, Dr. Eugene Bruder, John Cantwell, Tim Cartwright, Xan Chamberlain, Dr. George Conger, Dr. Ira Davidoff, Marvin Erickson, Dr. Sheldon Freed, Dr. Thomas Fore, Lee Gong, Quent Hansen, Doug Hill, Kenneth Hill, Paul Houck, Alan Kreuzer, Sam Lukes, Mark McWherter, Alan Meghrig, Ron Neuman, Lynn Ourso, Bob Pedlosky, Vernon Sebby, Ronald A. Sirna, Dr. Stanley Spurgeon, Dr. Thomas Turrissini, Mark Van Deusen, William O. Walker, Mark Watson, Alan Williams,** and **Jerry Wysong.** I'm sure there are many others who contributed greatly but I've failed to mention; to those I'd also like to give a heartfelt "Thank you."

Mike Ellis (of Oklahoma), and **Dr. Tim Larson** both reviewed early transcripts of this text. **Kenneth Bressett**, editor of Whitman's *Guide Book of United States Coins* (the *Red Book*), offered suggestions.

Numismatic expertise was given generously by **John Dannreuther, Julian Leidman, Bill Fivaz, J.T. Stanton, Thomas K. DeLorey, Jack Beymer, R.W. Julian, Saul Teichman, Andrew Lustig,** and **P. Scott Rubin**.

The staff of **Whitman**, a very talented group, have my thanks.

American Numismatic Rarities provided a coin photograph. **Miguel Colón Ortiz** contributed historical essays and images. **Dalmatian Press, LLC**, provided an illustration. **Charles Daughtrey** illustrated the frontispiece. **H.E. Harris & Co.** provided a postage stamp image. **Steve Hayden** and **Steven Tanenbaum** provided Civil War token images.

I'd like to give very heartfelt thanks to **Brian Wagner** for all his help over the years. The late **Elliott Goldman**, of Allstate Coins, was very instrumental in getting access to the richness of talent that abounds in this hobby.

About the Author

Rick Snow

Rick Snow has had a passion for coins since 1972, when a local coin dealer in his hometown of Whippany, New Jersey, ignited his interest. After ten years in the hobby, being a local coin club president, small–coin shop counter-person and active collector, Rick fell out of collecting to work in the real world. This departure endured only six years. In 1986 he became senior numismatist to a Tucson coin dealer, Allstate Coin.

While working for Allstate Rick developed an interest and expert knowledge in Flying Eagle and Indian Head cents. This quickly translated into the development of a national coin club devoted to these coins—The Flying Eagle and Indian Cent Collectors Society, or Fly-In Club (www.fly-inclub.org). The club is still going strong more than 35 years later. Rick also wrote the first book devoted to these coins in 1992. That book transformed into The Flying Eagle and Indian Cent Attribution Guide and in 2014 was published in its third edition. It is the official listing of all varieties of these series and is a two-volume 900-page book.

In 1993 Rick began his own coin dealership, Eagle Eye Rare Coins. In its first year it was based in Tucson, Arizona, but between 1993 and 2000 it was based in Seattle, Washington, with Brian Wagner as a partner. Since 2000, Eagle Eye has been based back in Tucson. You can usually catch Rick at any major show around the country with his Flying Eagle and Indian Head cents. You can visit his business online at GreatCoins.com.

Eagle Eye Photo Seal was the first certified-holder acceptance system. It was begun in 1996 and has been hugely successful in labeling correctly graded Flying Eagle and Indian Head cents. Eagle Eye makes a market in Photo Sealed coins. After 20 years (in 2016), Eagle Eye Photo Seal has become the accepted standard in the Flying Eagle and Indian Head cent community. It assures that full-red coins are really full red and coins are graded correctly by the major grading services. This has helped prevent the abuse of overgrading by grading services.

In 2016 Rick announced a new grading system. The PDS grading system, as it is called, is detailed in this book. The system uses the Official ANA Grading Standard's adjectival grades with a Planchet-Die-Strike qualifier rating the quality of each of those aspects on a particular coin. The benefits can be seen when comparing coins graded with the 70-point Sheldon system. For many years collectors have seen the problem of grading inflation in certified holders take control of the market. Hopefully the PDS grading system will help reverse this trend.

Index